TRACING YOUR ANCESTORS' CHILDHOOD

FAMILY HISTORY FROM PEN & SWORD

Tracing Your Army Ancestors
Simon Fowler
•

Tracing Your Pauper Ancestors
Robert Burlison
•

Tracing Your Yorkshire Ancestors
Rachel Bellerby
•

Tracing Your Air Force Ancestors
Phil Tomaselli
•

Tracing Your Northern Ancestors
Keith Gregson
•

*Tracing Your Black Country
Ancestors*
Michael Pearson
•

Tracing Your Textile Ancestors
Vivien Teasdale
•

Tracing Your Railway Ancestors
Di Drummond
•

*Tracing Your Secret Service
Ancestors*
Phil Tomaselli
•

Tracing Your Police Ancestors
Stephen Wade
•

*Tracing Your Royal Marine
Ancestors*
Richard Brooks
and Matthew Little
•

Tracing Your Jewish Ancestors
Rosemary Wenzerul
•

*Tracing Your East Anglian
Ancestors*
Gill Blanchard
•

Tracing Your Ancestors
Simon Fowler
•

Tracing Your Liverpool Ancestors
Mike Royden
•

Tracing Your Scottish Ancestors
Ian Maxwell
•

*Tracing British Battalions on the
Somme*
Ray Westlake
•

Tracing Your Criminal Ancestors
Stephen Wade
•

*Tracing Your Labour Movement
Ancestors*
Mark Crail
•

Tracing Your London Ancestors
Jonathan Oates
•

*Tracing Your Shipbuilding
Ancestors*
Anthony Burton
•

*Tracing Your Northern Irish
Ancestors*
Ian Maxwell
•

*Tracing Your Service Women
Ancestors*
Mary Ingham
•

Tracing Your East End Ancestors
Jane Cox
•

Tracing the Rifle Volunteers
Ray Westlake
•

Tracing Your Legal Ancestors
Stephen Wade
•

Tracing Your Canal Ancestors
Sue Wilkes
•

Tracing Your Rural Ancestors
Jonathan Brown
•

Tracing Your House History
Gill Blanchard
•

Tracing Your Tank Ancestors
Janice Tait and David Fletcher
•

*Tracing Your Family History on
the Internet*
Chris Paton
•

Tracing Your Medical Ancestors
Michelle Higgs
•

*Tracing Your Second World War
Ancestors*
Phil Tomaselli
•

*Tracing Your Channel Islands
Ancestors*
Marie-Louise Backhurst
•

*Tracing Your Great War
Ancestors DVD*
Pen & Sword Digital &
Battlefield History TV Ltd
•

*Tracing Your Prisoner of War
Ancestors: The First World War*
Sarah Paterson
•

*Tracing Your British Indian
Ancestors*
Emma Jolly
•

Tracing Your Naval Ancestors
Simon Fowler
•

*Tracing Your Huguenot
Ancestors*
Kathy Chater
•

Tracing Your Servant Ancestors
Michelle Higgs
•

*Tracing Your Ancestors from
1066 to 1837*
Jonathan Oates
•

*Tracing Your Merchant Navy
Ancestors*
Simon Wills
•

*Tracing Your Lancashire
Ancestors*
Sue Wilkes
•

*Tracing Your Ancestors through
Death Records*
Celia Heritage
•

*Tracing Your West Country
Ancestors*
Kirsty Gray
•

*Tracing Your First World War
Ancestors*
Simon Fowler
•

*Tracing Your Army Ancestors -
2nd Edition*
Simon Fowler
•

*Tracing Your Irish Family
History on the Internet*
Chris Paton
•

*Tracing Your Aristocratic
Ancestors*
Anthony Adolph
•

*Tracing Your Ancestors from
1066 to 1837*
Jonathan Oates
•

TRACING YOUR ANCESTORS' CHILDHOOD

A Guide for Family Historians

Sue Wilkes

Pen & Sword
FAMILY HISTORY

First published in Great Britain in 2013 by
PEN & SWORD FAMILY HISTORY
an imprint of
Pen & Sword Books Ltd
47 Church Street
Barnsley
South Yorkshire
S70 2AS

ISBN 978 1 78159 166 6

Typeset in Palatino and Optima by
CHIC GRAPHICS

Printed and bound in England by
CPI Group (UK), Croydon, CR0 4YY

Pen & Sword Books Ltd incorporates the imprints of
Pen & Sword Archaeology, Atlas, Aviation, Battleground, Discovery,
Family History, History, Maritime, Military, Naval, Politics, Railways,
Select, Social History, Transport, True Crime, and Claymore Press,
Frontline Books, Leo Cooper, Praetorian Press, Remember When,
Seaforth Publishing and Wharncliffe.

For a complete list of Pen & Sword titles please contact
PEN & SWORD BOOKS LTD
47 Church Street, Barnsley, South Yorkshire, S70 2AS, England
E-mail: enquiries@pen-and-sword.co.uk
Website: www.pen-and-sword.co.uk

CONTENTS

For Nigel, Lizzie and Gareth

ACKNOWLEDGEMENTS

Once again I must express my gratitude to the many archivists and librarians who have patiently assisted with my enquiries, including Martine King (Barnardo's), Edward Ratcliffe (Children's Society Records and Archive Centre), Martin Rayment (Norwood), David Springer (NSPCC), Susan Gentles, the Red Cross Collections Officer, Simon Fenwick (Shaftesbury Young People) and Steven Spencer (Salvation Army International Heritage Centre).

Also of great assistance were Phaedra Casey (Brunel University Archives), Anne Clarke (Cadbury Research Library, University of Birmingham), Lisa Greenhalgh (Cheshire Archives and Local Studies), Karen Millhouse (Derbyshire Record Office), David Tilsley (Lancashire Archives), Laura Taylor (London Metropolitan Archives), Mike Bevan (National Maritime Museum), Jonathan Draper (Norfolk Record Office), Margaret Page (Quaker Family History Society), Heather Johnson (Royal Naval Museum Library), Jacqui Burgin (State Library of Queensland), Sarah Maspero (Hartley Library, University of Southampton), and Jennie Kiff (West Yorkshire Archive Service). Apologies to anyone I have inadvertently omitted.

I would also like to thank Bryony Partridge (Ancestry), Debra Chatfield (Findmypast) and David Osborne (The Genealogist) and Martin Brayne and Guy Etchells and (Parson Woodforde Society).

All TNA records quoted are Crown Copyright. Records held by Lancashire Record Office and Cheshire Archives and Local Studies, to which copyright is reserved, are reproduced by kind permission.

Information about the Society of Genealogists' resources quoted from their website by kind permission of Else Churchill. Information from the Staffordshire BMD website quoted by kind permission of Ian Hartas. Information on the Navy League and Sea Cadets quoted by kind permission of the National Museum of the Royal Navy.

Any mistakes in the text are my own.

Every effort has been made to trace copyright holders for images used in this work. The publishers welcome information on any attributions that have been omitted.

I would also like to express my gratitude to Simon Fowler and Rupert Harding of Pen & Sword Books for their help and encouragement. Last but not least, I must once again thank my husband Nigel, and my children Elizabeth and Gareth, for their untiring help and support.

LIST OF ABBREVIATIONS

BMDs	Birth, marriage and death certificates
BFSS	British and Foreign School Society
BTs	Bishops' Transcripts
CALS	Cheshire Archives and Local Studies
COS	Charity Organisation Society
DANGO	Database of Archives of Non-Governmental Organisations
FFHS	Federation of Family History Societies
FWA	Family Welfare Association
GRO	General Register Office (St Catherine's House indexes)
HMI	Her Majesty's Inspector(ate)
LA	Lancashire Record Office
LEA	Local Education Authority
LMA	London Metropolitan Archives
NCVCCO	National Council of Voluntary Child Care Organisations
NLW	National Library of Wales
NRA	National Register of Archives
NSPCC	National Society for the Prevention of Cruelty to Children
PCC	Prerogative Court of Canterbury
PCY	Prerogative Court of York
QFHS	Quaker Family History Society
SPCK	Society for Promoting Christian Knowledge
TNA	The National Archives
UCL	University College, London
UCLAN	University of Central Lancashire
WYAS	West Yorkshire Archives Service

LIST OF ILLUSTRATIONS

All illustrations are from the author's collection, and photos are by the author, except where otherwise credited.

1. Map of England and Wales.
2. Photo postcard of a baby, dated Christmas 1915.
3. Photo postcard of the Sandford family, Christmas 1915.
4. Photo postcard of mother and baby, *c.* 1910.
5. Family life for poor people in the 1860s.
6. 'Cabinet card' of a well-to-do family photographed in a Southsea studio, *c.* 1890.
7. Oliver Twist's narrow escape from being apprenticed to a chimneysweep.
8. The Apprentice House at Quarry Bank Mill, Styal.
9. The Lower Cotton Mill, Holywell, owned by Douglas & Co.
10. Police try to hold back an angry mob in Giltspur Street, London as George Sloane is taken before the magistrates.
11. Oliver Twist asks for more gruel in the workhouse.
12. Boy working as a domestic servant.
13. 'Who'd be a "nuss"!'
14. Child worker using a machine for combing worsted.
15. School exemption certificate for Sarah Jane Dickman dated 27 September 1893 permitting her to work full-time.
16. Boy leading a pit pony.
17. The old schoolroom, Harrow.
18. Macclesfield Sunday School, now a heritage centre.
19. Howarth National School, Church Lane, Haworth.
20. The Lambeth Ragged Schools opened on 5 March 1851.
21. Postcard of a class of schoolgirls with their teacher, *c.* 1910.
22. A school board visitor testing children's knowledge.
23. Pupil teacher apprenticeship indenture for William Butler Cowap from Leftwich.
24. Schoolteacher with a cane.
25. The Artful Dodger picks a pocket.
26. Prisoners including child felons.

27. A very young-looking offender, Michael Daley (16), in 1892.
28. Sydney, New South Wales, south view in 1824.
29. The Philanthropic Society's farm at Redhill.
30. The Foundling Hospital.
31. Homeless street-sweepers sleeping under a railway arch in London in the 1880s.
32. Mud-larks on the Thames trying to earn a living by scavenging.
33. Postcard of the Babies' Castle, Hawkhurst, Kent, a Dr Barnardo home, postmarked 1911.
34. Shoe-black boy.
35. Postcard of the children at the Royal School for Deaf and Dumb Children, *c.* 1910.
36. Great Ormond Street Hospital for Sick Children.
37. Nurse and children at Cromwell House, Great Ormond Street Hospital's convalescent home.
38. Postcard of the Children's Hospital, Birmingham, *c.* 1906.
39. Jack Cornwell's second funeral in 1916.
40. Naval cadets learning woodwork.
41. Royal Naval Schools, Greenwich.
42. A boy training at Watt's Naval School, North Elmham, Norfolk, 1920s.

Part 1

CHILDHOOD AND EDUCATION

Map of England and Wales. *Barclay's Dictionary*, Bungay edn (T. Kinnersley, 1813).

Chapter 1

BEGINNING YOUR SEARCH

Tracing your family history is an absorbing hobby which has become increasingly popular in recent years. There has never been a more exciting time to be a family historian: there are books, magazines, online genealogy services, family history or local history societies, online forums, reunion websites and even TV programmes exploring past lives.

However, to date, there has not been a genealogy title that surveys the many archival sources available for children and young people living in earlier times.

Your ancestors' formative years were immensely important for their futures, and those of their offspring. Were your ancestors born to rich parents? Were they perhaps merchants, craftsmen or labourers? Did your ancestors follow their parents into the same trade or profession?

Maybe your ancestors were destitute, or came from a broken home: their chances in life would have been extremely limited. Poverty and poor nutrition had consequences for their health and that of their children. Literacy skills provided opportunities for poor people to 'better themselves': but could they afford to go to school?

Tracing Your Ancestors' Childhood focuses primarily on records for England and Wales from 1750–1950. The first part of the book explores your ancestors' childhood experiences from birth until 16 years of age.

The second part is a research guide with a directory of contact details for the archives and repositories mentioned in the book. The other sections in the research guide list sources such as useful websites, online databases of children's records, addresses of children's societies, military sources and museums.

In this chapter, some basic family history sources are briefly reviewed for the benefit of those readers completely new to genealogy. Birth and baptism records are discussed, and other potential methods of discovering your ancestor's date of birth are explored. Later chapters discuss childhood records in detail: Poor Law records, apprenticeship indentures, school

Photo postcard of a baby, dated Christmas 1915.

registers, criminal records, wartime records and so on. Suggestions are given for exploring these topics in greater depth elsewhere and specialist archives are noted where appropriate.

Some topics, e.g. schools, are dealt with in more than one chapter, because more than one type of organisation ran schools: Poor Law guardians, churches, charities, local councils and so on. Signposts are given to other chapters where necessary to explore a particular subject further; you should also use the index to help you.

Sources relating to childhood are particularly important for exploring our ancestors' lives for demographic reasons. During the nineteenth century, children and young people formed a far higher proportion of the population than the present day. In 2009, 29 per cent of the UK's population was under 16 years old. In 1841, 36 per cent of England's population was under 15 years old.

Many thousands of children lived in institutions: in 1840, 22,300 children aged 9 to 16 were workhouse inmates. Hundreds of organisations and charities were dedicated to helping destitute, poorly and disabled children.

Your child ancestors may have migrated overseas. Thousands of young offenders were transported to America (until the 1770s) and Australia (until 1868), where they were used as a cheap labour force as punishment for their crimes.

Many churches, charities, Poor Law officials and local authorities sent impoverished children to begin a new life in Australia, Canada and South Africa, and this practice did not cease until 1967, when the last group of children was flown to Australia by Dr Barnardo's charity.

During the Second World War, hundreds of child evacuees were sent to America and the British Dominions to keep them safe from bombing raids and a possible German invasion. This book suggests starting points, using transportation and emigration records, to help you find child ancestors who emigrated.

In order to trace the childhood of a particular ancestor, we need to establish when and where they were born. The primary sources for dates of birth are birth certificates and baptismal records in parish registers.

Civil Registration

The 'magic year' for genealogists is 1837, when civil registration began. Every birth, marriage and death was recorded at local register offices, and you can order copy certificates of the entries made by the registrar.

Birth certificates show the date and place where a person was born, name, sex, father's name, mother's maiden name and residence, father's occupation, date when the birth was registered and name and address of the person who registered the birth.

Marriage certificates give the date when the couple married, place where the marriage was solemnised, name and occupation of bride and groom, residences at the date of marriage and name and occupation of bride's and groom's father. The bride and groom sometimes gave their planned future address to avoid paying for two sets of banns. A marriage certificate should show all of a bride's earlier surnames if she was previously married.

Death certificates give the person's age and occupation, date of death and residence, cause of death, date when the death was registered and name and address of the informant. After 1837 it was illegal to bury a body without a death certificate unless the deceased was a stillborn child (this exception was lifted in 1875).

Two sets of indexes are available for birth, marriage and death certificates (BMDs). The indexes compiled by local registrars are the most accurate. Indexes for some civil registration districts are available online; follow the links from the UKBMD website, www.ukbmd.org.uk.

Civil registration districts did not necessarily follow county boundaries. A list of civil registration districts and index of place names is available on the GENUKI website, www.ukbmd.org.uk/genuki/reg.

Every three months, local registrars' records of births, marriages and deaths were copied and sent to the General Register Office (GRO), which compiled its own indexes.

A mother's maiden name was not included in the birth indexes until 1911. For marriage indexes, the surnames of husband and wife (maiden name) were not listed together until 1912.

After 1866, a person's age at death was included in the GRO indexes (not local ones), so you could use this information to infer an approximate date of birth without the expense of ordering a death certificate, if you are certain you have found the correct person.

Photo postcard of the Sandford family, Christmas 1915.

The GRO indexes are divided into quarters for each year and give the place where the event was registered. You can order a copy certificate from the GRO (Section B) using the volume and page number references in the index. Local record offices and reference libraries may have microfilm copies of the GRO indexes.

The local register office indexes are not the same as the GRO indexes; you cannot use a local register office reference number to order a GRO certificate, or vice versa.

You can search the birth, marriage and death indexes, formerly called the St Catherine's House indexes, of the GRO free on the FreeBMD website (the whole index has not yet been transcribed), www.freebmd.org.uk.

Case Study

The marriage certificate dated 29 September 1890 of the author's great-great-grandfather Arthur Lomas to Sarah Ellen Frith at the Church of St James, Higher Broughton, Salford, gives his age as 21; hence he was born sometime around 1869.

Always allow some leeway for birth dates when searching just in case your ancestor mistook the date (or told a fib!) when filling in forms.

A search of the FreeBMD birth indexes for 'Arthur' plus 'Lomas' from March 1868 to December 1869 elicits six results including an Arthur Lomas born at Leek in October–December 1868.

The author knew from family information that the Lomas family came from Longnor, in Staffordshire, so this was a promising lead. The FreeBMD index gives the GRO reference as Volume 6b, page 261, and the author could have used this to order a birth certificate.

Alternatively, a search of the Staffordshire BMD index site (www.StaffordshireBMD.org.uk) for 1868 confirms that an Arthur Lomas was born that year and the author used the reference found to order his birth certificate from Newcastle-under-Lyme Register Office.

The certificate gives Arthur's date of birth as 24 October 1868 at Reapsmoor, Fawfieldhead, Staffordshire. His father was John Henry Lomas, joiner; his mother was Elizabeth and her maiden name was Fowler. Elizabeth registered Arthur's birth on 16 November 1868 at Longnor, in the registration district of Leek, Staffordshire. She signed her name with an 'X' (so she was illiterate), and gave her residence as Reapsmoor.

Many people did not bother to register their child's birth. After 1875 fines were introduced for non-registration. If you have a common surname, and there are many likely births for an ancestor in the civil registration indexes, it can be prohibitively expensive to buy a certificate for each one in the hope of finding your ancestor.

If you cannot find a birth or death certificate for your child ancestor, or there are several possibilities for a particular ancestor, then check parish registers from the churches where they lived. Parish registers can also be used to trace ancestors born long before civil registration.

Parish Registers

From 1538 the clergyman of each parish recorded every baptism, wedding and burial in his church. The quality and quantity of information gathered varies according to date. Early registers just give the child's name; later, fathers' names begin to appear. From the mid-1600s, names of both parents may be noted, and possibly a brief address.

From 1812, when a child was baptised, the clergyman noted a parent's occupation and residence as well as names of parents and child. Until this date it was rare for the father's name to be recorded when an illegitimate child was baptised.

A child may have been baptised several weeks (sometimes even years!) after its birth, so a baptismal record is only a rough guide to a child's date of birth.

Case Study

The Church Stretton parish register records the baptism on 18 August 1776 of Elizabeth, 'an illegitimate daughter of Hannah Urwick' in St Lawrence's Church. The burial of 'Elizabeth Urwick, infant' is recorded on 1 November 1778 (W.G.D. Fletcher (ed.), *Shropshire Parish Registers, Diocese of Hereford, Vol. VIII* (Shropshire Parish Register Society, 1911)).

You may be able to find the father or 'putative' father of an illegitimate child using Poor Law records (Chapter 2) or quarter sessions records (Chapter 5). Illegitimate children may be referred to as a 'base' son or daughter, or just plain 'bastard'. See Ruth Paley, *My Ancestor was a Bastard* (Society of Genealogists, 2011).

Some churches (particularly Methodist) kept 'cradle rolls' or 'cradle roll registers' in addition to baptism registers. Cradle rolls were lists of infants.

Parents entered their child on the roll, usually when it was christened. The child was sent a birthday card annually, and when old enough, invited to attend Sunday school. Parents were given a cradle roll certificate recording the child's date of birth and date of enrolment. Cradle rolls, registers and sometimes certificates can be found with parish records.

In 1754 Hardwicke's Marriage Act required parishes to keep records of banns and marriages in specially printed books. This Act also required everyone's marriage (unless a Quaker or Jew) to be solemnised in an Anglican church; this requirement lasted until 1837. If you cannot find a record of a marriage in a parish register, the couple may have been married by special licence. Record offices may hold copies of marriage licences and supporting paperwork such as marriage bonds and allegations.

Until the Age of Marriage Act of 1929 increased the marriage age to 16 years, boys aged 14 and girls aged 12 were permitted to marry, although in practice it was unusual for children this young to wed. Parents' consent was needed for minors under 21 to marry. See Rebecca Probert, *Marriage Law for Genealogists* (Takeaway Publishing, 2012).

If your ancestors were Roman Catholics, they may have been baptised or married twice: once in an Anglican church, and again secretly in a church of their own faith. Roman Catholic records may include registers of children's sacrament.

Other parish records for children include lists of candidates for first communion and confirmation, confirmation registers, and communion and confirmation certificates.

Infant mortality was extremely high for both rich and poor families during the nineteenth century. Sadly, this means that your ancestor's childhood may have been extremely brief; check burial registers and civil registration death indexes. Burial records in early registers were entered in the same volume as baptisms, and just give the child's name and date. After 1812, burials were recorded in a separate register, and the child's name, age, residence and date of burial were noted. Names of parents were sometimes included.

The Federation of Family History Societies (FFHS) has compiled a National Burial Index for England and Wales. It includes Nonconformist and other burials as well as Anglican, but not monumental inscriptions. Your local archives or reference library may have a copy. You can buy it on CD-ROM: www.ffhsservices.com/National-Burial-Index-Ed.-3-23.

Parish registers and Bishops' Transcripts (BTs) are deposited with the current diocesan record office (usually the local record office), but parish registers still in use will be at the church.

Photo postcard of mother and baby, *c.* 1910.

Parish registers for several counties have been published by parish register societies, family history and local history societies. The Society of Genealogists library has the largest collection of copies of parish registers in the UK.

Every year, Anglican parishes sent copies or transcripts of their registers to the bishop of the diocese. BTs are very useful if the original register has been lost. BTs are usually, but not always, kept at the diocesan record office; local record offices may have copies on microfilm.

For some counties such as Cornwall, Lancashire and Somerset, volunteers ('online parish clerks') have transcribed parish registers and other genealogical information and put it online free to view. Some online parish clerks will answer email enquiries, www.genuki.org.uk/indexes/OPC.html.

The FreeReg website has free transcripts of millions of baptism, marriage and burial registers, www.freereg.org.uk.

Several genealogical publications are available including Stuart A. Raymond, *Birth and Baptism Records for Family Historians* (Family History Partnership, 2010), Colin D. Rogers, *The Family Tree Detective* (Manchester University Press, 2008) and David Annal and Audrey Collins, *Birth, Marriage and Death Records* (Pen & Sword, 2012).

If you are searching parish registers dated before 1752, remember that prior to that date, the new year began on 25 March, not 1 January. See Cliff Webb, *Dates and Calendars for The Genealogist* (Society of Genealogists, 1989).

Stillbirths

There was no national register for stillbirths in England and Wales until 1 July 1927. Copy certificates for stillbirths cannot be ordered using the usual procedure: the Registrar General has to give permission first. Certificates can only be ordered by the child's mother or father, or a sibling if the parents are deceased. The dates of the parents' deaths must be submitted with the application. A certificate can be ordered by telephone or by writing to the GRO at Southport, bit.ly/zDt0Nu.

The Historic Stillbirths Register 1551–2005 is a new and growing resource available on CD-ROM. Currently, the register contains over 10,000 transcriptions of records of stillbirths.

For example, the Wakefield Borough Burial Ground (West Yorkshire) register includes the burial on 11 December 1869, in grave no. 789, of a stillborn child of the Craven family, residence Bridge Street. Coverage varies from county to county and not all years are included yet. Updates are available as more records are added to the register, http://anguline.co.uk/stillbirths.html.

FamilySearch

The FamilySearch website is a very good starting point for tracing your family tree in England and Wales. It hosts the International Genealogical Index compiled by the Church of Jesus Christ of Latter-Day Saints. The index includes transcripts from parish registers, Nonconformist register indexes, militia and workhouse records, school records, indexes to censuses, merchant navy service records, Chelsea Pensioners' Service records, etc. Images are available for some records, or alternatively a web-link to a subscription website where you can view the original record, https://familysearch.org, https://familysearch.org/search/collection/igi.

FamilySearch Record Centres (Section B) have copies of parish registers, censuses and other records on microfilm.

Nonconformist Registers

Baptists, Salvationists and members of the Society of Friends (Quakers) did not baptise their children, but they kept registers of births, marriages and burials. Nonconformist registers including Methodists, Wesleyans, Independents, Protestant Dissenters, Congregationalists and Quakers were surrendered to the Registrar General in the early 1840s, and more were transferred in 1857.

Nonconformist and non-parochial records can be viewed on microfilm at The National Archives (TNA) (series RG 4–8). These series are also indexed on the FamilySearch website.

The BMD Registers website (in partnership with TNA) is the official website for ordering copies of Nonconformist and non-parochial registers (fee payable). It includes some lying-in hospital records, www.bmdregisters. co.uk.

The Society of Genealogists has a guide to Nonconformist records at www.sog.org.uk/leaflets/nonconformists.pdf.

Quaker Records

Indexes or 'digests' were made of Quaker registers. These were arranged alphabetically and chronologically according to the initial letter of the surname (so if you are looking for a particular surname beginning with 'C', say, you will have to look through the whole 'C' section in case that surname crops up again later).

Digests are available on microfilm (some on CD–ROM) at FamilySearch centres, the Library of the Religious Society of Friends (which holds the originals) and the Society of Genealogists Library. Some local record offices also have copies for their area.

The Quaker Family History Society (QFHS) has published CD-ROMs of indexes to some digests, www.qfhs.co.uk/public_html/research/digest_mcf .htm.

'Monthly meeting' records such as minute books may include apprenticeships of Quaker children and 'settlement and removal' certificates (not to be confused with Poor Law settlement papers, see Chapter 2). When a Friend moved to another area, they took a certificate with them to show that they were of good character. These certificates included the names of a man's wife and any children under 16.

'Disownment' of a Friend occurred if they offended against Society rules, e.g. if a Friend had a child born out of wedlock. People who repented were 'reinstated' in the Society. Disownments and reinstatements are recorded in minute books.

Local record offices may hold Friends' minute books. The QFHS website has more detailed information. See E.H. Milligan and M.J. Thomas, *My Ancestors Were Quakers* (Society of Genealogists, 1999).

Salvation Army

Salvation Army babies receive a 'dedication' ceremony, not a baptism. A register of dedication includes register number, name of child, date of birth, place of birth (full address), date when dedicated, name of the hall where the ceremony took place, the name of the officer who conducted the dedication, the parents' names and the names of witnesses. The dedication certificate given to the family contains similar information to a baptismal certificate.

Registers still in use should be at the original hall (church). Many Salvation Army records were destroyed during the Second World War, but the Salvation Army International Heritage Centre in London holds some closed registers as well as dedication certificates and cradle roll certificates.

Jewish Records

Jews did not usually maintain specific birth records, so you must rely on the civil registration indexes. Births may have been announced in the *Jewish Chronicle* newspaper (1841 onwards).

A few local record offices (e.g. Tyne and Wear) hold a 'Bris Milah' (Brit Milah) or register of circumcisions carried out on boys eight days old, but you must obtain special permission from the depositor to view these records. The Hartley Library at the University of Southampton (Section A4) has some circumcision registers in its collections of Anglo-Jewish archives.

See Rosemary E. Wenzerul, *Tracing Your Jewish Ancestors* (Pen & Sword, 2008) and Anthony Joseph, *My Ancestor was Jewish*, 4th edn (Society of Genealogists, 2008).

Family life for poor people in the 1860s. John Leech, 'Pictures of Life and Character', *Punch* (Bradbury & Evans, 1863).

If you cannot find a birth or baptism, marriage, death or burial record for your ancestor, you could try checking Medical Officer of Health records or hospital records (Chapter 6).

Medical Officer of Health (MOH) Records

Infant mortality was particularly high in the crowded cities but even in rural districts, disease could spread quickly in places like schools. In the metropolis of London in 1839, even for genteel families, over 1 in 4 deaths were children under 10 years old. In rural Herefordshire, over one-third of deaths was children under 10. Edwin Chadwick, *Inquiry into The Sanitary Condition of the Labouring Population of Great Britain* (London, 1842).

Sanitation was poor in town and country; medical science was in its infancy, and the causes of disease only imperfectly understood. The Public Health Act (1848) saw the introduction of local health boards, but it was not compulsory for them to appoint a qualified medical practitioner as Medical Officer of Health until the Public Health Act of 1872.

The MOHs kept records and reported on infectious diseases. J.G. Bride, Medical Officer of Health for Runcorn, noted in 1882 that an epidemic of scarlet fever in the Frodsham and Halton townships, which had killed eight children (some were younger than 5), swiftly died down after the authorities closed all schools in the area (CALS LRR/19/1).

The Notification of Births Act 1907 required medical practitioners in local authorities to notify MOHs of each birth within 48 hours. When a MOH knew that a child had been born, he asked health visitors to visit mother and baby to check that both were well. This Act was not compulsory, however, and not all local authorities adopted the system.

Medical Officers of Health kept registers of the births notified to them (some kept their own unofficial registers of stillbirths). The MOH ledger for Nantwich Urban District Council records the birth of a 'male child' to 'Mrs Broomfield' of '32 Welch Row' at 3 am on 26 September 1910. The birth was notified by Mrs Platt, the midwife. No details are given for the boy's father (CALS LUN 52).

The Notification of Births Extension Act (1915) made it compulsory for MOHs to be notified of children's births, but some boroughs such as Camberwell refused to fund health visitors.

You can also estimate a date of birth from a secondary source such as a death certificate, burial record, memorial inscription, census return, pension record, etc.

Memorial Inscriptions

Memorial or monumental inscriptions are particularly useful because they sometimes record information not easily available elsewhere, especially before civil registration. The ages of relatives recorded on memorials may only be approximate, however.

Case Study

The author found the grave of her great-great-great-grandfather John Henry Lomas and his parents John and Ann Lomas in the graveyard of St Bartholomew's Church, Longnor, Staffordshire. The inscription records the names of John Lomas's first wife Sarah and three children, all previously unknown to the author:

> In memory of John Lomas of Reaps Moor who died Oct 6th 1865 age 60, also of Sarah his wife who died Oct 6th 1840 aged 38 years, also of Thomas their son who died Jan 21st 1835 aged 5 years, also of Asenath their daughter who died Jan 23rd 1835 aged 18 months, also of Adah their daughter who died Jan 30th 1835 aged 3 years. Also of Ann second wife of the above who died August 31st 1886 aged 76 years. Also of John Henry their son who died February 10th 1887 aged 44 years.

Civil Service

The Society of Genealogists' Library has a unique collection for the Civil Service. Civil servants needed to provide proof of their age for a pension. The collection (1752–1948) covers some 60,000 individuals. Proofs of age include testimonial letters and copies of birth certificates; sometimes the documents include family information. The collection is indexed on Findmypast, www.findmypast.co.uk/civil-service-evidence-of-age-search-start.action.

Adoptions

Until the 1920s, adoptions were usually informal arrangements; only the wealthy could afford complex legal proceedings in chancery. You may find children who were fostered or boarded out in Poor Law records (Chapter 2). There was no formal process for adoption until the Adoption of Children Act of 1926, which came into effect the following year. It is difficult to find adoption records prior to that date, although some charities such as the Children's Society arranged adoptions and kept records.

Adoption registers or records of relevant court proceedings may be in petty sessions records or local authority social service records in local archives. Further help on locating adoption records, birth relatives such as parents or siblings, or relatives through adoption can be found online (Section C) or via the addresses listed in Sections A2 and B. The official adoption register is on the government website, https://www.gov.uk/adoption-records/the-adoption-contact-register.

The Adoption Search Reunion website has a 'Locating Adoption Records' database (another contact register, AAA-NORCAP, closed in 2013).

Some genealogy subscription websites such as TheGenealogist offer an adoption search service (using a professional genealogist's expertise). Ancestry has an adoption queries online message board, http://boards.ancestry.co.uk/topics.adoption.adoption/mb.ashx.

Jewish adoption records, and certificates of evidence of Jewish birth, are held by the Ecclesiastical Court of the Chief Rabbi (Beth Din); a fee is charged for all enquiries.

Advances in scientific techniques such as deoxyribonucleic acid (DNA) testing have made it possible to trace the history of a particular surname, infer genetic links with other individuals (such as proof of paternity) and disprove genetic connections. This is a complex topic; see Debbie Kennett and Chris Pomery, *DNA and Social Networking: A Guide to Genealogy in the 21st Century* (History Press, 2011).

Friendly Society and Insurance Records

Before the National Insurance Act of 1911 and the advent of the National Health Service in 1948, poor people had little protection if they became ill. If the breadwinner did not work, he did not get paid, unless he was a member of a friendly society or trade union.

Some friendly societies provided sickness benefits; others were burial clubs for funeral expenses (a pauper's funeral paid for by the parish was considered shameful). Child workers occasionally paid contributions to friendly societies.

Parents enrolled their children in burial clubs (sometimes more than one). Following lurid claims that poor people were murdering their offspring to profit from their death, the Friendly Societies Act of 1846 banned the membership of children under 6 years of age in burial clubs (Anthony S. Wohl, *Endangered Lives: Public Health in Victorian Britain* (Methuen & Co., 1984)). From this date, friendly societies had to be registered (series FS at TNA).

Although friendly societies were numerous, not many records can be found in local record offices; surviving records may include rulebooks (deposited with the clerk of the peace), registers of members, death certificates, records of contributions with name and age of member, details of funeral expenses and so on.

People's life-insurance records may include names of dependent wives and children. Parents took out life-insurance policies for their children, such as fixed term policies and annuities. Some people took out education endowment policies to pay for a child's education fees. For example, the National Provident Society offered an endowment policy which paid a lump sum when a child was 14 (*Report from the Select Committee on Friendly Societies* (1852)).

Insurance policies or certificates may be at local record offices in family papers, or mentioned in legal documents such as wills or marriage settlements.

The records of the Aviva Archive at Norwich date back over 300 years. There is no specific series of records for policies related to children; survival for life-policy records is patchy. For some companies, no records have survived, but the archive has an excellent collection for others such as Norwich Union.

Information in the records typically includes policy number, name, address, age, occupation (e.g. 'scholar' for children), term, premium and so on. The Norwich Union collection includes a series of proposal forms and referees' letters with information on the life to be insured: place of birth, details of physical characteristics, medical and family history (not all records have survived for each policy).

Life-insurance policies at the Aviva Archive are organised by policy number, determined by the date the policy began. There is no surname index to the policies, so to trace an individual, you must know the policy number or date when the policy began. The archive holds registers of death claims for some years, so if you know a date of death and the archive has a register for that time then it is possible to find the claim, which gives the policy number, allowing one to find the policy in the register (if still extant).

If your ancestor had a policy taken out over 100 years ago with one of Aviva's constituent companies, contact the Group Archivist (Section A3). Search the Aviva website by insurance company name to check if the Archive holds its records, www.aviva.com/about-us/heritage/companies-and-countries.

Newspapers and Magazines

Newspaper announcements are a great way of tracing ancestors' births, marriages and deaths. Local reference libraries and record offices hold copies of local newspapers on microfilm. However, searching old newspapers has become much easier thanks to the Internet. Some library services subscribe to online resources such as *The Times* Digital Library, the *Guardian* and the *Observer* Digital Archive and the British Library 19th Century Newspapers Archive. This collection contains British national and regional newspapers from 1800 to 1900.

British Newspapers Archive, 1700–1949

This ever-growing online resource hosts digital images of local newspapers such as the *Birmingham Daily Post* or *Derby Daily Telegraph* (not all dates or publications are available yet). Search the archive by personal name, date or location. Searching is free but you must purchase 'time-limited' credits to view images, www.britishnewspaperarchive.co.uk.

Historical Magazines

Reference libraries may have copies of the *Gentleman's Magazine* (1731–twentieth century), which is extremely useful for ancestors born before civil registration. This journal printed birth, marriage and death notices for middle and upper-class people (working-class folk with unusual life stories are mentioned), obituaries of eminent people including writers or clergymen, and pedigrees for notable families.

Case Study

It is unusual to find an obituary for a child. The *Gentleman's Magazine* for February 1827 published a lengthy tribute to 7-year-old George-William Strong, son of 'the Rev. William and Susanna Strong, of Stanground, Hunts.', written by his grief-stricken father. This little 'angel', who was gifted with 'uncommon strength of intellect and unusual manliness of disposition', died at Woodbridge, Suffolk on 7 January and was buried 'in a pretty graveyard at Great Bealings'.

The Internet Library of Early Journals has some copies of the *Gentleman's Magazine* (1731–50) and *Annual Register* (1758–78), www.bodley.ox.ac.uk /ilej.

Wills, Probate and Legal Records

Wills and administration orders ('admons') may list children who were alive when the will was written. Although you are unlikely to find a child ancestor who left a will, it is not impossible. Prior to 1849 (when the law changed so that wills made by people aged under 21 were invalid), boys aged 14 and girls aged 12 could make a will disposing of their goods and chattels (personal property), but not land.

Solicitors' records deposited at local archives may include wills; if a solicitors' firm acted as executor for a person's estate, its records could contain details of payments or correspondence relating to children mentioned in the will.

Before 1858 wills were proved in the ecclesiastical (Church) courts. For southern England and much of Wales, the Prerogative Court of Canterbury (PCC) was used. The Prerogative Court of York (PCY) was used for probate in the northern counties. The court where a will was proved (archdeacon's, bishop's or archbishop's) depended on where a person died, the location of their property, and its value. TNA at Kew holds PCC wills (PROB 10, PROB 11) and death-duty registers; indexes are available online. The Society of Genealogists library and FamilySearch Centres also have indexes to wills. See TNA Guide to Wills and Probate Records, www.nationalarchives.gov.uk/records/research-guides/wills-and-probate-records.htm.

The National Wills Index (British Origins) for pre-1858 wills and probate documents in England and Wales is online. Subscribers can order a hard copy, www.nationalwillsindex.com.

In 1858 ecclesiastical courts ceased to have responsibility for probate. For England and Wales, wills and administrations after 1858 are held by the Probate Service. The National Probate Calendar, an index to these records, can be viewed at the Probate Search Room at the London Probate Registry. Partial indexes can be found at local probate registries, the Guildhall Library, the Society of Genealogists and on the Ancestry website.

You can apply for a wills search by post to Leeds District Probate Registry (Section B); give details of the deceased's full name, last known address and approximate date of death if known.

See Stuart Raymond, *The Wills of Our Ancestors* (Pen & Sword, 2012) and Karen Grannum and Nigel Taylor, *Wills and Probate Records: A Guide for Family Historians*, 2nd edn (TNA, 2009).

Children may be mentioned in legal records such as articles of agreement, tenancy agreements, estate or household accounts, property deeds or leases (to provide an income for a person's children), mortgages, guardianship papers and deeds of separation (between husband and wife). 'Leases for lives' ensured continuity of tenancy for a family, and these documents can cover several generations. Legal records may be found in solicitors' records, family or estate papers.

Census Records

From the early nineteenth century, the government carried out a census of the population every ten years. The census returns for 1841–1911 are an invaluable resource for exploring your ancestor's childhood.

Every householder filled in a form ('schedule') listing each person in the household, their name, age, occupation and place of birth. Officials or 'enumerators' visited each home, collected the schedules and compiled 'returns' for each area. The information gathered for each census became more detailed over time.

The 1911 census is the only one released to date for which the household schedules have survived; you can see your ancestor's handwriting on these forms. This particular census included a 'women's fertility' question. Women were asked how long they had been married, how many children were born alive during their marriage, how many were still alive and how many had died.

> ### Case Study
> In 1911 the author's great-grandparents William Kirkwood Dickman (53) and his wife Annie Mary (50) lived at 375 Bolton Road, Pendlebury, Lancashire. Annie had had fourteen children, but only ten were still alive. Four children still lived at home: miner Herbert (19), iron turner Albert (17), Frank (13) and Doris (8); the last two had no occupation (RG 14/23970/105, copyright TNA and courtesy Ancestry).

Sometimes the householder made mistakes when filling in the form. So, for example, a parent might have listed all the children of the marriage before realising that only the ones still living at home should be entered on the form. Or a widow might have mistakenly answered the 'fertility question', even though this information was not required from widows.

Use caution when inferring a date of birth from a census entry. A person may not have known their exact age. Whenever possible, you should check the date of birth against the civil registration indexes or parish registers. You may find a person's place of birth varying slightly from census to census, too, which can be confusing, so it's best to find the family in as many census years as possible.

The FreeCen website (www.freecen.org.uk) is a database of census transcripts from 1841–91. Some counties and census years are incomplete, but it is free, www.freecen.org.uk/statistics.html.

Several genealogy subscription services (e.g. Ancestry, Findmypast,

TheGenealogist, Genes Reunited) provide indexes to the censuses (by name, location and date) and digitised images of the records.

Indexes to transcripts of the 1881 census are available free from the FamilySearch, Ancestry and Findmypast websites (the latter two are free to search, pay to view images).

Tip

Indexes to censuses were compiled by volunteers. The original census schedules are sometimes illegible, so the names in the indexes are not always accurately transcribed. If you cannot find an ancestor or their family in the online indexes, try using a 'wildcard' search: the first few letters of a name plus an asterisk, e.g. a search for 'Hig*' would find all names beginning with those three letters such as Higginson, Higgs, Higson, Higginbotham, etc. Or search using a keyword such as a person's occupation, if this search facility is available. Alternatively, look for other members of the same family if known; they may be living in a nearby street. Some genealogy services have an address search facility.

Many guides to census records have been published, including Stuart Raymond, *The Census 1801–1911: A Guide for the Internet Era* (Family History Partnership, 2009) and Peter Christian and David Annal, *Census: The Expert Guide* (TNA, 2008).

Census records (dates and coverage varies) can be accessed on microfilm at TNA, local record offices and reference libraries. These institutions often offer free access on site to one of the genealogy subscription services.

Addresses can also be found from trade or street directories, telephone directories and electoral registers (local record offices). There are some examples on the Electoral Registers website, www.electoralregisters.org.uk.

Family Photographs

Do you have photographs in your family album, but no information about the sitters or the date when it was taken? If there is enough detail in the image, you may be able to use clues from people's hairstyles, hats and clothes to obtain an approximate date. Several guides to dating photographs have been published, including Jayne Shrimpton, *How to Get the Most From Family Pictures* (Society of Genealogists, 2011) and Robert Pols, *Dating Nineteenth Century Photographs* (FFHS, 2005) and companion volume *Dating Twentieth Century Photographs* (FFHS, 2005).

'Cabinet card' of a well-to-do family photographed in a Southsea studio, *c.* 1890.

Upper-Class Ancestors

If your ancestors were wealthy or of noble blood, then their family tree may have been printed in publications such as *Burke's Peerage and Baronetage* (1826 onwards) or *Debrett's Peerage*. Some library services offer their members access to the Oxford Dictionary of National Biography online.

The Society of Genealogists Library has a collection of peerages and publications such as Edward Walford's *County Families* (1860–1920) and *Kelly's Handbook to the Titled, Landed and Official Classes* (1880 onwards).

The College of Arms is the official repository for coats of arms and pedigrees in England and Wales. The Heraldry Society also has information on family pedigrees and coats of arms.

Burke's Peerage has an online database (subscription needed), www.burkespeerage.com/welcome.aspx. The Peerage website is free and has surname indexes, www.thepeerage.com.

Locating Archives

Family archives of personal papers such as letters, diaries or journals, estate papers, account books, bill payments, etc. may be deposited with local record offices. Family or business records may be held by more than one archive.

Several finding aids are available to locate archives for people, businesses and organisations.

The National Register of Archives (NRA) index can be searched by corporate name, family name, personal papers or alphabetical listings, www.nationalarchives.gov.uk/nra. The NRA index includes links to the ARCHON directory, a database of archives in the UK and elsewhere, with contact details, www.nationalarchives.gov.uk/archon.

The Access to Archives (A2A) search engine is easy to use, although it has not been updated for several years. You can search for the locations of parish registers, school records, Poor Law records, quarter sessions records, wage books, staff records, photographs and records of organisations such as youth clubs, Brownie packs, etc., http://nationalarchives.gov.uk/a2a/.

Use the Archives Hub to locate specialist collections, http://archiveshub.ac.uk.

However, that nugget of information you seek may not be available online. Not all archives have full online catalogues and you may need to search through an archive's card indexes, paper catalogues or finding aids to locate a particular record.

Access to Children's Records

Archives and repositories almost always restrict access to records relating to persons who are (or may be) still alive if they contain sensitive information as specified by the Data Protection Act. Each archive operates its own policy, and access may be at the archivist's discretion. There are no national guidelines. The archivist may request proof that the relative concerned is deceased.

School archives that still hold their own records such as admission registers may only operate a thirty-year closure rule. Local record offices may keep access to school or institutional records closed for up to 100 years, depending on their policy.

Many records mentioned in this book are subject to restricted access, and are likely to be closed for 100 years, particularly for children who lived in institutions, were in local authority care or were adopted.

An archive's catalogue normally specifies the length of time for which records are closed to public access. Contact the archivist if you are unsure whether a particular document is available, particularly if you live a long way from the relevant archive.

Tip

You may be able to gain access to a restricted record via a 'freedom of information request' under the Freedom of Information Act 2000. Local record offices may charge for this service.

Most files in the Home Office series at TNA that relate to individual children are closed for at least seventy-five years. If you wish to submit a 'freedom of information request' for access to a closed file held at TNA, Kew, there's guidance on its website, www.nationalarchives. gov.uk/foi/requests. htm.

Because the bulk of Britain's wealth and lands belonged to a minority of the population (and still do), it's far more likely that your ancestor was from the 'middling' or professional classes, or one of the millions of labouring poor. The poor have always been with us, and society's attempts to deal with this perennial problem have left a rich vein of records for 'paupers', especially children.

Chapter 2

CHILDREN AND THE POOR LAW

W ho should care for orphans, the old, sick and infirm, and unemployed persons? Does helping people discourage them from thrift and encourage them to breed? Whose money should pay for the burden of caring for the poor?

The way in which society addressed these problems had an immense impact, for good or ill, on our ancestors' childhoods. Until the twentieth century there was no welfare state funded by central government. Poor people's necessities were met by donations from charitable individuals or societies, or if in dire need, by the Poor Law authorities. Children's charities are discussed in Chapter 6.

The Old Poor Law

From the late sixteenth century, parish authorities (overseers and churchwardens) were responsible for looking after those people in their parish who could not afford, or were unable, to look after themselves. In some towns, such as Bristol, Hull and Norwich, boards of guardians (incorporations) were formed to care for the poor of several parishes.

Parish officials and boards of guardians levied rates from their wealthier inhabitants to pay for poor 'relief'. These officials decided which 'paupers' should receive relief. Children were directly affected by whether their families were classed as the 'deserving' or 'undeserving' poor.

Old people with no means of support, and the chronically sick, were given poor relief. Some people were deemed unable to work but deserving of help perhaps because they had a physical disability such as blindness, or because they suffered from a mental impairment ('imbeciles' or 'lunatics'). Widows with dependent children, orphans, children deserted by parents and illegitimate children were given relief.

Parish officials adopted a more robust attitude to unmarried pregnant females and the 'able-bodied' poor: unemployed workers (whether through illness or lack of work), workers whose wages were too low to support their families, beggars and 'vagrants' (tramps).

There were two forms of relief available. 'Out-relief' was dispensed to paupers in their own homes: gifts of food (e.g. bread, flour), money or the means for people to earn a living, such as a spinning-wheel. The parish also paid for medical care.

'Indoor relief' was given in the poorhouse or workhouse. The first workhouses or 'houses of industry' appeared in the late seventeenth century. The inmates, even children, worked in return for their bed and board. Child paupers at the Shrewsbury House of Industry (1784) learnt to read and write, but when they were 5 years old they were taught how to spin wool for the house's woollen factory.

Workhouses were sometimes 'farmed' out to an enterprising individual who agreed with the overseers to run the establishment for a fixed sum; the quality of the inmates' food, of course, was subject to his profit margins.

Parish officials devoted much time and effort to ensure that they only gave relief to 'their' paupers. A poor person could only receive relief in their legal place of 'settlement', where they had a 'right to remain'. Their settlement was not necessarily the place where they were born. Children (if legitimate) always took their father's settlement, even if he was not born in the parish where they lived.

A wife always took the same settlement as her husband, so if a widow remarried, her settlement became that of her new husband. Her children from her first marriage still kept their father's settlement, so if the family became chargeable to the parish (i.e. they needed help), her children could be taken away and sent back to their father's parish. An illegitimate child's settlement was in the parish where they were born.

A newcomer to a parish gained a settlement if they paid taxes, or paid more than £10 in rent, or held public office in the parish. Estate holders who lived in a parish for forty days gained a settlement. Travellers or tramps passing through a parish did not have to be removed to their place of settlement, as they were not staying permanently.

Unmarried servants, providing they lived in the parish for a year and received a full year's wage, gained a new settlement. Apprentices (over 7 years old) acquired a settlement after forty days' residence.

Newcomers to a parish could stay providing they had a settlement certificate from their 'home' parish. As soon as they became 'chargeable', people who asked for relief, such as a pregnant unmarried girl, faced removal to their 'home' parish. The parish overseers applied to local magistrates for a 'removal order'. If a person was ill, but had no settlement in the parish, their removal order was suspended until they were well enough to travel.

If parish officials did not believe that a poor person was entitled to relief, the person was examined before the magistrates. These 'settlement examinations' can include very detailed biographical information about a person and their family. Because apprenticeship conferred a settlement, details of apprenticeships may be found in examinations.

If a person convinced the magistrate that they had a legitimate settlement, they were permitted to stay and given a certificate (although some parishes, such as Leeds or Skipton, never issued certificates). Persons who could not prove they had a settlement were forcibly removed to their last known place of settlement.

Case Study

Kirkdale Quarter Sessions records include a settlement examination of Mary Ellen Jones 'single woman' and her son John Andrew Jones, who lived in Toxteth Park Union and were in need. The magistrates examined Mary on 18 November 1842. Mary, who was 'about 23 years old . . . the daughter of Richard and Margaret Jones' believed that she was born 'in Norfolk St, Liverpool'. In 1832 'she was hired by Richard St. Paul of the Queen's Dock Hotel at the bottom of Norfolk St . . . as a yearly servant at the wages of £5 per annum'. Mary was in service there for about fourteen months and since that time had not acquired a settlement 'in her own right' elsewhere. Her 'male illegitimate child' John was born 'on or about the 17th day of February 1841' in Bell Street, Toxteth Park.

The magistrates decided that Mary and John were chargeable to the Liverpool authorities, not Toxteth Park, and signed an order for her removal, which was suspended on 29 December because the baby was poorly (LA QSP 3190/26, QSP3196/35).

Disputes between parishes over settlement cases can be found in quarter sessions records; sometimes cases were referred to higher courts.

If a girl was pregnant, and the child's alleged father had a settlement elsewhere, parish authorities might force or bribe him to marry the girl so that she and her baby became the responsibility of the father's parish.

Parson James Woodforde of Weston Longeville recorded one of these 'gunshot weddings' in his diary (23 September 1794): 'I . . . married by Licence, One Daniel Tabble of Ling and Anne Dunnel of Weston – a forced match – she being very near her time, and he under custody of the Parish Officers ever since Yesterday morning'.

Sometimes the luckless groom was handcuffed to a parish officer to stop him running away until after the ceremony was over. One imagines that forced weddings like this were unlikely to result in a happy marriage.

Magistrates could order people to pay for their children's and grandchildren's upkeep. The converse applied, too: if a person's parent or grandparent was unemployed or could not work, magistrates could order them to maintain them, although in practice it seems that this power was not used very often.

If a woman had an illegitimate child, magistrates took out a 'bastardy order', 'bastardy certificate', 'filiation order' or 'affiliation order', that is, a maintenance order forcing the father to pay for the upkeep of his child and its mother. Sometimes maintenance orders were called 'memorandums of agreement'.

The parish overseers gave money to the mother for her child, irrespective of whether the father paid for its maintenance or not. A mother was asked to contribute to their child's upkeep if for some reason she could not look after it.

Case Study
Bastardy Order

On 8 April 1800, Thomas Blake, 'yeoman' of Barton in Cheshire, was ordered to pay £1 5s to the parish for the 'lying-in' of Mary Hewitt, 'single woman', who bore a 'female bastard child' on 17 March 1800. The baby was chargeable to Barton township. Blake was ordered to pay 1s 6d weekly for the baby's maintenance. Mary was also ordered to pay 6d per week to the parish 'in case she shall not nurse and take care of the said child herself' (CALS: PC 19/6/6).

If a parish ordered a father to sign a 'bastardy bond', he not only agreed to pay maintenance but also offered a surety to the parish – a large lump sum – in case of default. Other members of his family, perhaps the child's grandfather, might sign the bond, too, and agree to pay the surety. Fathers who refused to pay maintenance, or deserted their family, could be committed to the local house of correction or Bridewell.

Parish overseers gave relief to the families of men who served in the local militia, and these maintenance orders list dependent children.

Several archives such as Surrey History Centre have calendared and indexed their bastardy records, and family history societies such as Lincolnshire FHS have published indexes of Poor Law records such as settlement examinations and removal orders.

Until the mid-eighteenth century, 'great numbers' of infants in the care of the parish authorities died before their fifth birthday. In one parish alone, of the fifty-four poor babies taken into the workhouse in twelve months, not one child outlived its first year (Jonas Hanway, *An Earnest Appeal for Mercy to the Children of the Poor* (London, 1766)).

Jonas Hanway (1712–86) was governor of the London Foundling Hospital. He campaigned vigorously on behalf of the unfortunate infants consigned to parish 'care'. Thanks to his efforts, from 1762, every parish in the metropolis kept a register of all infants under the age of 4.

When a child was born and taken into the workhouse, it was baptised within fourteen days (if not already baptised), and its name entered into the workhouse register; its name was also entered in the parish register. This legislation was called the 'act for keeping poor children alive' by ordinary people. Poor Law guardians and churchwardens were made publicly accountable for maintaining the registers.

Hanway argued that if pauper babies were sent to a paid foster mother in the countryside, they were more likely to survive than if left in the workhouse; parish nurses were notoriously careless. Even if a child's mother cared for it in the workhouse, the baby rarely survived.

Hanway's Act of 1767 made it compulsory for all infants in parish care in the London area to be boarded with foster mothers out of town. In 1778 Hanway's Acts were extended to cover all parish infants, not just those in the metropolis. Poor Law guardians' minute books and churchwardens' accounts include lists of children boarded out.

Parish Apprentices

Parish overseers had a statutory duty to apprentice out children in their care. These children might be orphans, or abandoned by their parents, or their parents were receiving parish relief. Once a child was apprenticed, it was no longer a financial burden on the parish.

In theory children receiving 'out-relief' at home could be apprenticed, but in practice only workhouse or poorhouse children were bound to masters. Girls were apprenticed until they were 21, or until they were married, whichever came first. Until 1767, London boy paupers were apprenticed from age 9 or 10 until they were 24. Hanway's Act of 1767 reduced parish apprenticeships for London children to 7 years, or a maximum age of 21. The law did not change for children outside London parishes until 1778, when the end of parish apprenticeship was fixed at age 21.

Because an apprentice gained a settlement in his new parish after forty days, this encouraged parish officials to bind him outside his home parish. Parish overseers did not need parents' consent for these apprenticeships. Children might not see their families for many years. Parents who objected risked having their poor relief cut or withdrawn.

Parish overseers forced unwilling ratepayers to take an apprentice if not enough tradesmen wanted a child. People resented being forced to feed and clothe an apprentice for many years, and some treated them harshly. Many

Oliver Twist's narrow escape from being apprenticed to a chimneysweep. Illustration by George Cruikshank, *The Adventures of Oliver Twist* (Chapman & Hall Ltd and Henry Frowde, *c.* 1905).

children were beaten or given insufficient food. Elizabeth Brownrigg was hanged at Newgate in 1767 after parish apprentice Mary Clifford, one of two young girls apprenticed to Elizabeth's husband, died following months of abuse.

An 1815 enquiry discovered that of the 5,815 children from London parishes apprenticed between 1802 and 1811, over 2,000 apprenticeships were away from their home parish (*Annual Register*, 1815).

When investigators tried to discover the whereabouts of the 2,026 children sent away, they found only 644 children still with the same master. Around 200 children had finished their term of service, 80 were dead and 18 unfit to work. There were 26 children in parish workhouses. Over 400 children could not be accounted for at all.

Parish children were apprenticed into many different trades: textiles, coal mining, farm labour, domestic service, the navy, fishing, chimney-sweeping, etc. The early factories needed a ready supply of cheap labour. Robert Blincoe from St Pancras parish was just one of hundreds of London pauper children sent to textile mills in Lancashire, Cheshire, Derbyshire and Nottinghamshire and even Scotland during the late eighteenth century.

The Apprentice House at Quarry Bank Mill, Styal. The Styal mill children were treated more humanely than at Holywell and some other factories. (© Nigel Wilkes)

The Lower Cotton Mill, Holywell, owned by Douglas & Co. Engraving by W.C. Wilson, 1792.

Apprentices were housed near the mills. Some mill-owners like Samuel Greg at Quarry Bank Mill took care of his child apprentices, but other apprentices fared less well, like those at the Holywell Twist Co. in Wales. These children worked a 16-hour day.

In 1844 the law forcing ratepayers to take compulsory apprentices was repealed. Stricter legislation was introduced to prevent cruelty after several high-profile prosecutions involving parish apprentices. Orphan Jane Wilbred was apprenticed by the West London Union workhouse to Mr and Mrs Sloane in London as a domestic servant in 1851. She was starved and abused by the Sloanes. Later the Poor Law Board stopped children being apprenticed into domestic service.

Apprenticeship Records

When a child was apprenticed, a legal document or 'indenture' was drawn up. Indentures recorded the child's name and age, date of binding, name and brief address of new master, the premium paid by the parish and conditions and length of service. A 'premium' of a few pounds sweetened the bargain for the master.

Police try to hold back an angry mob in Giltspur Street, London as George Sloane (accused of 'frightful cruelty' against his teenage servant Jane Wilbred) is taken before the magistrates. *Illustrated London News*, 4 January 1851.

Indentures for parish and private apprentices followed a standard formula: each apprentice promised 'faithfully' to serve his or her master 'in all lawful business, according to his Power, Wit and Ability'. Apprentices were not allowed to marry during their apprenticeship; they could not indulge in 'fornication', 'adultery', gambling or visit ale-houses.

Local record offices hold many examples of parish apprenticeship indentures, e.g. Greater Manchester County Record Office holds apprenticeship indentures for parish children sent to Quarry Bank Mill, Styal, from the 1790s to 1847 (series C5/5).

Some county archives have indexed their parish apprenticeship records and put them online (Sections A3, C).

Case Study

An apprenticeship indenture dated 2 June 1802 records that James Stopford, a 'poor boy' of the township of Rufford, 'aged about ten years' was apprenticed to Henry Caunce, 'husbandman', for nine years (LA DDHE/104/38).

In 1802 cotton magnate Sir Robert Peel (1750–1830) piloted a Health and Morals of Apprentices Act through Parliament after a deadly fever struck apprentices in his own factories. This Act required parishes to keep registers of children apprenticed to mill-owners.

Magistrates were ordered to appoint two visitors (one a clergyman, one a justice of the peace) to inspect mills and factories that employed parish apprentices; the visitors' reports were entered in a book kept by the clerk of the peace. Owners of mills had to register their premises with the clerk of the peace (quarter sessions records). However, this law was widely flouted.

A parish apprentice broke the law if they ran away; if caught, they could be imprisoned for breaking their indentures. An apprentice who was ill-treated could complain to a local magistrate (children were often too afraid of their master to do this). Quarter sessions records include disputes about apprenticeships.

Wealthy folk sometimes gave money or left bequests to apprentice poor children. Parish overseers were often made responsible for spending this money and these apprenticeship indentures can be found in parish records. Solicitors' records sometimes include fees for drawing up parish or charity apprenticeship indentures, bastardy papers or dealing with Poor Law settlement disputes.

Registers of parish apprentices, registers of children receiving out-relief, apprenticeship indentures, settlement examinations or certificates, bastardy bonds or certificates, maintenance payments to militia families and removal orders can be found in parish overseers' records, parish vestry records and board of guardian records in local record offices.

The New Poor Law

By 1834 so many people claimed parish relief that the authorities suspected the system was being widely abused; the impact of economic conditions on unemployment was not fully understood. The 1834 Poor Law Amendment Act was designed to slash poor rates and curtail alleged abuses of the system. More workhouses were built and the payment of out-relief slashed.

Workhouses were feared and hated by poor people. Inmates were segregated by age and sex, so families were split up when they entered the workhouse. Children, men and women were put in separate wards, and forced to wear a special uniform. People would do anything to avoid going into the workhouse (exactly the result the Poor Law commissioners had hoped for) and some starved rather than apply for relief.

A distressing case at Hackney was reported in 1856. Bricklayer Edward

Oliver Twist asks for more gruel in the workhouse. Illustration by George Cruikshank, *The Adventures of Oliver Twist* (Chapman & Hall Ltd and Henry Frowde, *c*. 1905).

Harvey and his partner Harriet Ray were charged with the 'wilful murder' of two of Harvey's children, William (7) and Harriet (5), after they starved to death at home. Edward had two more children, who survived. Harvey and Ray claimed that they shared all their food with the children. Harvey had refused to go into the workhouse, even though he had been given a ticket of admission. At the inquest on the dead children, the coroner commented:

'People do not like to go into the workhouse, and lose their liberty'. Harvey was found guilty of manslaughter; Ray was acquitted (*The Times*, 4 January and 10 January 1856).

Children in the workhouse were not necessarily orphans. If their parents were inmates, they were only allowed to see them once a week. Sometimes parents put their children in the workhouse as a temporary measure because they could not cope. A typical meal for a child in the workhouse was gruel, or a mixture of bread, milk and water, or bread and butter – hardly adequate for growing children.

Poor Law Union Records

Several different classes of records are available for workhouse children: registers of births, baptisms, deaths, admission and discharge registers, punishment books, creed registers, registers of 'lunatics' and so on.

Registers of births show date of birth, sex of child, name of parent or mother (sometimes aliases for the mother are recorded), the parish from which the mother was admitted, when and where the child was baptised (e.g. 'in workhouse'), baptismal name and if the child died before being baptised. 'Remarks' may mention if a child was stillborn or one of a multiple birth. Registers of deaths include name of deceased, date of death, age, parish admitted from and where buried.

Case Study

The register of deaths for Great Boughton workhouse lists the death on 1 April 1869 of an infant surnamed Smith from Broxton parish. The baby, who only lived for 2 hours, was buried in Chester Cemetery (CALS ZHC/9). If we turn to the register of births for Great Boughton workhouse, we find that on 31 March 1869, Hannah Smith from Broxton gave birth to an unnamed female infant, who died before being baptised (CALS ZHC/7).

If you have obtained a birth certificate for your ancestor, you may not realise that they were born in a workhouse or former workhouse such as a hospital. After 1904 registrars put the street address (sometimes with a fictitious house number), not the name of the institution, on workhouse children's birth certificates (the same principle applied to death certificates, too). All reference to a workhouse was omitted. Some registrars continued this practice for several years after the Poor Law ended.

Workhouse admission and discharge registers were daily logs of people entering and leaving the institution. Child beggars or tramps formed a small proportion of workhouse inmates. On the night of Sunday 14 December 1845, from a total of 1,721 'vagrants and trampers' given aid in England and Wales workhouses, 121 boys and 77 girls were under 16 (*13th Annual Report of the Poor Law Commissioners* (1847)).

The Banbury Union Workhouse built separate wards for male and female beggars in 1838; those admitted were given a supper of bread and cheese and a bed for the night. Beggars were not given breakfast unless they performed 4 hours' work first. However, child vagrants and those unable to work were allowed breakfast without having to work.

It can take some detective work to follow a particular individual's comings and goings, especially the 'in-and-outs', i.e. regular visitors.

After 1868 institutions such as workhouses kept creed registers (recording inmates' religious faith) and these registers can be used as an index to the admission and discharge registers. Unlike admission registers, these records are arranged in rough alphabetical order, so they are easier to navigate.

The registers record a wealth of detail including: date when entry was made in the register, date of person's admission, name, date of birth, religion, occupation, where from, reason for admission, date when discharged (or died in the workhouse) and address of next of kin.

Case Study

On 29 January 1879, Thirza Ashton and her daughters Eliza, Jessica and Alice entered Chester Workhouse. The creed register (1860–80) shows that Thirza was born in 1839, Eliza in 1870, Jessica in 1873 and Alice in 1875. They were from Holy Trinity Parish; their religion was Church of England. Thirza was the wife of Henry, a 'chair-maker' who had deserted her: he 'worked for Mr Garner'. Mother and daughters were discharged the next day at Thirza's request.

On 7 April 1879, Thirza, Jessica and Alice (but not Eliza) were admitted again. A note says that Henry Ashton 'works at Mr Icke's, Watergate Row'. On 14 August, Thirza, Jessica and Alice were 'removed to London' (CALS ZTRU/18).

Each workhouse kept a 'punishment book' for inmates, even children, who were deemed to have misbehaved. These books recorded each instance where inmates had been 'refractory or disorderly', gave details of each offence, punishment given and the date, and noted whether the case had been reported to the Poor Law guardians.

Case Study

The story of one young lad's life in Chorley Union Workhouse can be explored in its punishment book. In 13 July 1872, John Silk and three other boys were 'severely punished with a rod, and sent to bed' because a few days earlier they 'repeatedly left the House for the purpose of bathing in the canal and brook'. On 3 October, John was 'severely caned' for 'soiling his clothes unnecessarily'.

The following year, John and another boy, Bernard Hodson, were 'caned by the Master' on 18 September for 'neglecting to make their beds and making a disturbance in the Bedroom' that day. A few weeks later, John was in hot water yet again on 4 December when he and two other boys were given dry bread for their meals for 'using bad language and fighting' (LA PUX/7).

Workhouse registers may be found in Poor Law union or hospital records (Chapter 6) because many former workhouses became hospitals after the Poor Law ended.

Poor Law guardians were responsible for overseeing the vaccination acts. Smallpox was a killer disease; as many as one in four of the people who caught it died. Children were most at risk. Survivors of this terrible illness were left scarred or disfigured for life. In 1796, Edward Jenner (1749–1823) experimented on a boy named Phipps, and proved that if a person was inoculated with cow-pox virus, they did not catch smallpox.

In the late eighteenth and early nineteenth centuries, some parish vestries such as Bozeat in Northamptonshire (1789) and Clifton in Bedfordshire (1825) inoculated their parishioners against smallpox.

A ghastly epidemic in 1837, which killed over 40,000 people in England and Wales, led to the 1840 Vaccination Act. Poor Law guardians paid doctors to vaccinate every person resident in their parish or union (not just workhouse children). Each child was vaccinated when 6 weeks old unless it was 'delicate' or poorly, in which case inoculation was postponed until the child was well enough.

There was no charge for vaccination: the first free medical service in England and Wales. Although the cost of vaccination was met from the poor rates, this was a public health measure, not parish 'relief'.

In each Poor Law union a vaccination officer compiled a report book or register of vaccination, using extracts from the registers of births for his area. The register included details of each child's name, sex, date of birth, place where born, name and surname of father (or mother if the child was illegitimate), parent's profession and the date of the medical certificate issued to confirm when the child was vaccinated.

If a child died before it could be vaccinated, its date of death was recorded in the register. In addition to the registers, you may discover certificates of 'successful vaccination' or of 'postponed' vaccinations.

Case Study

The vaccination register for Frodsham District in Runcorn Union, Cheshire for July 1875–January 1877 records the vaccination of Mary Ellen Clarke. Mary, the daughter of Robert Clarke, a stone getter, was born on 30 May 1875 at Five Crosses in the township of Frodsham Lordship, Cheshire. Mary's mother (not named) was issued with a vaccination order on 10 July 1875, and a medical certificate of successful vaccination was issued on 26 October that year (CALS LG3/3).

Some children were not vaccinated until they were 2 or 3 years old, which put them at risk. Following a damning report by Sir John Pakington into the extent of vaccination, compulsory vaccination was introduced in 1853, but authorities did not have sufficient powers to enforce the law. Gaps in vaccination coverage were thought to be a major cause of the smallpox epidemic of 1871–2.

Because so many children slipped through the net, they may not appear in vaccination registers. However, boards of guardians kept registers of children who were not vaccinated, perhaps because their family had moved, or could not be traced or their parents were 'conscientious objectors'.

A significant minority of parents refused to allow their child to be vaccinated, perhaps because they did not understand the necessity, or because they had genuine fears about the safety of the vaccine. Parents were taken to court and fined if they refused to comply with the law.

In 1898 a new law permitted parents to 'opt out' of having their child vaccinated on grounds of conscience, providing they could persuade a magistrate to permit exemption. The 1907 Vaccination Act made it easier for parents to refuse their children's vaccination, and at the outbreak of the Second World War, only about one-third of the UK's children were inoculated. Quarter sessions records may have records of parents' fines or penalties under the vaccination acts or certificates of 'conscientious objection' against child vaccination.

Workhouse Schools and Children in Care

Metropolitan Poor Law authorities 'farmed out' their child paupers to private contractors to save money. These 'farm schools' were supposed to educate their inmates, and this was a common practice before and after the 1834 reforms, until a major scandal broke in the late 1840s.

Over 140 children, including 5-year-old Bridget Quin and 6-year-old James Andrews from Holborn Union, died in a cholera epidemic at a 'baby farm' at Tooting during the winter of 1848/9. Drouet's Pauper Establishment housed nearly 1,400 children. The proprietor, Peter Drouet, was paid 4s 6d (22½p) for each child by various parishes, but the food and accommodation he provided was disgustingly inadequate. Children slept three or four to a bed, were dressed in rags and lived on food such as rotten potatoes. The inquest jury found Drouet guilty of manslaughter, but when he was charged with the manslaughter of James Andrews later that year at the Central Criminal Court, the jury acquitted Drouet.

Poor Law authorities set up schools in, or attached to, workhouses. Henry Morton Stanley (born John Rowlands) was brought up by his grandfather; his mother did not want him. After his grandfather's death, he was sent to St Asaph Union Workhouse. Henry (1841–1904) never forgot the vicious beatings he endured there from its schoolmaster, ex-miner James Francis.

One day Henry rebelled during a flogging from Francis and knocked him down. He ran away and a cousin gave him a place as a pupil-teacher at a National School at Brynford, near Holywell.

The quality of education in workhouse schools depended on how much the board of guardians was prepared to pay for tuition. Some schools taught reading but not writing. Industrial training was much favoured, such as agricultural labour for boys and domestic skills for girls.

However, some workhouse schools, such as the one at Atcham in Shropshire in the mid-nineteenth century, educated their children to a higher standard than local elementary schools.

'Barrack schools', sometimes called 'district schools' or 'industrial schools', were sizeable residential institutions for workhouse children set up by large unions or a combination of several unions, like the school at Upper Norwood in Surrey.

Swinton Industrial School (1846) was one of the first large separate institutions for pauper children. In 1850 this 'palace' housed 630 children, of whom over 300 were orphans and 124 were 'deserted by their parents'. The junior section of the school had a playground where children 'were enjoying themselves in the sunshine . . . some were playing at marbles'. The children alternated school lessons with industrial training. The boys were taught shoe-making or tailoring; they made clogs and clothes for the schoolchildren. Girls were trained as domestic servants. (*A Day in a Pauper Palace, Household Words*, 13 July 1850.)

In 1853 the Poor Law Board reported that 33,766 children attended workhouse and district schools. Only about 900 of these children attended district schools (*5th Annual Report of the Poor Law Board* (1853)).

Table 1

Average Number of Children Attending Workhouse Schools During the Half-year Ended Lady Day, 1852	
Boys under the age of 10	8,016
Boys over the age of 10	9,273
Girls under the age of 10	8,572
Girls over the age of 10	7,067
Average Number of Children Attending District Schools During the Half-year Ended Lady Day, 1852	
Boys under the age of 10	229
Boys over the age of 10	296
Girls under the age of 10	157
Girls over the age of 10	216

In 1855 boards of guardians were given powers to pay school fees for children receiving outdoor relief, but this measure was not adopted with enthusiasm. Later (1873) elementary school attendance for children aged 5 to 13 was made a condition of outdoor relief.

Records for workhouse schools include admission and discharge registers, creed registers and classification registers. If a school was attached to a workhouse, there may be separate admission and discharge registers for school and workhouse, and separate indices for each institution's records.

> **Case Study**
> **Swinton Industrial Schools**
> The boys' school admission and discharge register (not in alphabetical order of surname) notes the child's admission number, age, religion, parish chargeable to, date of admission, whether previously in the workhouse school or another school and how long for, date of discharge and 'observations' on the child's conduct and reason for discharge. For example, Thomas Philbin (admission no. 4610), a Roman Catholic aged 9 from Manchester parish, was admitted to the school on 29 September 1892. He was discharged from the school on 6 February 1894: 'given up to Mother' (LA PUG 2/1).

Classification registers include each child's name, date of birth, where born, parents' names and occupation, whether illegitimate, orphan, deserted, etc., and other details such as date when admitted or discharged, if the child ran away, was apprenticed, placed in service or died and general remarks.

Workhouse school records (see below) may be with Poor Law union records, or archived with county council education department collections.

The Industrial Schools Act of 1857 gave magistrates the power to sentence child beggars and vagrants to spend time in an industrial school; see Chapter 5 for more information on certified, industrial, reform and approved schools. Institutions and hospitals for blind, deaf, disabled and children with a mental disability are discussed in Chapter 6.

'Boarded-out' Children

After the mid-1870s, a more humane approach was gradually adopted for pauper children. Instead of the monotony of industrial training or Bible reading in a workhouse school, children were 'boarded out' either with foster parents or in 'cottage homes'. Cottage homes were establishments run by married couples who looked after up to forty pauper children; the children attended local schools.

Poor Law union records in local record offices include 'registers of boarded out children' or 'registers of orphan children' which give the child's name, age, the address of the foster parent or cottage home and dates when the child was living there. Sometimes further information is given on the child's later whereabouts, e.g. if they returned to the workhouse or went into domestic service.

Poor Law officials had other duties to perform as well as disposing of workhouse children. The Elementary Education Act of 1876 required Poor

Law union officials to enforce school attendance in areas that had no school boards (Chapter 4).

Following some shocking cases of 'baby farming' in which child-minders killed children in their care, the Infant Life Protection Acts of 1872 and 1897 were passed. Inspectors were appointed to inspect child-minders' and foster parents' homes where more than one child was boarded and their report books can be found in Poor Law union (later public assistance committee) records. (The Acts did not apply to children in hospitals or workhouses.)

Inspectors' report books include information such as the address where the infant was kept, name of person receiving infant, date of visit, name of infant, etc. Records may include registers of foster parents' addresses.

The Children's Act of 1908 required foster parents or child-minders who boarded just one child privately for a fee to register with the local authority, and these registers can be found in Poor Law union records. In some areas, such as the London County Council, the Public Health Department was responsible for Infant Life Protection (after 1917).

Several local record offices have catalogued and indexed their Poor Law records and put databases online (Section C). London Metropolitan Archives (LMA) have produced an information sheet on Poor Law records in the London and Middlesex area, including children's records and workhouse school records: www.cityoflondon.gov.uk/things-to-do/visiting-the-city/ archives-and-city-history/london-metropolitan-archives/Documents/ visitor-information/04-poor-law-records-in-london-and-else where.pdf.

Workhouse inmates were listed in the nineteenth-century censuses, although sometimes their full names are not given, only their initials.

For children's living conditions in workhouses, see Frank Crompton, *Workhouse Children* (Sutton, 1997) and Simon Fowler, *Workhouse: The People; The Places; The Life Behind Doors* (TNA, 2007), which has appendices on workhouse records, and Simon Fowler, *Poor Law Records for Family Historians* (Family History Partnership, 2011). The Family History Partnership has published *Poor Law Union Records* by Jeremy Gibson and other authors (various editions, 1997–2008) in three volumes (plus a gazetteer) and notes which records have survived for each union.

Peter Higginbotham's *Workhouse Encyclopedia* (History Press, 2012) has several articles relating to pauper children, cottage homes, barrack schools, boarding out, etc. The *Encyclopedia* includes a directory with street addresses of many workhouses. Higginbotham's Workhouses website (www.work houses.org.uk) lists details of surviving archival sources for each workhouse.

You can search and download records for over twenty Poor Law unions from TNA's Discovery online catalogue. These records sometimes mention individual workhouse inmates.

The system of parish apprenticeship did not end with the new Poor Law. Board of guardian minutes may mention individual apprentices. Poor Law Board correspondence with individual Poor Law unions (MH 12 at TNA) may include information on parish apprentices, sometimes with brief biographical information. This correspondence was published in parliamentary papers (Chapter 3).

For example, a letter dated 29 December 1859 from Halifax Poor Law Union to Bristol Union includes a list of seventeen boy apprentices (with ages) sent from Bristol workhouse to Whitworth's mill at Luddenden Foot, West Riding of Yorkshire. Michael Cusick (13) was of Roman Catholic parents but 'while he was in this workhouse (a period of seven years), he was brought up in the religious persuasion of the Established Church' (*Correspondence between the Poor Law Board and Guardians . . . Pauper Children to the Factory Districts*, [259] (House of Lords, 1861)).

At this date, pauper children were not supposed to be apprenticed more than 30 miles from their home parish. In January 1851 there was a public outcry when news broke that over twenty children from St Pancras Workhouse had been sent to Bermuda (then a penal colony). Poor Law guardians were still apprenticing children until the early twentieth century. TNA holds the official records of the Poor Law Commissioners (later the Poor Law Board).

The Poor Law Board was renamed the Local Government Board in 1871 and given some additional duties. The Poor Law Boards were dissolved in 1929 and their duties taken over by county councils and borough councils. Public assistance committees now cared for the poor and they took over responsibility for workhouse schools, cottage homes and similar institutions. In 1948, the National Assistance Act finally stamped out the last smouldering embers of the Poor Law, and people's fear of the workhouse was lifted forever.

Tip

Before 1991, local authorities did not have a statutory duty to retain case files for children under the care of social services or living in local authority children's homes once the child reached the age of 21. Many case files were destroyed.

The Care Leavers' Association has produced a guide to accessing children's case records, www.careleavers.com/accesstorecords.

Chapter 3

GROWING UP AT WORK

W orking-class children were expected to contribute to the family income. For parents on the breadline, each child's wages was vital.

Charles Lamb wrote that a working-class child 'had no young dreams' but was born 'into the iron realities of life . . . it is only another mouth to be fed, a pair of little hands to be . . . inured to labour' (*The Works of Charles Lamb Vol. III* (W.J. Widdleton, 1866)).

Children helped their parents with their work in the home (e.g. handloom weavers) or in the family business. They worked in factories, down the mines and on the land. They made lace, silk, hosiery, worsted, pins, nails, glass, iron, tobacco, bricks and so on.

Domestic service was the largest employer for young girls. At the time of the 1841 census, in the county of Middlesex and London area alone, some 28,500 girls and women under 20 worked as domestic servants, as did 9,000 boys in the same age group. By 1871, over 89,000 girls aged 10 to 14 were in domestic service.

Servants' working hours depended on their mistress. A 'slavey' or maid-of-all-work was up before the rest of her mistress's household and worked long after they were tucked up in bed. She did all the cooking, cleaning, washing and waited on the family. Board, lodging and clothes were part of her wages if she 'lived-in'. Boys worked as page-boys or perhaps in the stable or garden.

Many young children looked after younger siblings whilst their parents were out at work, or if their mother worked at home making gloves or similar handicrafts. Eliza Cotton (13) worked as a 'nurse' before she began packing tobacco at Huxley & Co., a tobacco manufacturer in Whitechapel Road, London: 'I am 14 on the 11th of next February. I have not worked a year yet [here]. I can read a little. Before I came here I went out to nurse the baby. I got 2s 8d per week for nursing. I go to school now on four nights a week. I go to Buck's Row. I pay nothing'. Eliza worked from 8.30 am until 5 pm each day, sometimes until 8 pm at night; she packed about 60lb of tobacco each day. (*Children's Employment Commission (1862), Fourth Report of the Commissioners, with Appendix* [3] (1865)).

Boy working as a domestic servant. John Leech, 'Pictures of Life and Character', *Punch* (Bradbury & Evans, 1863).

'Who'd be a "nuss"!' Little girls often cared for younger members of their family while their parents worked. John Leech, 'Pictures of Life and Character', *Punch* (Bradbury & Evans, 1863).

The work children did depended on what was available locally. In 1851 agriculture was the largest employer for boys and adult men. In rural districts like Dorsetshire, boys 'are generally sent out to work at the ages of eight or nine, sometimes as young as seven' (*Reports of Special Assistant Poor Law Commissioners on the Employment of Women and Children in Agriculture*, XII (1843)). Their first task might be scaring birds away from the crops (a lonely job) or minding cattle. When they were big and strong enough, boys helped lead the horses when ploughing.

It was unusual for girls to work regularly in the fields before they were 13, although from the 1820s in East Anglia girls as young as 6 worked for long hours under the notorious 'gang' system, doing jobs like pulling turnips miles from home (this was exceptional, however).

Traditionally girls and boys from the age of 10 'lived-in' with another family as farm servants, but this system gradually died out as yearly hirings became less popular with farmers, and they switched to employing workers by the day.

Alternatively, young children in rural areas worked in domestic industries: lace-making, straw-plaiting, button-making, etc. In lace-making or straw-plaiting 'schools' in places such as Bedfordshire and Hertfordshire respectively, children performed a set amount of work each day, which was then sold: the money went to their parents. Straw-plait was used to make hats or decorate bonnets.

Around 13,000 children and young people were listed in the 1861 census as straw-plaiters, but government investigator J.E. White believed that 'many children under 5 years of age' doing this work had not been recorded as such by their parents.

Boys and girls made straw-plait from about the age of 4 under the watchful eye of the 'school' mistress, who acted like 'an overlooker from the factory' to check that they did their work. At Houghton Regis, 4-year-old Jane Fowler said that she made ten to twelve yards of plait per day. (*Second Report of the Children's Employment Commission 1862: Lace, Hosiery &c.,* [3414], XXII (1864).)

During harvest time, rural schools were deserted because every hand was needed in the fields. The logbook (Chapter 4) for Knowle Green British School in Lancashire for 5 July 1872 records teacher Miss Taylor's frustration at her charges' poor attendance:

During the last week the attendance have [sic] been much less. Most of the more advanced scholars having been taken home to assist their parents who are engaged at [sic] the hay. I have had much difficulty to persuade their parents to promise their presence at the examination which is to take place on Wednesday before H.M. Inspector Mr Steel. (LA SMRB 1/1)

Some schools closed for a week or two longer than usual if the harvest was late owing to bad weather.

The Agricultural Children's Act of 1873 banned children under 8 years old in rural areas from working on the land; this measure rescued them from the 'gangs'.

Most child workers never saw the inside of a factory, but the Industrial Revolution changed the scope and intensity of child labour. In the 1790s the early water-powered textile mills in remote districts, manned by pauper apprentices like Robert Blincoe, became notorious for their long working hours.

Child worker using a machine for combing worsted. *Pictorial Gallery of Arts Vol. I* (Charles Knight, *c.* 1862).

The introduction of steam power meant that factories could be sited anywhere with access to coal, and parish apprentice labour became less common. 'Free labour' children like Gerald Massey were employed instead.

Massey (1828–1907) was the son of a poor canal-boatman at Tring, Hertfordshire. His family of six lived in a 'little stone hut'; their rent was 9*d* (4p) weekly. When in work, his father earned 10*s* (50p) per week. If his father was unemployed, the family survived on the children's earnings. When Gerald was 8 years old, he and his siblings went to a nearby silk factory from 5 am until 6.30 pm. 'I had no childhood', he wrote many years later: 'Ever since I can remember, I have had the aching fear of want throbbing in heart and brow'. Gerald earned from 9*d* to 1*s* 3*d* per week; the children's wages totalled 5*s* 9*d* per week. (Samuel Smiles, *Brief Biographies* (Ticknor & Fields, 1861).)

Child labour was considered essential for the nation's prosperity. From the 1830s, campaigners tried to introduce legislation to limit children's working hours so that they could go to school. But many manufacturers and politicians were convinced that any interference with industry would be ruinous for the economy. Universal education for young children was not enshrined in law until 1870, and even then school attendance was not compulsory.

Several government investigations found evidence that children became 'crippled' from lengthy factory shifts (15 hours a day in Bradford in 1833). Some children were beaten to keep them awake, or were killed or injured by factory machinery. The factory reform movement was born.

Early attempts at regulatory legislation proved ineffective. The 1833 Factory Act was the first to have some impact on child mill-workers' lives. Night work was banned for all persons under 18. 'Young persons' aged 13 to 18 were limited to a 69-hour working week. The minimum working age in textile factories (except silk) was set at 9 years, and 'children' (9 to 13-year-olds) were limited to a 48-hour week. Children were entitled to a set number of annual holidays.

This Act was primarily an educational measure. Factory children must have at least 2 hours' schooling per day, and for the first time, factory inspectors were appointed to ensure that they went to school. Some factory owners set up their own schools near the works: the North Shore Mill in Liverpool had a day school and Sunday school for its child workers.

Prior to civil registration, a doctor or surgeon certified that a child or young person appeared to be old enough for factory work under the 1833 Act. These 'age certificates' may have survived in factory records, plus books of age certificates signed by the surgeon noting each child's name, parents' names, residence and date when the child was examined.

Successive legislation limited children's hours, increased the number of hours spent at school, and extended the factory inspectorate's remit. The 1844 Factory Act introduced the 'half-time' system for children: they must go to school either each morning or afternoon, and work the other half of the day. (Or they could work three alternate days for a maximum of 10 hours, and go to school for two days). This Act required firms to keep registers of children and young persons. School certificate books list dates when the children attended school.

For example, Derbyshire Record Office holds records for cotton-spinning firm W.G. & J. Strutt at Belper (series O1). Records relating to their child (and teenage) workers (O1/14) include school certificate books, age certificates, registers of children under 13, registers of young persons, 'general registers' and accident and poisoning registers. Belper Mill School records (O1/15) include admission registers, class registers, night school records and a 'forfeits' book (for bad behaviour).

Case Study

Lancashire Record Office (LA) holds records for William Thompson & Company Ltd's Galgate Silk Mill including factory registers and certificates under the Factory and Workshop Acts. The company specialised in silk spinning and doubling; the mills were steam-powered.

The 'List of Children Employed in This Factory' includes James Howarth of Galgate, date of first employment 2 August 1879. James's parents were James and Jane Howarth. His date of birth 'as ascertained by production of certificate of birth' was 13 June 1867. (If a birth certificate was not shown, but other evidence produced instead, this was noted in the register.) The certifying surgeon signed the register to say that James junior was fit for factory work on 10 August 1879.

When a child stopped working at the factory, then 'Left' was noted in the 'Remarks' column of the register, as in James's case. If a youngster remained at the factory until they were old enough to be classed as a 'young person', then 'Young Person' was noted instead (LA DDX 2743/MS7612/1).

Following lengthy campaigning by Lord Shaftesbury and others, in the early 1860s a royal commission on children's employment investigated unregulated industries such as lace-making, straw-plaiting, glass-making, metals manufacture and 'sweated' trades such as millinery.

William Barratt worked in a forging shop at E. Wilk's screw-bolt works, Darlaston in the 1860s: 'I am going 11 [under 11, i.e. age 10]. I've worked three years. I get 3s [15p] per week. There are seven of us at home, besides father and mother. Father is a navvy. I am the only one that works. Mother doesn't. I can't read. I never went to school' (*Children's Employment Commission (1862), Third Report of the Commissioners, with Appendix*, [3] (1864)).

The Factory Act Extensions Act of 1867 and Workshops Regulation Act of the same year limited children's working hours in more industries and more employers became subject to inspection by Her Majesty's Inspectorate (HMI).

Factory inspectorate reports (1834 onwards) contain much information about working conditions, factory schools and include records of prosecutions against employers and parents for infringements under the factory acts, e.g. for underage or illegal working. These reports are parliamentary papers (see below).

Factory inspectorate reports can be found in firms' records or public-health records in record offices. For example, Wiltshire and Swindon Archives hold factory inspection records (series 1387) for woollen manufacturer Samuel Salter and Co., Trowbridge. Firms also kept records of accidents or cases of poisoning (if noxious chemicals were used on-site) and these should include personal details of the person injured or killed.

TNA has several series related to the factory inspectorate, including registered papers, correspondence and accounts: HO 43, HO 45, HO 81, HO 87 and LAB 14–15. LAB 15 includes administration and inspection records, factory registers, certificates of employment and files relating to young persons' employment.

The Elementary Education Act of 1870 permitted any child aged 10 to 13 who reached a set educational standard to be wholly or partly exempted from school attendance. 'Labour certificates' were issued by educational

School exemption certificate for Sarah Jane Dickman dated 27 September 1893 permitting her to work full-time.

authorities such as school boards. These certificates may have birth certificates attached. Labour certificates may be in school board or local education authority (LEA) archives or family papers.

> ## Case Study
> A Manchester School Board certificate dated 27 September 1893 gave William Dickman of 15 Ashworth Street, Manchester, the author's great-grand-father, permission to exempt his child Sarah Jane from school attendance so that she could work full-time. Another Manchester School Board certificate in the author's possession, dated 4 April 1894, gave William permission for his son William to be exempt from school one day per week so that he could work.

Table 2

Age When Children Began Full-time Work (Minimum School Leaving Age)		
Year	Legislation	Age
1870	Forster's Education Act	10
1893	Elementary Education (School Attendance) Act	11
1899	Elementary Education Amendment Act	12
1918	Education Act	14
1936	Education Act (start date of 1939 not enforced – wartime)	15
1944	Education Act	15

Another landmark law that restricted child labour was the 1842 Mines Act. A royal commission that year uncovered horrific working conditions underground, especially in districts with very narrow coal seams. Children as young as 4 dragged or pushed heavy loads of coal. The Act banned all females and boys under 10 years of age from mines. Indentures for parish apprentices bound to miners now ended at age 18 instead of 21.

In 1861, the age limit for boys in mines was raised to 12, but boys aged 10 to 12 could work underground if they had a school certificate proving they could read and write proficiently.

Even if your child ancestor attended school full-time, they may have delivered milk or newspapers before school or run errands after school. The Education Act of 1918 imposed fresh restrictions on the employment of children under 14, because in some places children worked up to 40 hours per week.

Boy leading a pit pony. This is a very large coal seam. Charles Knight, *Pictorial Gallery of Useful Arts* (London Printing and Publishing Company), *c.* 1864.

New byelaws, such as a system of employment cards, were introduced by several local authorities for children working outside school hours. At Portsmouth in 1919, over 1,500 children aged between 7 and 14 worked for long hours, but following the new regulations, just 170 children were employed. In several other local authorities, the number of children at work dipped markedly, and their hours fell to between 7 and 15 hours per week (*2nd Report of the Children's Branch* (HMSO, 1924)).

Employment Records and Occupational Sources

Unfortunately there is no guarantee that you will find employment records for a particular firm, business or shop, even for an industry in which large numbers of people were employed. For example, few staff records have survived for the coal mining industry in south Wales. Use the NRA index, ARCHON database and A2A search engine to find company, personal or business records.

Historical trade or street directories list addresses of businesses, manufacturers, grocers and shops, traders, firms, schools and other organisations (or for more recent times, telephone directories). Local record offices and reference libraries have copies of trade directories. Some directories have been digitised and can be browsed online by county, www.historicaldirectories.org/hd/index.asp.

Local record offices may hold apprenticeship indentures (see below) and employment records for businesses, firms or farmers. Cash or wage books may have payments to regular or casual child workers; employee records may include date of birth. Colliery records may include lists of boys employed underground or payments to boys in wage books. Family household accounts may include servants' wages or cash payments to children doing casual jobs.

Many books have been published on children's working conditions including Jane Humphries, *Childhood and Child Labour in the British Industrial Revolution* (Cambridge University Press, 2011) and Sue Wilkes, *The Children History Forgot* (Robert Hale, 2011), which includes parish apprentices and factory reform. B.L. Hutchins and A. Harrison, *A History of Factory Legislation* (Frank Cass & Co. Ltd, 1966) covers 1800–1910.

For occupational sources, see Stuart A. Raymond, *Trades and Professions: A Family Historian's Guide* (Family History Partnership, 2011). The Society of Genealogists has published several titles on occupations in the 'My Ancestor Was A . . .' series. For domestic and farm servants, see Michelle Higgs, *Tracing Your Servant Ancestors* (Pen & Sword, 2012).

Occupations in the Censuses

Census returns (Chapter 1) are one of the best ways to research your ancestor's occupation.

Case Study

At the time of the 1861 census, the author's great-great-great-grandfather James Thompson (56) and his wife Betty (55) lived at 4 Marriot's Place, Salford with four of their children. Their home was in the parish of St Stephen, civil registration district of Salford, sub-district Greengate. James's birthplace is listed as Manchester and his occupation as shoe-maker. Betty was born in Newton Heath; her occupation is 'wife'.

Their son John (16), born in Newton Heath, was a 'van driver'; another son, Robert (12), born in Manchester, was a 'bobbin turner'. Daughter Mary (19), born in Manchester, had 'no business'. The youngest child, Nancy (Ann), age 10, had 'no business'; she was born in Sandbach, Cheshire. From the children's birthplaces, it appears that the family had at least three different addresses before moving to Salford. (RG 9/Piece 2912/Folio 75/p.1, copyright TNA and courtesy TheGenealogist.)

A bobbin turner made wooden bobbins for cotton spinning; Robert (the author's great-great-grandfather) is unlikely to have owned his own lathe, and therefore probably worked in a bobbin mill. Several bobbin turners are listed for the Salford area in Slater's *Directory of Manchester and Salford* (1863) which could be possible places of work for Robert.

If a child is 'missing' from the census, they may be staying with a relative, or 'living out' in another household if working as a farm servant, domestic servant or apprentice. If a child worked night shifts (not uncommon for bleaching, calico printing, glass, foundry or furnace workers) they may be found listed at work. If the family worked together, e.g. at open-pan salt-works or down the mine, parents and children may be found at the workplace.

When a householder filled in the census form, they were asked to record a child as a 'scholar' if he or she attended school or was taught at home. A child's occupation had to be recorded if they attended work regularly. This brings us to the problem of half-time working and underage working.

There has been much scholarly debate over whether wives' and children's occupations were under-reported in the censuses. A parent might have hesitated to record a child's occupation if they only worked part-time or were working illegally.

Many householders appear to have recorded their children's occupations honestly, e.g. 'half-time rope-maker', 'half-time labourer' or even 'half-time weaver scholar'. The author's great-great-grandfather Arthur Lomas (12) is listed in the 1881 census as a 'halftime silk picker and scholar' at Leek (RG 11/2738/55/p.23, copyright TNA and courtesy TheGenealogist).

However, it is best to keep an open mind if you see a child recorded as a 'scholar'; the child may only have attended Sunday school and worked all week.

The way in which census data was collected for ships, fishing vessels and canal boats varied over the years, and coverage is imperfect for some censuses, so if your youthful ancestor worked on one of these vessels they may be hard to find. See Edward Higgs, *Making Sense of the Census Revisited* (University of London, Institute of Historical Research, 2005).

Trade Unions

Whether your child ancestor was a trade-union member depends on the union membership rules. For example, in the early 1870s the National Agricultural Labourers' Union admitted boys aged 13 to 17 years half-price (Pamela Horn, *The Victorian Country Child* (Alan Sutton, 1990)).

Some youthful workers made history by their fight for better wages. The Bryant & May match-girls' strike hit the headlines in 1888. Activist author Annie Besant contrasted the girls' low wages with the firm's high dividends. The workers (mostly teenagers) formed a union and went on strike for three weeks. The strike was a public relations disaster for Bryant & May, which gave in to the girls' demands for better wages.

The TUC History online website has digitised images of the match-girls' strike-fund register, with names and addresses for the match-girl and boy workers, and images of other documents relating to the strike, www.union history.info/matchworkers/matchworkers.php.

The Modern Records Centre at Warwick University library holds records for trade unions (and publications relating to youth clubs). It holds union records for many different industries including miners and transport workers, but membership records are not always included.

There's a guide to the genealogical sources available at the library, http://www2.warwick.ac.uk/services/library/mrc/explorefurther/subject_guid es/family_history/.

Parliamentary Papers

The sessional and 'Command' papers published by Parliament (Blue Books) are packed with information on children's employment, education, working and living conditions (all ages), HMI reports on education, factories, mines, prisons, and so on. Amongst the most interesting for researching child labour are the Children's Employment Commission Reports of the 1840s and 1860s, which include interviews with children. Some parliamentary papers are referred to in this chapter and others; see the Bibliography.

Large reference libraries may hold copies of Blue Books, which are indexed. The Parliamentary Archives have copies, and digitised versions can be viewed at TNA reading room. A select number of parliamentary papers are available free on Google books (http://books.google.co.uk) and the Victorian Times website, http://victoria.cdlr.strath.ac.uk.

Apprenticeship Records

For hundreds of years, the Statute of Artificers and Apprentices (1563) governed the rules by which young people learned a 'craft, trade or mystery'; they had to serve an apprenticeship first. Apprenticeship indentures and agreements are another wonderful resource for genealogists. The Statute of Artificers was repealed in 1814, but apprenticeships (of varying value) have continued into modern times as a means of training young people.

Middle-class parents paid hefty premiums to apprentice their children into trades and professions such as banking, brewing or the law (it cost over £100 in the mid-1740s to be bound to an attorney). It was traditional for the better-paid artisans to pay a sizeable premium to apprentice their children into a skilled craft such as shipbuilding or carpentry. Private apprenticeship indentures followed a similar legal formula to those used for parish apprenticeships. The survival rate for private apprenticeship records is not as good as for parish apprenticeships, but indentures may be found in business, estate or family papers. For example, the Ogden of Stanley papers at Derbyshire Record Office Local Studies & Archives Centre include an apprenticeship indenture dated 1801 for William Chandler, aged 10, to Joseph Hogton, framework knitter of Denby (D331/9/12).

If your ancestor was a militiaman, his attestation papers (WO 96 at TNA) will give his date of birth, and note if he was an apprentice when he enlisted, with the name of his master and date of indenture.

Many trades and industries such as factory work which sprang up during the Industrial Revolution were not covered by the Statute of Artificers, although parish overseers still used apprenticeship indentures to ensure that their pauper children were safely off their hands.

It was quite common for a child to be informally apprenticed to his father or another family member such as an uncle, in which case there is unlikely to be a record of the 'apprenticeship'. But some families drew up formal indentures, for example, Josiah Wedgwood was apprenticed to his brother Thomas for five years in November 1744 to learn the art of throwing and handling clay to make pots. The indenture was signed by Thomas and Josiah, and their mother Mary, and witnessed by Josiah's Uncle Abner and Samuel Astbury (L. Jewitt, *The Wedgwoods* (London, 1865)).

'Indoor' apprentices 'lived in' with their master or mistress, who provided their clothes, food and board. Depending on the type of indenture, the apprentice received no wage, or perhaps a small wage which increased as they became more proficient. Some masters paid a portion or all of the apprentice's wage to his parent as part of the deal.

'Outdoor' apprentices, like those bound to potters in the Potteries, and children working in metal trades in the Wolverhampton area in the 1840s, lived at home but went to work with their master each day; these were usually informal arrangements and no premium was paid.

From 1710–1811 tax was paid on apprenticeship premiums, and these payments were recorded by the Commissioners of Stamps in the Apprenticeship Books at TNA (IR 1). Parish and charity apprenticeships were exempt from this tax.

Taxes for London were recorded in the 'City' Apprenticeship Books, and places outside the capital (including towns) in the 'Country' books. The tax was sometimes not paid until several years after the child was apprenticed. Each record includes the name of the child and their master, date of indenture, date when the tax was paid, the amount of the premium paid and length of apprenticeship. Sometimes brief details of the indenture terms are included. The registers cover England, Scotland and Wales.

The IR 1 series can be searched online at the Ancestry website, and you can view free digital images of the apprenticeship books.

Case Study

Jane Austen's aunt, Philadelphia Austen (1730–92), was apprenticed to a London milliner when she was 15 years old. The IR 1 register shows that 'Phila Austin' was apprenticed for five years on 9 May 1745 to Hester Cole of Covent Garden, Middlesex for a premium of £45. Tax on the indenture was not paid until 12 November 1748, however. (IR 1/8/p. 146, copyright TNA and courtesy Findmypast.)

The Society of Genealogists has indexed part of the IR 1 register in two alphabetical series, 1710–62 and 1762–74, http://www.sog.org.uk/library/upper.shtml app.

You can download a 'Digital Microfilm' (not indexed) copy of IR 1 from TNA website, www.nationalarchives.gov.uk/records/digital-microfilm.htm.

Several local record societies and local history societies have published transcripts of sections of IR 1 relevant to their area. This TNA guide to apprenticeship records includes the IR 1 series, merchant navy apprentices, apprentices in Admiralty dockyards and more, www.nationalarchives.gov.uk/records/looking-for-person/apprentice.htm.

The archives of the City of London Livery Companies (guilds) are held at Guildhall Library. If you do not know which Livery Company your ancestor belonged to, try checking the City of London freedom papers first (an apprentice who served out their time could become a freeman). Online catalogues and guides are available. See *City livery companies and related organisations: a guide to their archives in Guildhall Library*, 3rd edn (Guildhall Library, 1989).

Cliff Webb has compiled indexes to the apprenticeship registers (up to the early nineteenth century) of over forty City of London livery companies; copies are kept at the Guildhall Library.

Access the Guildhall Library guide to apprenticeship records at www.cityoflondon.gov.uk/things-to-do/visiting-the-city/archives-and-city-history/guildhall-library/Documents/18-apprenticeship-records-in-england.pdf.

You can search for London apprentices and freemen on a new online searchable database: Records of London's Livery Companies Online

(ROLLCO). The database currently has details of apprentices and freemen registered with the Companies of Clothworkers (1545–1908) and Drapers (c. 1400–1900), with some Goldsmiths records (1600–1700). Mercers' Company records will be added in 2013, www.londonroll.org.

Large employers may have kept lists of apprentices or ledgers of apprenticeship agreements. Stuart Raymond's *My Ancestor Was An Apprentice* (Society of Genealogists, 2010) is a comprehensive guide to the different types of apprenticeship records.

Merchant Navy Apprentices

The merchant navy has always been vital for the UK's prosperity, and boys joined at an early age. Merchant ships carried cargo or passengers in peacetime and wartime, and aided Royal Navy operations if necessary in wartime. Sean Longden has estimated that over 500 casualties serving on merchant navy vessels in the Second World War were under 16 years of age.

The Marine Society, one of Britain's earliest maritime charities, played a key role in training men and boys for the sea services.

The Marine Society

In 1756, England's Royal Navy faced a manpower crisis on the eve of war with France. A naval captain asked London magistrate John Fielding if he could find some poor boys to crew his ship, saying he would pay for their clothing himself. Fielding was impressed by the idea, and set up a subscription, which raised enough money to clothe 300 boys for the King's navy. Landsmen were recruited and outfitted, too.

Philanthropist Jonas Hanway put Fielding's scheme on a firm footing by founding the Marine Society. When the war ended, the Society suspended its operations for a short time. After its funds were boosted by a large bequest by merchant William Hickes in 1763, the Society began apprenticing boys to the merchant navy.

The Society, incorporated in 1772, had powers to kit out boys for the Royal Navy, or alternatively apprentice them to the merchant navy for seven years. Some boys served with the East India Company. If the boys had parents living, they had to give their consent first. Under the terms of the Hickes bequest, in peacetime the Society also apprenticed poor girls aged 12 to 16 years into domestic service.

In 1786 the Marine Society set up a training ship (the first in the UK), the *Beatty*, moored on the Thames near Deptford. Before the boys went to sea, they were taught naval skills and 'reading, morality, and the principles of the Christian religion'.

When a boy went to sea, he was given a comb, knife, needles and thread, a Bible and a set of clothes including 'leather cap, one blue jacket and trowsers [sic], two check shirts, one canvass frock, two pair[s] of shoes' (*The Byelaws and Regulations of the Marine Society*, 6th edn (1820)).

The Caird Library, National Maritime Museum holds a major collection of Marine Society records including apprenticeship registers. The Marine Society at Lambeth only holds records from 1977 onwards. DANGO (Database of Archives of Non-Governmental Organisations) (Chapter 6) lists archive details for some local branches of the Marine Society.

Boys could be apprenticed to a merchant vessel's master voluntarily (because they wanted a career at sea) or compulsorily by the Poor Law authorities. Parish apprentices usually went to sea when they were 13 years old.

The Merchant Shipping Act of 1835 ordered compulsory apprenticeships for boys entering the merchant navy. Each apprenticeship was registered with the General Register Office of Merchant Seamen in London, or if at another port, with the customs officer. Until 1849 the number of apprentices on each ship was determined by its tonnage: vessels between 80–200 tons carried one apprentice, vessels of 200–400 tons had two apprentices, and so on up to a maximum of five apprentices for vessels over 700 tons.

After compulsory apprenticeship was abolished in 1849, the numbers of apprentices fell sharply and continued to decline yearly. In 1845 there were 15,704 apprentices enrolled on merchant ships; by the late 1890s roughly 2,000 apprentices enrolled annually (R.J. Cornewall-Jones, *The British Merchant Service* (Sampson Low, Marston & Co., 1898)).

In the late 1850s boys were apprenticed for five years to merchant ships when they were about 14. For their first year their wage was £5 p.a., rising to £10 for the final year of their apprenticeship: hardly enough to pay for their clothes. By comparison, a 14-year-old '2nd class boy' in the Royal Navy earned £9 2s 0d p.a. (*Reports of the Assistant Commissioners . . . into the State of Popular Education in England, Vol. III* (1861)).

There was no statutory minimum age for working on board a ship until 1920, when boys under 14 were not permitted to serve on vessels (except training ships), unless they worked for a relative.

Living accommodation in merchant ships could be cramped and smelly. William Schaw Lindsay (1816–77), an apprentice in the 1830s, slept between decks in the forecastle in a space only 5ft high, 21ft wide and 20ft long. The sleeping area was shared with the cook, ten seamen, two other apprentices, water casks, rope and other equipment. Food was salt pork or beef and maggoty biscuits. Rats scampered over the crew and into their hammocks whilst they slept (R.J. Cornewall-Jones, *The British Merchant Service* (Sampson Low, Marston & Co., 1898)).

The Royal Greenwich Hospital (Chapter 7) trained boys for the merchant navy, too. Boys also trained at naval schools and on Poor Law and reformatory training ships (Chapter 5).

A training ship for merchant navy officers, the HMS *Conway*, moored on the River Mersey at Rock Ferry, opened to pupils in 1859. It was founded by the Mercantile Marine Service Association. There were also privately run nautical or navigation schools.

On the River Thames, the training ship HMS *Worcester* (for merchant navy officers) was set up by a wealthy merchant in 1861; in the 1870s the original ship was replaced by the *Frederick William*, and the establishment renamed the Thames Nautical Training College.

If a family wanted their son to train as an officer in the merchant navy, this ambition did not come cheap. In the 1890s it cost between £50–£150 for an apprenticeship premium for one of the bigger shipping companies, plus the boy's uniform (£20). Smaller firms wanted a premium of £30, sometimes less. The cost of sending a boy to one of the training ships such as HMS *Conway* or HMS *Worcester* was allegedly beyond a middle-class income.

These private apprentices, who hoped to become captains one day, often found themselves doing the same kind of work (scrubbing decks, cleaning brass-work, cleaning out the bilges and so on) as the pauper apprentices, who expected to become able seamen at the end of their training.

The Maritime Archive and Library at Merseyside Maritime Museum holds some records for training ships HMS *Conway* and TS *Indefatigable* (Liverpool Sea Training School for Boys). Its website has a guide, http://bit.ly/WfJw5y.

From 1747 masters of vessels kept crew lists or muster rolls (BT 98) and these can be found at TNA, which also holds transcripts of registers of shipping and seamen from the customs records of London and Edinburgh (BT 107).

Muster rolls record the ship name, master's name and place of residence, ship's tonnage, port of departure and arrival, and the name of each crewman. Details for individual crewmen include their name, age, place of birth, residence, first ship and master served with, length of service on current ship, when and where discharged, killed, or wounded and the pension fund payments collected (every seaman paid sixpence into a disabled seamen's pension fund to support widows and dependent children).

Trinity House supervised this fund for the Humber area and the muster rolls (crew lists) for 1747–1851 are held at Hull History Centre (C DSTR). An index of ships' names is available.

There's an example of a Trinity House muster roll on the Hull History Centre website, http://bit.ly/P9hbx8.

Records of merchant seamen, including apprentices and cabin boys, are in the Registers of Seamen 1835–1857 (several series) at TNA, also available at Findmypast. The registers include name, age, date of birth and position held on ship: the amount of information varies according to the date of the record.

TNA has records of Merchant Navy apprenticeships 1824–1953 (BT 150); indexes are available in BT 151 and BT 152. Series BT 113 is a register of seamen's tickets 1845–53. There are several guides to merchant seamen's records on TNA website.

The Crew List Index Project (CLIP) is a finding aid for merchant seamen on British registered ships for 1861–1913, www.crewlist.org.uk/index.html.

For help navigating the records, see Simon Wills, *Tracing Your Merchant Navy Ancestors* (Pen & Sword, 2012), Kelvin Smith, Christopher T. Watts and Michael J. Watts, *Records of Merchant Shipping and Seamen* (Public Record Office, 2001) and Christopher T. Watts, *My Ancestor was a Merchant Seaman*, 2nd edn (Society of Genealogists, 2002).

Chapter 4

AN EDUCATIONAL PRIMER

The question of where (and if) your ancestor went to school during the eighteenth and nineteenth centuries is inextricably linked to their family's income. A good education was generally available only for upper and middle-class children. Working-class children's educational opportunities were limited by the cost of school fees and the need to work.

Many people believed that the provision of education was not the State's responsibility. School attendance was not compulsory until late in Queen Victoria's reign, and elementary school fees in State schools were not abolished until the end of the First World War.

Wealthy parents educated their children at home. They engaged a tutor for the boys, and tutors or governesses for the girls; in 1851 an estimated 50,000 children were taught at home. Sometimes a tutor or governess was engaged for a child's early years, after which they went to a private school like Eton, Harrow or Westminster.

For example, the future poet Percy Bysshe Shelley (1792–1822), son of the well-to-do Sir Thomas Shelley of Field Place manor near Horsham, was taught at home from the age of 6 by the Revd Edwards of Warnham. When Percy was 10 he attended Sion House Academy at Brentford for two years, then went to Eton so he could make the right social and aristocratic connections.

The daughters of well-heeled parents were expected to make a good marriage to someone of their own class. Georgiana Spencer (1757–1806), daughter of Earl and Countess Spencer of Althorp, had several tutors: she learnt writing, languages, geography, deportment and how to play the harp. Her brother George had a private tutor to prepare him for Harrow School.

Family papers deposited at local record offices may include records of payments to tutors, receipts or correspondence related to tuition; solicitors' archives may contain similar records.

Children did not necessarily board at the school they attended. When George Bryan ('Beau') Brummel and his brother William went to Eton in 1786, they lodged with Dame Yonge nearby. At Harrow in the 1760s,

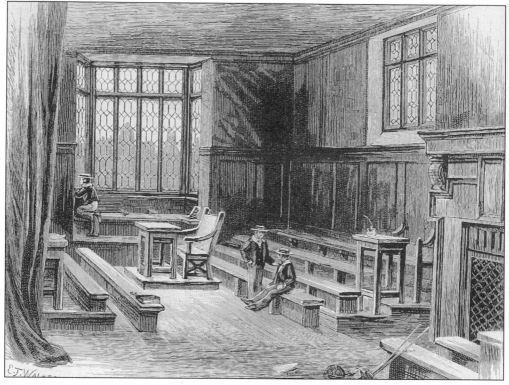

The old schoolroom, Harrow. Engraving by E.J. Walker, *Our Own Country* (Cassell & Co. Ltd, *c.* 1882).

headmaster Revd Dr Sumner set up boarding houses for his pupils to crack down on their boisterous behaviour.

Upper middle-class parents such as manufacturers and professional men either sent their sons to grammar schools or private boarding schools, or apprenticed them into professions (Chapter 3). 'Proprietorial' schools like Cheltenham and Rossall, which offered a similar (but less rigid) curriculum to public schools, became increasingly popular with the middle classes from the 1840s. Lower middle-class parents generally sent their children to the British and National schools (see below).

Dissenters sent their boys to schools or academies (such as Warrington Academy) to kit them out for a career in commercial life. They learnt subjects such as geography, mathematics and science. The sons of Anglicans often attended Dissenting academies, too, as the subjects taught there were of more practical use than schools where the classics still held sway like Eton and Harrow.

Middle-class girls were expected to become wives and mothers. Few 'genteel' careers were open to them apart from being a governess (or after the mid-nineteenth century, a teacher). Girls were educated at home until they were about 10, then depending on their parents' means, attended a local day school, seminary or an 'honest, old-fashioned boarding school . . . where girls might be sent to . . . scramble themselves into a little education without any danger of coming back prodigies' (Jane Austen, *Emma* (Smith, Elder, 1815)). Many boarding schools taught a smattering of 'ladylike' accomplishments rather than a good, all-round education. There were few girls' grammar schools.

Middle-class parents in straitened circumstances who did not want their children to mix with working-class children, but could not afford a decent school, found them a place at a charity school.

Case Study

The Revd Patrick Brontë (1777–1861) and his wife Maria Branwell (1783–1821) had one son, Patrick Branwell, and five daughters. Patrick senior had a very limited income. Branwell (as he was known) and his sisters were educated by their father at home during their early years.

After their mother Maria's tragic death, Patrick sent his daughters Maria, Elizabeth, Charlotte and Emily to the Clergy Daughters' School, Cowan Bridge, a charity school with subsidised fees. The school's regime was spartan, with poor quality food. The two older Brontë sisters, Maria and Elizabeth, who were already in poor health, died in 1825. Charlotte never forgot her sisters' early deaths and later immortalised her experiences in *Jane Eyre* (Smith, Elder, 1847).

A search of the NRA index for 'clergy daughters' elicits three results, one of which is for Casterton School, formerly the Clergy Daughters' School, Cowan Bridge: the school entrance (admission) book is held by Cumbria Archive Centre, Kendal.

Working-class parents who wanted their child to learn were limited to dame schools, common day schools, 'voluntary' or 'public' schools or charity schools. ('Public' in the historical sense means 'publicly funded' by charitable societies or subscribers, not today's 'public schools' such as Eton and Harrow).

Working-class adults were often quoted as saying they wished they had gone to school, and wanted better opportunities for their offspring. The famous engineer George Stephenson was illiterate until he was 19 years old; he learnt to read at night-school.

George was determined that his son Robert (1803–59) would not suffer the same disadvantages. The local parish clerk at Long Benton (the Stephensons lived at nearby Killingworth) taught Robert to read and write. Meanwhile, George spent his evenings after work mending clocks and watches so that he could fund Robert's education. When Robert was 12 years old, he went to Mr Bruce's school at Percy Street, Newcastle, and rode there and back each day on a donkey.

Dame schools were for very young children (2 to 7 years old). These were really child-minding services, usually run by an old man or woman, who used a large stick or cane to maintain discipline (there were sometimes up to fifty children in a class). Dame schools did not keep registers; fees were a few pence weekly.

Privately run 'common day' schools were of doubtful educational value. Anybody could run one, regardless of qualifications (some schoolmasters and mistresses had had no training whatsoever).

Although these schools were often of extremely poor quality, if an impoverished child learned to read, it could awaken a real thirst for knowledge. The poet Gerald Massey learnt to read at a 'penny-school' (fees were a penny per day) before his family fell on hard times. The only books available to him were the Bible, Bunyan's *Pilgrim's Progress* (which he assumed was a history book) and some Wesleyan tracts.

But when Gerald went to London at the age of 15 and started work as an errand boy, a wealth of literature was suddenly within his reach. He peeked into books on bookstalls, or went hungry so that he could afford a book: 'the crown of all desire, and the sum of all existence, was to read and get knowledge' (Samuel Smiles, *Brief Biographies* (Ticknor & Fields, 1861)).

There were also factory schools and 'schools' which were really workshops where crafts like straw-plaiting were taught (Chapter 3).

Charity, Endowed and Voluntary Schools

Charity schools have a long and honourable history in the UK. Children were educated, fed, clothed and boarded free of charge in 'blue-coat' or 'green-coat' schools (named after the uniform) in cities such as Chester and Liverpool and London. The larger blue-coat schools gave their pupils a free uniform and apprenticed out the children when they left.

For example, Christ's Hospital in London was founded by Edward VI in 1552 to educate poor local children; by 1821 it had 1,150 pupils. The Hospital had a Royal Mathematical School affiliated to it, which trained boys for the navy, and, unusually, a free girls' school at Hertford from 1778.

Writers Samuel Taylor Coleridge, Charles Lamb and Leigh Hunt were all 'blue-coat' boys at Christ's Hospital. Parents of would-be pupils had to prove that they could not afford to pay fees, and some of these 'presentation papers' have survived. Christ's Hospital also apprenticed boys into the sea service. LMA holds records of Christ's Hospital for up to 1911 for boys, and 1890 for girls; write to the Clerk of Christ's Hospital for records after those dates.

Endowed grammar schools such as Manchester Free Grammar School (1515) date back to the sixteenth century. For example, St Paul's in London was founded by Dean Colet in 1509; it was left in trust to the Mercers' Company.

Grammar schools did not give elementary instruction; the original founders usually specified that pupils should learn classical subjects such as Greek and Latin so that they could qualify for Oxford or Cambridge Universities. Depending on the foundation, some boys were taught free of charge.

At Witton Free Grammar School in Cheshire (later Sir John Deane's Grammar School), all pupils, including poor scholars, paid an entrance fee of 4d. Boys were admitted from the age of 6; the school was restricted to local children. Some grammar schools like Sir John Moore's, Appleby (Leicestershire) took day pupils and boarders.

By the early nineteenth century many grammar schools (including the mis-named 'public' schools), had moved a long way from their founders' precepts. Free places for poor pupils (e.g. at Eton), were squeezed out to make room for fee-paying pupils because schools' original endowments were insufficient to keep them solvent.

From the end of the seventeenth century onwards, many schools for poor adults and their children were founded by the Society for Promoting Christian Knowledge (SPCK) and other charities. Education was considered a useful social tool. If the working classes were given Christian instruction, they would be industrious and less likely to rebel against their 'betters'.

Sunday Schools

Despite the SPCK's efforts, many children could not attend school because they worked all week; Sunday was their only day of rest. Robert Raikes (1735–1811) of Gloucester is usually credited with founding Sunday schools, although there are other contenders, such as the Revd Joseph Alleine at Taunton, Somerset almost a century earlier.

Gloucester's poorest inhabitants sent their children to work in pin factories. One day in 1780, Raikes was 'struck with concern at seeing a groupe

Macclesfield Sunday School, now a heritage centre.

[*sic*] of children, wretchedly ragged, at play in the street'. Raikes believed these children would end up as criminals unless they were educated and taught right from wrong. In July 1780, Raikes and the Revd Thomas Stock, headmaster of Gloucester Cathedral school, set up three Sunday schools.

After Raikes publicised the Gloucester schools, Sunday schools spread like wildfire. Nonconformists in particular picked up the ball with enthusiasm. The Revd Thomas Charles at Bala founded the first Sunday schools in Wales in 1785. Classes were attended by many adults keen to learn, as well as children.

Charles helped found the British and Foreign Bible Society in March 1804 after he discovered that Bibles written in Welsh were very scarce. One little girl, Mari Jones, walked several miles each week so that she could read a Welsh Bible.

Raikes 'raised Sunday teaching from a fortuitous rarity into a universal system' (Alfred Gregory, *Robert Raikes, Journalist and Philanthropist* (Hodder & Stoughton, 1880)). By 1851 there were over 2.3 million scholars; over 935,000 attended Anglican Sunday schools.

National Schools and British Schools

Many more schools were needed for the growing population, however, and some form of education 'on the cheap' was required.

The National Society for Promoting the Education of the Poor in the Principles of the Established Church was founded by Andrew Bell in 1811. The 'monitorial' system was very simple and cheap; one teacher gave the subject matter for a lesson to several older pupils or 'monitors'. Each monitor then taught the same information to a group of pupils. It was the factory system in miniature, but since it depended on the children learning everything 'by rote', they did not always understand what they were taught.

Bell's method was also known as the 'Madras system' and you will sometimes see references to 'Madras schools' in contemporary publications. National Schools used the Bible as their most important textbook.

The National Society took over the SPCK's charity schools and became the major provider of education for ordinary children. Children as young as 3 attended these schools, usually run by the local church. Rural areas in particular were dominated by National schools.

At Haworth in Yorkshire in 1832, clergyman Patrick Brontë set up a Sunday school with the National Society's help, and his son Branwell and daughters Charlotte and Emily taught in the school. Twelve years later, Patrick persuaded the National Society to build a new schoolroom. As well as taking day scholars, the school held evening classes for local factory children.

Dissenters, naturally, did not want their children educated by the Established Church. A rival organisation, the Lancasterian Society, was founded by Quaker Joseph Lancaster in 1808. It became the British and Foreign School Society (BFSS) in 1814. The Society's schools used a variant of the monitorial system, and these 'British schools' were sometimes known as 'Lancasterian' schools in honour of their founder.

For much of the nineteenth century, the question of working-class schools was bedevilled by religion. Successive government investigations showed that charitable and voluntary societies could not afford to provide enough schools for all poor children. But religious groups were vehemently opposed to any State aid for schools unless it was linked to religious instruction.

From 1833 onwards the government gave building grants for schools funded by religious bodies and public subscription. The National Society received the lion's share of the money.

In 1851 the only schools supported by the State or local rates were the

Howarth National School (on left), Church Lane, Haworth. Charlotte Brontë taught here.

military and naval schools, workhouse schools and prison schools. There were 10,595 Church-run schools, with over 1 million pupils: 569,300 boys and 479,551 girls. This compares with 3,125 endowed schools (including grammar schools) which had 206,279 pupils: 138,459 boys and 67,784 girls.

After 1853 (in country parishes) and 1856 (in towns) schools received 'capitation grants' according to their attendance figures and other requirements. To reduce government spending, in 1861 the 'Revised Code' made capitation grants for schools dependent on attendance figures, *and* children's examination results for the '3 Rs' (reading, writing and arithmetic). Children under 6 did not have to take these exams. This 'payment by results' system meant that teachers focused their energies on the '3 Rs' and other subjects fell by the wayside.

By 1843 Dissenters (including Baptists and Congregationalists) realised that they could not overcome the Established Church's opposition to a national secular system of education (for which they had been campaigning) and they helped fund BFSS schools. Other denominations such as Roman Catholics, Jews and Quakers set up their own schools.

There was a growing movement to educate very young children (up to 6 years old) in kindergartens, nursery or infant schools in their own right, distinct from dame or elementary schools. Robert Owen's school for his factory workforce at New Lanark in 1816 was an early experiment in infant education: it took children as young as 18 months.

In England, the Home and Colonial Society for infant education was founded in 1836. This Society founded a teacher training college at Gray's Inn Road, London. Other promoters of the infant school movement were Joseph Wilson, who founded an infant school at Spitalfields, and the school's teacher, Samuel Wilderspin (1792–1866), who publicised the Infant School Society (1824).

Ragged Schools

Vast numbers of children did not attend any kind of school because they were penniless. Even some Sunday schools would not accept poor children as pupils if their clothes were too ragged.

The first 'ragged school' is said to have been founded by Portsmouth shoemaker John Pounds (1766–1839) in 1818. Pounds brought up his nephew, who was disabled like himself, and educated him at home. He thought the lad would find learning more congenial if he had a companion, so a poor neighbour's son joined the 'class' in John's workshop on St Mary Street. Soon there were nearly forty 'little blackguards', including twelve girls

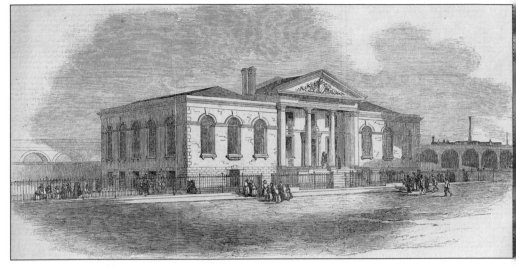

The Lambeth Ragged Schools opened on 5 March 1851. *Illustrated London News*, 8 March 1851.

in the class. Pounds taught the children how to mend shoes, and cook their own meals, as well as introducing literacy skills.

The ragged school movement owed a great deal to Lord Shaftesbury's support. In the early 1840s, Sunday school teachers from the London City Mission set up ragged schools in the metropolis. St Giles' Rookery Ragged School (later Shaftesbury Young People) was formed in 1843. When the Ragged School Union (later the Shaftesbury Society) was founded the following year, Lord Shaftesbury became its chairman, and maintained a life-long interest in its work.

The schools' mission was to 'reclaim and civilize a child, and . . . place it in some honest calling' (*Report from the Select Committee on the Education of Destitute Children* (460) (1861)). Children learnt their Bible and received industrial training so that they could earn a living.

Many ragged schools gave destitute children somewhere to sleep, so pupils may be listed as residents or 'inmates' in census schedules. These schools suffered from a chronic lack of funding, and some later became certified industrial schools or reformatories (Chapter 5).

Although there were numerous Sunday and ragged schools, in 1861 it was estimated that there were 60,000 working-class children in London alone who still had no access to any education.

A national system was needed. Forster's Education Act of 1870 set up 'school boards' with powers to build schools in areas where there were no Church or voluntary schools. The new schools were non-denominational but offered simple Bible teaching. As a sop to secularists, a 'conscience clause' excused children from scripture classes if their parents wished.

These 'board schools' were funded by rate-payers. The Education Act of 1880 made school attendance compulsory (but still not free). Some working-class parents were not keen on losing their children's wages, so school boards appointed truancy officers.

Voluntary schools that were struggling financially could opt to be taken over by school boards. Series ED 16 at TNA has files relating to the transfer of voluntary schools, ragged schools, industrial schools, evening schools, higher elementary schools and school savings banks to school boards after 1870.

A census of schools was taken in 1871 following the 1870 Act, and the returns for this census are held at TNA (lists of schools, not individual pupils).

Secondary Education

Very few children attended 'secondary' schools: in 1851, less than 4 per cent of children aged 14 and over were still at school. Eventually people realised that if the UK was to compete with other imperial powers such as Germany, youngsters required more than just basic literacy and numeracy skills.

Endowed and grammar schools were revamped following the Taunton Commission (Schools Enquiry Commission) of 1868. It discovered that some schools, such as Queen Elizabeth's Grammar School, Mansfield, had not had *any* pupils for several years, and the schoolroom was hired by a private schoolmaster. Perkins' Grammar School at Barrow-on-Soar only had two pupils. The Endowed Schools Act of 1869 set up special commissioners with powers to change grammar school endowments.

The Taunton Commission found that the vast majority of educational endowments had been appropriated by boys' schools. Many more girls' high schools were set up following the report.

After 1870 several school boards including Leeds, London and Sheffield began providing school places beyond elementary level ('higher grade schools'). However, the infamous 'Cockerton Judgement' of 1899 set a legal precedent that stopped school boards spending public funds on secondary education.

There were some local initiatives. Several schools, like Ribchester National School, ran evening classes for youngsters who had left day school to work but wished to continue their education. This school, which opened on 2 October 1899, offered book-keeping, commercial correspondence and domestic economy courses, and had sixty-three boys and twenty-three girls on its roll (LA SMRB/2/8).

By the late nineteenth century three government departments were partially responsible for secondary school provision: the Education Department (higher grade schools, evening classes), Department of Science and Art (technical schools, science schools) and the Charity Commission (endowed schools). In 1899 a newly created Board of Education assumed control of these three bodies. Three years later, Balfour's landmark Education Act made local government responsible for elementary and secondary school provision in England and Wales.

School boards and school attendance committees disappeared, and were replaced by LEAs controlled by county councils, county-borough councils, district councils and urban or rural district councils, depending on the area. London had its own separate education authority.

Board schools (now known as Provided Schools) and Church schools (Non-Provided Schools) received assistance from the rates via the LEAs. The new LEAs had powers to set up secondary schools (county or municipal).

Teacher training was one form of higher education available even for children from 'very humble' homes (*Minutes of the Committee of Council on Education 1853–4 Vol. 1* (1854)).

By 1846 it was clear there were not enough good-quality teachers; some teachers were even illiterate. An early initiative to improve teacher training was a school for teenagers founded in 1840 at Battersea by Poor Law commissioners Dr James Kay (later Kay-Shuttleworth) and E.C. Tufnell. St John's College, as it became known, was taken over by the National Society in 1843.

After 1847 the government paid the salaries of pupil-teachers; schools received additional funding for each one they trained. 'Pupil-teachers' (boys and girls) aged about 13 years served an apprenticeship to a schoolteacher whilst still at school themselves. They received extra instruction outside school hours. Older pupil-teachers taught classes whilst supervised by a senior teacher.

Each year the pupil-teacher sat an exam and received a stipend if successful. When a pupil-teacher finished their apprenticeship, they sat another exam. Those who passed became a 'certificated teacher'; the best examinants won a Queen's (or King's) scholarship so they could go on to further education at a training college.

Some school boards such as Liverpool (1876) set up special pupil-teacher training centres where youngsters received instruction after school or on Saturdays. After 1905, pupils who wished to train as teachers had to stay in secondary school until they were 16.

In 1907, secondary education for working-class children was further boosted when government funding for secondary and municipal grammar schools was made dependent on them providing a quarter of their places free for children from elementary schools ('Free Places').

Children had to pass a 'scholarship' exam to gain a place. Even so, many bright working-class children were forced to turn down free places because their parents could not afford school uniform, or because they wanted them to work. In the early 1930s these free school places became means-tested ('Special Places').

The Hadow Report of 1926 recommended reorganising elementary schools into infant and junior sections, and fixing the age at which elementary school ended at 11 years. After that age, children should move up to secondary schools regardless of academic achievement. But just before the Second World War, less than half of all children over 11 years old attended a secondary school (Paul Wilding (ed.), *In Defence of the Welfare State* (Manchester University Press, 1986)). Butler's Education Act of 1944 at last made secondary education free for all children.

School Records

The most useful records are school registers and 'logbooks'. These become more plentiful after 1861, because teaching establishments kept detailed records to ensure that they received their capitation grants. However, there is no guarantee that these records have survived.

Admission registers (sometimes indexed) should contain the children's names, date of admission to school, and previous school attended (if any). The date when they left the school should be included and a reason given, e.g. moved away, or 'exempt' (because they had reached a high enough standard to go to work), or 'age limit' (the age when attendance was no longer compulsory).

You may have to search each page of the register to find a child's siblings if no index is available, or if it was not maintained properly. Sometimes parents' occupations are included. In general, the later a register is in date, the likelier it is that it will include more detailed information such as the child's date of birth and address. NB Admission registers are not the same as class registers kept by teachers to monitor pupils' daily attendance.

Case Study

James Bradshaw (admission number 351) was admitted to Knowle Green British School near Ribchester on 24 May 1882. His father was also named James Bradshaw, and the family's address was 'The Bottoms'. Young James's date of birth was 3 April 1879 (so he was only 3 years old when he joined the school!) and he was not 'exempt from religious instruction'.

No date of discharge is given in the relevant column, but the register notes that James passed his Standard IV examination on 1 March 1892, so this is the date when he left school. The reason for leaving was 'working at home'.

This admission register has an alphabetical index at the beginning. It does not seem to have been kept very meticulously. Another child, Mary E. Lund (born 26 October 1885), was admitted to the school on 2 May 1892; there is no record of a parent's name or address. In the 'Remarks' column of the register for Mary's name, 'Dead' is written in red ink, but no further details are given (LA SMRB/1/4).

Case Study

Darnhall School

Attendance registers recorded which children were in school each day, sometimes with additional comments by the teacher. The attendance register for Darnhall School, Cheshire for August–September 1770 comments that William Acton 'hath not been since Xmas last', but he was not the only back-slider: several other children had not attended for several months (CALS D4720/17).

Many schools taught boys and girls separately and kept separate admission registers and logbooks for the sexes. There may also be separate records for infant and primary sections of the same school. If schools underwent internal administrative changes, e.g. changing from separate boys and girls to 'mixed' infants, then registers, logbooks or other records may overlap in date.

'Logbooks' are diaries or journals for each school that recorded events such as change of schoolmaster, exceptionally poor attendance or good examination results. Logbooks record visits by HMI (see below) and include copies of or quotes from HMI reports.

Case Study

The logbook for Hambleton Board School records the school's first opening on 8 March 1880. The logbook was updated every few days. On 26 September 1882, the schoolteacher listed the 'object lessons' which the infant classes were studying for their approaching examinations: 'The Horse', 'The Cow', 'The Sheep', and so on. (In an object lesson, teachers explored a topic with the children using pictures, cards or samples or specimens of the object, e.g. an animal's horn). On 5 October 1882 pupil John Hodginson was punished with 'one rap on the hand' for 'disobedience'.

Children's examination marks were sometimes noted in the logbook, e.g. on 30 January 1885, William Bee, Elizabeth Ann Hull, Robert Hull, Thomas H. Hall and Margaret Parkinson received a 'Good' mark for their 'Freehand' examination (LA CC/EXTF/11/1).

Other school records include punishment books, examination results, school magazines (sometimes with photos of pupils) and photograph albums for each class or school year. School sports records (football teams, hockey teams, etc.) may include photographs.

Postcard of a class of schoolgirls with their teacher, *c.* 1910.

Some schools had savings clubs or 'penny banks' to encourage thrift, and individual account books, cash books, pass books or account ledgers may have survived.

Few records have survived for some types of school, especially small private nursery, kindergarten, day, proprietorial or boarding schools. Private school records include pupil record cards, books or registers of tuition fees paid by parents with date of admission, name and age of child when admitted, and address.

Sunday school records such as attendance registers, admission registers, cash books, class registers, minute books, cradle rolls (Chapter 1), prize-giving books and roll books can be found with Church records in the diocesan record office. Some Sunday schools published their own magazines; the British Library has a collection. You may also find Band of Hope or temperance registers (Chapter 7) with Sunday school records.

If no registers or logbooks have survived for a Sunday or ragged school, try checking the managing committee, trustees' or governors' minute books for mentions of individual pupils.

Case Study

Chester Ragged Schools

The Chester Ragged Schools Society was founded in 1851. Its minute book (which has newspaper cuttings on the Society pasted in) records the foundation in January 1852 of two schools in the city: the Boughton Ragged School and the St Olave's Ragged School. The Boughton Ragged School was built on land donated by the Shropshire Union Railways and Canal Company; St Olave's was initially situated on Lower Bridge Street, but later moved to a building near St Olave's Curch).

The minutes for 26 April 1852 give a report by Felix Thomas, the Boughton schoolmaster. School lessons were from 9 am until 12 am, and 2 pm until 4 pm. Evening classes were held at another location.

There were forty-one boys and seventy-nine girls admitted to the school at Boughton; by April twenty-five of these children had left ('gone begging', found work or changed schools).

Only the most destitute children were admissible, so the committee ordered the master to note down the names of children who applied so that they could be approved by the committee. Schoolchildren who attended regularly were treated to milk and currant bread during race week (a major social event locally).

The minutes for 28 May 1852 list the names and brief addresses of the latest children who had applied, and those names on suspension (pending further investigation) or rejected. William Bowles (Seville Street), Mary Evans (Barker's Lane) and Henry, Joseph and John Bradley (Canal Side) were amongst the lucky ones admitted. Mary Shaw (Edward's Entry) was 'suspended'. Jane and Eliza Sunder from Love Street and Anne Jones from Barker's Lane were refused admission (CALS DES/23/1).

Schools were subject to government inspection from 1839, and HMI reports and school inspectors' notebooks may include comments on individual schools, classes, pupil-teacher standards, etc.

HMI inspectors did not visit National, British or Roman Catholic schools, which had their own system of inspection: 'diocesan inspectors' or 'school visitors'. The Home and Colonial Infant School Society had its own inspectors, too. Visitors' reports (county archives) can help you explore classroom life.

A school board visitor testing children's knowledge. *Punch*, 26 August 1882.

Case Study
The visitor to Mill Hill Ragged School noted that on Sunday 30 September 1888:'I had the opportunity of seeing all the classes at work . . . I saw mothers in one class, younger women in another, and so on with every stage of womanhood down to infants ranged in classes. Similarly there is a like range on the men's side'. There were sixty-five boys and sixty-five girls at the school 'and very good they were too, they say [*sic*] very nicely for me "Gentle Jesus"' (LA DDX 1617/22).

Locating School Records

First, you need to work out which school(s) your ancestor may have attended. You will need the family's address, e.g. from a census schedule, birth, marriage or death certificate, or electoral register. A local street or trade directory should list schools in the immediate vicinity, although these directories can be out of date. If street maps are available for the relevant time period, you can check which schools were within walking distance (or on a bus route for more recent times).

Don't assume that your ancestor attended the school closest to home. For example, if the family was Anglican, and the nearest was a Roman Catholic school, it seems logical to start with the closest Anglican school. However, because most parents paid for their children's education, they may have sent their child to a school of the 'wrong' denomination if its fees were cheaper.

The Taunton Commission found that many grammar and day private schools attracted pupils from up to 5 miles (sometimes as far as 7 miles) away, but boarding school pupils could be from anywhere in the country. Census returns may help you find boarding school pupils.

When you have produced a shortlist of possible schools, find out where their records are located. Most State school records are not included in the NRA index and you should check your local record office catalogue first, or the A2A database.

National schools were usually supervised by the local Anglican church. Records such as school registers and logbooks for day and Sunday schools may be with parish records. British schools run by the BFSS managed their own records.

Records of National schools or British schools later taken over by school boards (or LEAs) may be with school board, LEA, municipal or county council collections at local record offices. Records for schools run by other denominations may be held locally, too.

Similar records are held locally for ragged schools: minute books, logbooks, correspondence, photographs and so on. Local reference libraries may have photos or newspaper cuttings for ragged schools.

Any surviving records for private nurseries and kindergartens may be held locally. If a nursery was attached to a school, its records may be with the school's archive; if run by a council, check the relevant collection.

If your local record office has not got the school registers or logbooks you seek, they may still be at their original school. Access to the registers will be at the principal's discretion, and probably subject to a closure period.

Elementary and secondary school records can sometimes be a nightmare to research because over the years schools were subject to administrative changes. Perhaps their premises became too small and they changed location, or they were taken over by the local authority. Schools have sometimes split into smaller schools or merged with others.

Even if you know which school which your ancestor attended, its records may not necessarily be catalogued under that name if it underwent successive name changes. So this is something to be aware of when researching schools; you may have to 'turn detective' and check through directories or phone books to discover other possible names for the establishment.

The same research principles apply for Welsh school records. Some Welsh school admission registers are held by the National Library of Wales (NLW), which holds over a hundred logbooks for Cardiganshire schools, and some National schools (Non-Provided) in St David's diocese. See Sheila Rowlands, *Cardiganshire school log books and registers in the National Library of Wales* (Dyfed FHS, 1985).

Several archives such as Manchester Archives, LMA and the City of Westminster Archives have put catalogues of their school records online, which can be a real time-saver. Some databases are listed in Sections A3 and C.

For the London area see Cliff Webb, *An Index for London Schools and Their Records* (Society of Genealogists, 2007), which lists London schools with dates of foundation, maps and relevant archives.

Records for long-established charity, endowed, grammar and public schools could be at more than one repository; use the NRA index as a finding aid. Several public and grammar schools, like Eton, Harrow, and Manchester High School for Girls, have their own archives. It is beyond the scope of this work to list contact details for every historic school archive; a select few are listed in Section D.

> **Case Study**
>
> Ackworth is a famous Quaker boarding school founded in 1779 at Pontefract, West Yorkshire. The Internet Archive has a copy of *List of boys and girls admitted into Ackworth school: during the 100 years from 18th of 10th month, 1779, to the centenary celebration on the 27th of 6th month, 1879* (1879) (NB Quakers use numbers, not names for months and days of the week). Another useful source is Isaac Henry Wallis, *List of Ackworth Scholars 1879–1930* (privately published, 1932), available from genealogy suppliers.
>
> A search of the NRA index for 'Ackworth School' reveals that minutes, administrative records and photographs are held at the school, with more collections at West Yorkshire Archives Service (WYAS), Hull University Archives (now Hull History Centre) and the Record Office for Leicestershire, Leicester and Rutland. There's a bibliography for Ackworth records in the Handlist of Schools on the 'Quakers in Britain' website, www.quaker.org.uk/schoolsdoc.

Registers for many public and grammar schools have been published; some are available on the Internet Archive. For example, registers for Charterhouse, Derby School, Eton, Leeds Grammar, Harrow, Merchant Taylors' School, Repton School, Rugby School, Shrewsbury School and Tonbridge School can be downloaded free, www.archive.org.

Published registers sometimes comprise lists of pupils compiled from several sources, particularly if earlier registers have been lost, and include brief biographical details. For example, the Honourable Robert Barlow Palmer Byng was at Tonbridge School from 1825–9. The second son of the sixth Viscount Torrington, he 'entered the 62nd Bengal Native Infantry in 1833 and rose to the rank of Major'. Byng was later 'killed in action against the mutineers at Lucknow in 1857' (W.O. Hughes-Hughes (ed.), *The Register of Tonbridge School from 1820 to 1886* (Tonbridge, 1886)).

The Society of Genealogists' Library has an excellent collection of school registers, particularly for public schools, catalogued and indexed by county; see *School, university and college registers and histories in the library of the Society of Genealogists*, 2nd edn (SOG, 1996).

FamilySearch Centres have copies of some school registers and logbooks on microfilm. Several genealogy subscription websites offer searchable indexes to school and college registers. Ancestry's educational collections include over 800 schools in the London area. The FamilySearch website has some indexes to Cheshire school registers, including Stockport Sunday School.

Pupil-teacher apprenticeship indenture for William Butler Cowap from Leftwich, apprenticed on 1 May 1860 as a pupil-teacher to Samuel Cooke, schoolmaster of Davenham National School, until 31 December 1864. CALS P6/14/70.

Familyrelatives.com has some online searchable indexes to registers for schools including Charterhouse, Harrow, Sherborne, etc. (free search, pay per view). Few Welsh schools have published lists of their pupils, but Welsh folk may be found amongst the alumni of English public schools and universities.

Records for pupil-teachers, including apprenticeship indentures or memorandums of agreement, may be found in school archives at local record offices. LEA records may include registers of pupil-teachers; pupil-teacher training centre records include logbooks.

Case Study

On 1 May 1860, William Butler Cowap from Leftwich was apprenticed as a pupil-teacher to Samuel Cooke, schoolmaster of Davenham National School, until 31 December 1864. His father John Cowap was a surety for the indenture, which was signed and witnessed by William and John Cowap, the schoolmaster and three other witnesses on 29 June 1860 (CALS P6/14/70).

If your ancestor was a teacher, check the Teachers Registration Council Registers collection (1914–48) at the Society of Genealogists Library. Registration began in 1914, but the registers include teachers who had worked since the 1870s, so former pupil-teachers may be listed. The registers should give the teacher's address or establishment where they were teaching, college or institution where the teacher gained their qualifications, and for female teachers, their maiden name if married.

The registers have been indexed and can be searched on Findmypast, www.findmypast.co.uk/search/teachers-registrations.

TNA holds some files related to teacher-training, www.nationalarchives. gov.uk/records/research-guides/teachers.htm.

University Registers

Biographical and matriculation registers of colleges and universities such as Oxford and Cambridge have been published. They usually list a student's birthplace and other biographical information such as father's occupation.

Sometimes several siblings or several generations of the same family can be tracked if they attended the same university. The registers often include the names of other publications with contain biographical information on the person mentioned.

Cambridge colleges noted the names of students' former schools from an early date, but it appears that some Oxford colleges did not follow suit until the mid-nineteenth century.

The Ancestry and Familyrelatives.com websites have databases (free search, pay per view) compiled from registers of students, graduates and officers who attended Oxford University from 1500–1886.

A Cambridge Alumni online database with biographical details of past students (deceased persons only) is under construction, http://venn.lib.cam. ac.uk/Documents/acad/intro.html.

Case Study

Choosing an example at random, the Oxford matriculation register lists two Behrens brothers from Manchester:

'Behrens, George Benjamin, 3s, of Edward, of Manchester, gent. Corpus Christi Coll., matric. 19 Oct. 1883, age 18 . . . Behrens, Oliver Philip, 2s, of Edward, of Manchester, arm., Oriel Coll., matric. 30 Jan., 1882, age 18, B.A. 1885' (Joseph Foster (ed.), *Alumni Oxonienses, The Members of the University of Oxford 1715–1886, Later Series A–D* (Parker & Co., 1888)).

> From this we can infer that Edward Behrens, a gentleman of Manchester, had at least three sons: Oliver was the second son ('2s'), born in 1864, and George was the third son ('3s'), born in 1865. Seemingly George did not take his degree, as no date or qualification is mentioned, but many upper-class parents sent their sons to Oxford and Cambridge purely for the experience.
>
> The abbreviation 'arm.', which means 'armiger', means that Edward Behrens had a coat of arms, in which case the College of Arms could supply more information.

Official Records

LEA records (county archives) deposited at local record offices may include records of the school boards that preceded them; sometimes school board records may be catalogued separately.

LEA and school-board collections include lists of schools, school attendance records or returns, registers of children exempt from full-time school, registers of cases reported to the school attendance committees or brought before local magistrates, and registers of births in the local area (to enable truancy officers to check which children should be at school).

School attendance committee records include attendance returns with lists of pupils, usually with each child's age and address. School Attendance Officer notebooks and report books include lists of children not attending school, with details of parents' occupations. Wartime LEA records may include evacuees' attendance registers.

In 1907 LEAs were given powers to provide free or cheap school meals for children in need, and provide grants for some free secondary school places. In the same year, the Board of Education set up a School Medical Service. School meals records include registers of children eligible for free meals and records of payments for school meals.

Fisher's Education Act of 1918 ended the half-time system (Chapter 3): it was finally compulsory for all children aged 5 to 14 years to attend school full-time. School fees ceased for elementary schools. LEAs were given powers to set up special schools for children with disabilities. The LEAs also paid maintenance allowances to poor pupils or scholarship students to enable them to continue their education. In the same year, regulations for the medical inspection of school children were tightened up.

Itinerant children such as gypsies, or those living on canal boats, found it difficult to get a good education because their families were always on the move. You may find pupils appearing and disappearing in school registers on the routes that they travelled along.

Some LEAs made special provision for canal-boat children, e.g. Greenway Road School at Runcorn (later Victoria Road School), founded in 1886. Surrey Education Committee opened a school for gypsies at Hurtwood, Shere, in 1926 (no admission registers have survived).

If a family lived near the boundary of an LEA's jurisdiction, their children may have attended schools in the adjoining LEA's control, if that was their nearest school. Children may also have attended schools in another LEA if the tuition they needed was not available, e.g. a grammar school place. Therefore, LEA records may include registers of children attending schools in other areas.

In Wales, joint education committees were set up by county authorities following the Welsh Intermediate Education Act of 1889, which empowered them to part-fund schools from the rates. These secondary schools were inspected by the Central Welsh Board.

A separate department for Welsh schools was set up at the Board of Education in 1907, and surviving files relating to the Welsh department are held at TNA. Some inspectorate records for Welsh schools (1912–92), including pastoral visits, working notes, correspondence, etc., can be found in Welsh Office records at TNA, BD 50.

Specialist Archives and Sources for Educational History

The archives of the SPCK are held at Cambridge University Library. The Society's annual reports and publications include information on the schools they founded.

The Church of England Record Centre at South Bermondsey holds administrative records for Church schools (including National Schools), but not school registers.

The BFSS archive, in the care of Brunel University, does not have any pupil records. However, the archive holds lists of schools, school returns (similar to census returns), grants, etc., which sometimes give school addresses, names of teachers and so on. The BFSS archive has some annual reports for the Home and Colonial Society (also known as the Home and Colonial Infant School Society).

The University of Southampton has collections for Anglo-Jewish organisations, including schools such as the Jews' Free School at Spitalfields in London, which educated 1,200 boys and girls in the early 1850s.

The Cadbury Research Library at the University of Birmingham holds records of the Local Christian Education Councils (LCEC) and the National

Sunday School Union, now the National Christian Education Council (NCEC), and related organisations. This important archive was formerly known as the Robert Raikes or Sunday School Movement collection.

The NCEC collection includes minutes, annual reports, finance committee minutes, magazines such as the *Sunday School Chronicle*, teaching materials and photographs. The LCEC collection includes records for individual Sunday school unions, mostly comprising minutes and annual reports, youth and children's committees and more.

The Shaftesbury Society Archives are part of the British Library's collections at Boston Spa. This collection includes magazines published by the Ragged School Union, mostly concentrating on ragged schools in the London area. Names of individual children are not usually mentioned, but the magazines contain information such as updates on emigration work, progress on new schools, their location and sometimes maps.

For example, the *5th Annual Report of the Ragged School Union* (1849) lists the ships (e.g. the *Osprey*) which took child migrants to Australia, and the names of the ragged schools that sent them, including Streatham Street School, Grotto Passage School and the Agar Town School.

Numerous parliamentary papers (Chapter 3) were published on education. You are unlikely to find an ancestor mentioned in them, but they can be used to trace a school's history. HMI school reports were parliamentary papers.

The reports of the Committee of the Council of Education, Taunton Commission and Newcastle Commission into the State of Popular Education (published in 1861) have information on individual schools; see also reports by the Charity Commission.

The Charity Commission

By the early nineteenth century, so many charities were in existence that there was great scope for maladministration. Some educational charities had become out of date or cared for a tiny number of children, but their endowments could not be altered to benefit the community more widely because it was difficult to overset a founder's will.

The *Select Committee of the Education of the Poor in the Metropolis* of 1816–17, headed by Lord Brougham, examined London school charities such as Christ's Hospital and St Paul's. Its findings prompted the government to set up an extremely wide-ranging survey of charities in general. The Charity Commission's remit was confined to educational charities for the first two years.

The commissioners published details of the charities they surveyed in the *Reports of the Commissioners for Inquiring Concerning Charities* (1817–41).

Later, *Digests of Endowed Charities*, compiled by the Charity Commissioners, were published in 1867–8 and 1912–13. These *Digests* can help you establish which charities and endowed schools existed in a particular location (assuming the survey was complete at that date).

Schools were not necessarily reliant on one source of funding; some endowed schools received grants from religious bodies as well as income from school fees, and some Church-supported schools were partly funded by endowments.

You can use trade directories and the Charity Commissioners' reports to trace the history of schools in a particular location.

Case Study
Holy Trinity National School, Over Darwen

For example, *The History and Directory of Mid-Lancashire* (Mannex & Co., Preston, 1854) notes that in Over Darwen, Lancashire: 'Here are schools conducted on the British and National plans; an operative children's free school; Church and Dissenters' day and Sunday schools, and infant schools'. The directory lists three National schools linked to Holy Trinity Church, one of which was a 'Sunday School' at Culvert (1832).

The *Reports of the Charity Commissioners: Endowed Charities, Lancashire* (1899) has more information on the school: 'By an indenture dated 4 September 1832, and enrolled in Chancery (3 Will. IV., Part 50, No. 4) Richard Hilton granted to James Greenway and three others a plot of land fronting on the south side the land from Calvert [*sic*] to Sough upon trust for the erection of a school in connexion with Trinity Church for the instruction and benefit of the poor . . . in union with the National Society'.

On 24 April 1871 a new plot of land on Watery Lane was rented under the School Sites Act and another school built; the vicar of St John's Church, the Revd Henry Headley Moore, was a trustee. The old school at Culvert was closed: no date is given for its exact closure, but the vicar of Holy Trinity Church and his successors were released from the office of trustee for the old school by an order of the Charity Commissioners dated 24 August 1883.

By the time of the Charity Commissioners' Report: 'The premises [on Watery Lane] are now used . . . as a Sunday School, and on weekdays as a young men's institute in connexion with the church of St. John' (LA Local Studies Library Q57 GRE).

Many books have been published on the history of education: some are listed in the Bibliography and more are listed in the 'Further Reading' section of the TNA guide to education history sources for the UK, www.national archives.gov.uk/records/research-guides/education.htm.

W.B. Stephens and R.W. Unwin, *Materials for the Local and Regional Study of Schooling 1700–1900* (British Records Association, 1987) contains a useful overview of parliamentary papers on education and elementary and secondary education sources at TNA. Some addresses given by Stephens for specialist archives are now out of date. W.B. Stephens, *Sources for English Local History* (Cambridge University Press, 1994) has a chapter on sources for education.

The *Victoria History of the Counties of England* (various volumes and dates) is an excellent resource for information on charities and schools. Your local reference library should have copies. These county histories generally review the history of education in their area of interest, with short historical accounts of some schools, and discuss the charities that were extant. Detailed source references are included.

Some volumes of the *Victoria History* have been published on the British History Online website (www.british-history.ac.uk) and on the Internet Archive (www.archive.org). Unfortunately, some counties have only been partially covered, and others not at all. See the Victoria County History website, www.victoriacountyhistory.ac.uk.

Schools, particularly private and boarding schools but also voluntary schools, advertised for pupils in local and national newspapers. These adverts may show if a particular school admitted boys or girls, or both, sometimes the age range of the pupils taught, the address, the name of the master or headmistress (which could help you find the school in the censuses), the address and types of subject taught. Schools also advertised the dates and times of scholarship examinations. Charity school advertisements are generally for staff vacancies rather than pupils.

Local newspapers reported events such as new school foundations, term dates, school prizes or scholarships won by pupils, examination results, anniversaries such as Sunday school outings, school reunions, extracts from HMI reports and so on.

Specialist magazines such as the *Scholastic Register and Educational Advertiser* printed news on schools and headteachers and changes of premises. For example, the *Register* for 8 July 1869 reported that new buildings were being erected for Dorset County School at Charminster. A news item sheds light on the brutality with which some children were

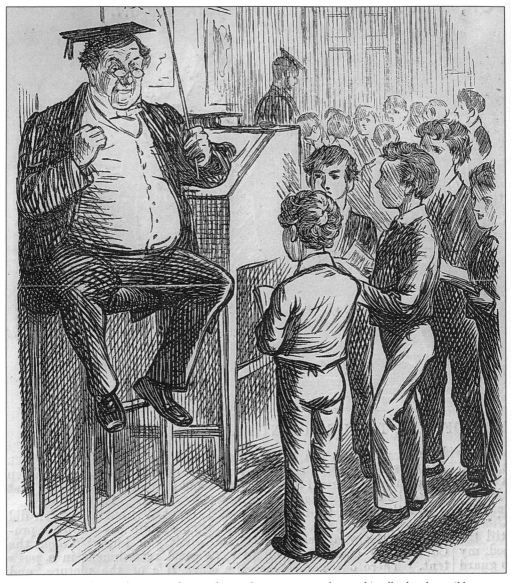

Schoolteacher with a cane. Corporal punishment was not banned in all schools until late in the twentieth century. *Punch*, 22 July 1882.

treated at that date. On 10 June magistrates had dismissed a summons for assault against the Revd G.E. Jepp, master of Ashbourne School, who had 'savagely flogged Richard Marley' because 'they considered an assault was not committed, even though the beating was too severe'.

Trade, street directories and telephone directories listed schools. There were also specialist directories such as John Crockford's *Scholastic Directory* (1861) and *The Educator's Guide* (Dean & Son, 1866) which featured information on private and independent schools.

Reference libraries and local record offices may have copies of the *Public Schools' Year Book*, published from 1910 onwards (after 1945, the *Public and Preparatory Schools' Year Book*) with listings of boys' independent and public schools. The *Girls' School Year Book* (1912 onwards) is a similar publication for independent girls' schools.

For London, the Charity Organisation Society (Chapter 6) published the *Charities Register and Digest* (1882 onwards – after 1897, the *Annual Charities Register and Digest*). The *Register* has information on industrial and charity schools, e.g. Wellington College, a boarding school for 'the education of the sons of deceased officers who have borne commissions in Her Majesty's army, or in the army of the East India Company' (*Charities Register and Digest*, 1890).

The *Official Year Books* of the Church of England contain reports on its educational work including Sunday school associations, and elementary, higher grade and grammar schools. The *1884 Year Book* has a table listing Anglican schools offering higher education (full addresses are not given). Later yearbooks contain additions and updates to this information, e.g. the *Year Book* for 1897 gives names and addresses and brief descriptions of Church schools (it also includes the names and addresses of children's hospitals and convalescent homes run by the Church). A similar publication, the *Catholic Directory* (1835 onwards) has information on Roman Catholic schools.

Please note that the Museum of the History of Education (University of Leeds) mentioned on some websites is currently closed and its collections are not accessible to visiting researchers.

Chapter 5

'SPARE THE ROD'

Our child ancestors grew up in a violent society. Corporal punishment was widespread at home, in schools and in the judicial system. Child convicts were flogged, sentenced to hard labour or transported overseas.

The age of criminal responsibility was 7 years; when a child became 14 years old (later 16), he or she was treated as an adult in the eyes of the law. Capital punishment for children under 16 was not abolished until 1908 (and for under-18s, not until 1932).

Most children were convicted for petty offences like larceny. In September 1818 pickpocket Uriah Sanders (12) was sentenced to a whipping and two months in the House of Correction at Chester for stealing a silk handkerchief (*Chester Chronicle*, 4 September 1818).

In the early 1800s over 160 offences, including stealing, were capital crimes (the 'Bloody Code'). Transportation for life replaced hanging as the maximum punishment for stealing in 1808.

Some children committed more serious crimes. John Bell (14) was tried at Maidstone Assizes on 4 May 1831 for the murder of 13-year-old Richard Taylor. Richard lived at Stroud, and his father had sent him to collect the family's parish relief from the overseers. John Bell and his brother James saw Richard returning from his errand, and realised he was carrying money. The boys waylaid Richard, saying they knew a shortcut home, and then took him into a wood. John cut Richard's throat and robbed him. John was convicted of murder and hanged on 31 May: 'this wretched boy paid the penalty of his crime at Maidstone' (*Gentleman's Magazine*, August 1831).

Until the late eighteenth century prison sentences for children were uncommon, although they endured lengthy periods in jail awaiting trial at quarter sessions, or the assizes. When the number of capital crimes was reduced, juries became more willing to convict children and more were jailed.

From 1838 onwards, hanging was reserved for murder and attempted murder. In general it was rare for sentence of execution to be carried out on

The Artful Dodger picks a pocket. Illustration by George Cruikshank, *The Adventures of Oliver Twist* (Chapman & Hall Ltd and Henry Frowde, *c.* 1905).

a young person. In most instances, the youngster was 'recommended to mercy' and the sentence commuted to transportation or imprisonment.

The number of children under 16 committed to jail rose sharply in the 1830s owing to new legislation such as the police Acts and vagrancy Acts. On average over 3,000 children (mostly boys) were jailed annually in the London area. Cold-bath Fields House of Correction and Clerkenwell Prison (formerly the New Prison) housed the largest number of child convicts (*Third Report of the Inspectors Appointed . . . To Visit the Different Prisons of Great Britain: I: Home District* (1838)).

Criminal Records

Records for young offender cases before the introduction of juvenile courts will be found in quarter sessions, assizes and petty sessions in local record offices. Birmingham had the first children's law court in Europe (1905). Three years later, the Children's Act of 1908 introduced special juvenile courts in Britain. Child criminals were now tried separately from adult criminals. The records of juvenile and youth court cases heard by local magistrates are held locally, not at TNA.

The Old Bailey was the central criminal court for the City of London and Middlesex. Transcripts of trials held at the Old Bailey from 1674–1913 are online. You can search the database by surname, crime, punishment and date, www.oldbaileyonline.org.

The most serious criminal cases were heard in the assize courts (ASSI at TNA). TNA holds many records of criminal trials, www.nationalarchives. gov.uk/records/looking-for-person/criminal-trial-or-conviction.htm.

The palatinates of Lancashire, Cheshire and Durham had their own courts. Cheshire joined the assize circuit in 1830; Durham and Lancashire remained outside the assize circuit until 1876. Palatinate court records, too, are kept at TNA. The main series for criminal trials from 1559–1971 are listed online, www.nationalarchives.gov.uk/records/research-guides/assizes-key-criminal-1559-1971.htm.

In Wales, the court of Grand Sessions heard civil and criminal cases, except for Monmouthshire, which was on the Oxford assize circuit. Minor (petty) offences were heard at quarter sessions, and as in England, these records are held at local record offices.

The NLW holds records for the court of Grand Sessions, and a database of crimes, criminals and punishments for 1730–1830 has been published online, www.llgc.org.uk/sesiwn_fawr/index_s.htm.

After 1830, criminal and civil cases for Wales were heard by English assize

Prisoners including child felons: 'stopping at the Baptist's Head in St John's Lane on the day of removal from the New Prison (Clerkenwell) to Newgate'. Illustration by Dodd, engraved by T. Smith, *c.* 1790.

judges (ASSI at TNA), www.nationalarchives.gov.uk/records/research-guides/assizes-key-welsh-1831-1971.htm.

Police records at local record offices include registers of criminals (sometimes indexed). These registers may include name and address of person convicted, physical characteristics, photographs (dependent on the date), details of their conviction and additional remarks.

Case Study

Lancashire Constabulary's 'register of persons arrested' contains some fascinating stories, including those of teenagers. Michael Daley (16), who had 'hazel' eyes and 'dark brown' hair, with a 'fresh' complexion, was 4ft 9 in tall. Daley, a mill-hand from Leeds, was convicted in July 1892 and sentenced to one month's hard labour for 'stealing boots'. Michael had several tattoos: 'D. B. and a dot on the right arm, and a cross and a dot on the left arm'. The 'Remarks' section notes that Daley 'states he has worked for Messrs Penny & Beck Cloth Finishers & Dyers north of Leeds'.

Some people in the register do not have any conviction noted, or details of any offence; they may have been arrested but not charged. One of these is 13-year-old Llewelyn Turner, born and resident in Skerlow and a 'labourer' by trade. Llewelyn had brown hair, blue eyes, and a 'fair' complexion (LA PLA 16/1).

Prisons

There were no separate detention facilities for children and young people until the late 1830s. Life in prison was no picnic. Boys and girls performed hard labour such as picking oakum, or useless 'work' such as climbing the tread-wheel (tread-mill) or turning a 'crank' for several hours daily.

After the early 1840s, the tread-wheel for females and boys under 14 was discontinued. Instead, youngsters were deprived of meals or given a greatly reduced diet if they did not do their work, or misbehaved. Adults and children were given religious instruction and taught how to read and write in prisons and houses of correction. There were thirty-four prison schools in 1851.

Solitary confinement was used as a punishment or as a proportion of a prisoner's sentence. Samuel Jones (11) was convicted of stealing linen in July 1828 and given six months in the Knutsford House of Correction; the last week of each month was spent in solitary confinement.

A very young-looking offender, Michael Daley (16), in 1892. LA PLA 16/1.

Prisons were grossly overcrowded, and to relieve the pressure, former naval vessels – the 'hulks' – were pressed into service in the 1770s. The hulks, which were cramped, insanitary and riddled with vermin, were supposed to be a temporary measure. Over the years thousands of men and boys were imprisoned in these notorious hell-holes, which held convicts awaiting transportation. Bullying was rife amongst the inmates onboard, who suffered from diseases such as scurvy.

The *Bellerophon* at Sheerness was briefly used as a boys-only hulk, with no adult prisoners. In 1824 John Henry Capper, the superintendent of the hulks, reported that the prison ship *Bellerophon* housed 320 inmates: 'the greater part of whom are under fourteen years of age' (*Two Reports of John Henry Capper, Esq., Superintendent of Ships and Vessels Employed for the*

Confinement of Offenders Under Sentence of Transportation, Vol. 162 (1824)). The boys made clothes and shoes for the prisoners.

On the Thames, the 'mast-less Hulks, with their grim-looking barred port-holes' held almost 900 prisoners under 15 in 1851: 20 boys were under 10 years old (Henry Mayhew, *The Great World of London, Part IX* (David Bogue, 1856)).

New prisons were built such as Millbank Penitentiary in London, also used as a place of detention prior to transportation, but some child convicts were distressingly young even by contemporary standards.

Reformers such as Mary Carpenter believed that prison was wholly inappropriate for young children; it did not reform them. At Liverpool Borough Gaol in 1841, 'R.H.', age 11, said that he had already been in prison 'seven times . . . When I first began to steal my brother used to send me into shops to take money or anything I could get hold of'. (*Sixth Report of the Inspectors Appointed . . . To Visit the Different Prisons of Great Britain,* XXX (1841)).

In June 1846, John Nicholls (7) was sentenced to seven years' transportation for stealing money at Warwick; he was sent to Millbank first. Dominick Rafferty (8) was found guilty at Preston of stealing 9*d* in coppers; he too was committed to Millbank to await transportation for seven years. John was later given a conditional pardon and sent to a house of correction instead; Dominick was pardoned by the Secretary of State.

Parkhurst Prison on the Isle of Wight (1838) was the first penal institution for juveniles only: it housed over 300 boys. The inmates were given a good education and industrial training. The idea was to reform the boys, then send them to settle overseas to Australia with a conditional pardon, or to New Zealand (not a penal colony).

Over 100 boys from the hulks were transferred to Parkhurst when it opened (child convicts were still kept in local gaols elsewhere in the UK). Discipline in Parkhurst was very strict; at first the prisoners wore leg irons, and the diet was extremely sparse. Conditions were later relaxed slightly and the leg irons removed.

When a boy arrived in the prison, he was kept in a separate cell for four months; if he misbehaved, he was kept in a separate cell for up to twelve months. Parkhurst's military style regime was savagely criticised by reformers like Mary Carpenter, however. The Parkhurst experiment was overtaken by the success of reformatories run by charities (see below) and it closed in 1864.

Records of Prisoners

Calendars of prisoners (quarter sessions records) list those awaiting trial, those already sentenced and the court's verdict and sentence against them. Calendars of prisoners were sometimes published locally, too.

Where possible, check the calendars for the assizes after a person was sentenced, which may give details of what happened next: whether the prisoner was discharged, transported or sentenced to a further term of imprisonment, etc.

Case Study

The calendars of prisoners tried at Chester Assizes 1828–42 show that in August 1828 William Casey (15) and James Riley alias Hatfield (18) were sentenced to death at Chester Summer Assizes for stealing gloves and silk handkerchiefs from John Heys' shop at Stockport (CALS D7734/1). The register of criminals at the Home Office for the county of Chester also records a sentence of death against Casey and Riley (HO 27/35/72).

However, if we search the calendar of prisoners at Chester, we discover that William's and James's sentences were commuted to transportation for life, and on 17 November that year they were transferred to the hulks at Woolwich to await their passage (CALS D7734/1).

We can use the Hulks' letter books to trace William and James's story a little further. The index to the register of prisoners has an entry for William Casey (no. 3320). It gives his destination as 'NSW' (New South Wales) and notes that he is a 'very bad' character, who has been convicted before (HO 9, piece 5, folio 51). James Riley (no. 541) was bound for New South Wales, too. The gaoler's report comments that James was imprisoned several times before, and his character was 'of the worst [type]'.

The register of prisoners confirms what we know but adds more detail: William and James were both convicted for 'life' at Chester Assizes on 28 August for 'burglary', and they arrived at the *Justitia* on 18 November 1828. But James's age is given as 19, not 18. They were put on the transport ship on 30 March 1829 (HO 9, piece 4, folio 146, copyright TNA and courtesy Ancestry).

A search on the Convict Transportation Database (State Library of Queensland) reveals that William and James were 2 of the 176 convicts transported on the ship *America* on 4 April 1829 (HO 11/7, folio 28), www.slq.qld.gov.au/info/fh/convicts.

Sydney, New South Wales, south view in 1824. *Gentleman's Magazine,* May 1824.

Prison records include registers of prisoners, with physical descriptions of them and details of their offences. Misconduct books, fines and penalties books, prisoners' property books and prisoners' denomination registers may prove useful. Prison governors' account books may contain payments made for work done by the prisoners. Prison chaplains compiled 'character books' on inmates.

TNA holds prison registers (indexed) for Parkhurst and Millbank prisons (HO 24) which show each prisoner's age, whether they can read or write, occupation, when and where convicted, crime, sentence, previous offences and more. TNA guide to looking for a prisoner, www.nationalarchives.gov.uk/records/looking-for-person/prisoners.htm.

The LMA website has an information leaflet cataloguing the prison records in its collections including the young offenders' institute at Feltham, and Wormwood Scrubs.

For the hulks, TNA Digital Microfilm online has copies of HO 9 (Registers of convicts in the hulks 1847–9) which include each inmate's name, year of birth, age, year, place where convicted, offence committed, name of the hulk and character reports.

Also on TNA's Digital Microfilm is series HO 10: records of settlers and convicts, New South Wales and Tasmania, with lists of male and female convicts and former convicts in the colonies. Series HO 11 (convict transportation registers) lists convicts transported with dates of their convictions.

Section C lists some websites for researching child prisoners, hulk registers and transported convict ancestors online.

Some children lived in prisons, not because they had committed an offence, but because they were born to a female convict or were with a parent awaiting trial. When prison reformer Elizabeth Fry visited Newgate Prison in 1813, she discovered 300 women and children incarcerated together without even the most basic necessities such as blankets.

Living conditions in these establishments were not ideal and prison death records, like the County Gaol register held at Surrey History Centre, may include prisoners' children. Prisoners and their children (if in jail) will be listed in census returns, but full names are not always given, just their initials.

Reformatories and Industrial Schools

People began to question the severity of the treatment meted out to juvenile offenders and child convicts. Many children had never learnt right from wrong, and did not know how to make an honest living. If they were taught habits of industry, and given religious instruction, they might avoid a life of crime and an ignominious end on the gallows. And once a youngster had been in prison, it was difficult for them to get a job.

The first reformatories were not State run; they were charities like the 'Temporary Refuge' attached to the London Refuge for the Destitute. The Refuge helped boys and girls like 13-year-old 'S.W.', committed to the Borough Compter for stealing a necklace from a child. After being admitted to the Temporary Refuge, she, 'conducted herself with honesty and propriety' (*Report of the Committee for the Society for the Improvement of Prison Discipline and the Reformation of Juvenile Offenders* (London, 1818)).

The Philanthropic Society, Redhill

The Philanthropic Society was founded in 1788 to prevent crime by reforming criminal boys and girls, and providing religious and moral education for convicts' children. Initially, the Society (incorporated in 1806) had a house at Cambridge Heath, Hackney, before moving to St George's Fields, Southwark in 1792.

The Society took children between 9 and 12 years old. The emphasis was on practical help for the children (or 'objects' as the Society described them in its reports). Convicts' sons who had not committed an offence were given industrial training in the 'Manufactory'. They learnt skills such as bookbinding, copperplate engraving, tailoring, shoemaking, etc.

Convicts' daughters were trained as domestic servants in another building

The Philanthropic Society's farm at Redhill. *Illustrated London News*, 14 June 1851.

near the Manufactory, separated from the boys by a high wall. They learnt needlework and plain sewing, made their own clothes and those of the boys, and did all the washing and mending for the Manufactory.

Criminal girls were only admitted for the first few years of the Society's inception; after 1817 no more were admitted, seemingly because it was difficult to stop them giving the convicts' daughters bad habits.

Boys who had previously committed an offence were sent to the 'Reform' building on arrival; some boys were sent there from the New Prison at Clerkenwell (*An Account of the Nature and Present State of the Philanthropic Society* (London, 1816)). The 'Reform' was originally at Bermondsey (1802), but later moved to the St George's Fields site. 'Reform' boys were given religious and moral instruction, and could attend the Manufactory when the chaplain deemed them sufficiently reformed to mix with other children.

By the late 1820s: 'in this institution upwards of 200 children are rescued from prison, the retreat of villainy, or the haunts of prostitution' (Thomas Allen, *A New History of London, Westminster and the Borough of Southwark* (London, 1829)).

In 1845 the Society stopped taking in convicts' children and girls. It concentrated on rehabilitating young male offenders. Four years later, the Society moved from Southwark to Redhill, where it founded a farm so that boys could learn agricultural skills to prepare them for emigration. The inmates cultivated the land and cared for cows, horses, sheep and pigs. Produce from the farm was sold to help defray its costs.

There were no walls to stop the boys escaping, but seemingly few ran away. The chief punishments were 'loss of diet, forfeiture of their small weekly earnings, and short solitary imprisonment' (*Illustrated London News*, 14 June 1851).

Other pioneering reformatories were Elizabeth Fry's School of Discipline for criminal girls at Chelsea (1828) and the Hardwicke Reformatory School (1852) in Gloucestershire. Mary Carpenter set up Kingswood Reformatory (1852) for boys and Red Lodge (1854) for girls in Bristol.

The good work done by reformatories persuaded the government to confer official status on those institutions approved by the Secretary of State. The first HMI of reformatories, Sydney Turner, was appointed to inspect certified institutions.

Under the Juvenile Offenders Acts of 1853 and 1854, magistrates could send convicted children over 10 years old to certified reformatories for two to five years instead of imposing a long prison sentence. (They had to serve a prison sentence of at least two weeks first). The parents of children sentenced to detention in reformatories had to contribute to their fees; if they could not find the money, the State paid.

However, it was up to individual magistrates to decide whether to impose a prison sentence and children were still sent to prison for their whole sentence. Magistrates could also order non-custodial punishments such as fines or corporal punishment.

By the mid-nineteenth century, charities had founded so many reformatories and children's homes that the Reformatory and Refuge Union (1856) was formed to help co-ordinate relief work. The Union campaigned for the introduction of juvenile courts. This organisation became the Children's Aid Society in 1933.

Following the 1854 Act, the Farm School at Redhill became a certified reformatory. In December 1857 there were 257 inmates: 149 boys were admitted that year. In the same year 129 youngsters were discharged: 66 emigrated, 52 found jobs in the UK, 8 went to the training ship *Akbar*, 1 lad died 'after a lingering illness' and 2 absconded.

An emigrant lad, 'T. M.', wrote to the chaplain at Redhill, Sydney Turner, on 17 March 1857 to let him know that he was now married and asked if Turner could contact his father: 'you know I never heard from him nor seen him [sic] but once all the time I was in the school' (*The Philanthropic Society's Farm School for the Reform of Criminal Boys* (London, 1858)).

In 1953 the organisation was re-named the Royal Philanthropic Society. Its records, including admission registers, are held by the Surrey History Centre, which has a database of registers for Redhill on its website (Section A3).

Some reformatories were 'training ships' like the *Akbar* on the River Mersey, founded by the Liverpool Juvenile Reformatory Association, and the *Clarence*, also on the Mersey, which took Roman Catholic boys. Discipline was not always easy to impose on the self-willed boys sent to the training ships and mutinies were not unknown.

The *Akbar* at Liverpool was no longer suitable by 1906. A new purpose-built reformatory, Heswall Nautical School, was constructed. The school received unwelcome publicity in 1911 following reports of cruel punishments inflicted on inmates which allegedly resulted in the deaths of some boys (*The Times*, 24 February 1911, *Manchester Guardian*, 24 February 1911).

Some children became ill, or were not sturdy enough to cope with the hard physical labour in reformatories. Deaths and illnesses were recorded in the institution's minute book or logbook. The managers' minute book of Bradwall Reformatory School, Sandbach reveals that in 1889 Thomas Cartwright, who had been suffering from 'Hooping cough' [sic] was given permission by the Home Secretary to be discharged and released into his parents' care (CALS D4304/1).

Case Study

An entry in the Heswall Nautical School logbook (15 July 1910) notes that the doctor was called to see a lad surnamed Severn admitted to the infirmary that afternoon. The next day, 'the boy Severn' was taken to the Royal Southern Hospital. On 17 July, 'no. 3360 Severn died at Royal Southern Hospital at 11.15 a.m.'. Three days later, the log records that a memorial service was held at the school for the youngster at 11.30 am, and 'Mr Smith and 5 boys attended Severn's funeral – 2 boys subsequently absconded!' (LA DDX 824/3/1).

The State later set up its own reformatories, named 'borstals' after the first one at Borstal in Kent (1895), as an alternative to prison for boys over 16 years old.

According to a Home Office report in 1924, a significant proportion of young men who were sent to borstal had appeared in juvenile courts several times before they were 16 years old. The criminal career of 'Case B' began when he was 10; he was cautioned for stealing. For later offences he received: 'for stealing a fowl at 12, six strokes [of the birch]; for stealing pencils at 14, six strokes; for stealing rabbit-skins at the same age, six strokes; for warehouse-breaking at 14, sent to a reformatory; for stealing a watch, etc., at 15, sent back to reformatory'.

The repeated birching of this youngster clearly did not deter him from theft. The use of the birch was declining, however: in 1913 magistrates ordered 5.4 per cent of offenders (2,079 children) to be birched. Most children's convictions were for larceny, for which they were fined (11,805 children). Over 1,000 children were sent to reformatories that year.

Ten years later, just 1.7 per cent of those convicted were given corporal punishment (*2nd Report of the Children's Branch* (HMSO, 1924)). Magistrates increasingly used probation as an alternative for young offenders.

Most offenders were boys: in 1916, 3,698 boys and 532 girls were committed to reformatories. Only about 10 per cent of boys and girls re-offended after leaving reformatories in the 1920s. After their discharge (or if they were allowed out on licence), boys chiefly entered the armed forces and merchant navy, or found work on the land or as labourers. Girls were more likely to enter domestic service.

Newspapers often give detailed reports of trials, and may include biographical information about a young offender's family. As late as the mid-1920s, details of juvenile court proceedings and the names of young offenders were still published in the press. The Home Office was concerned that this could lead to youngsters losing their jobs, pushing them into a criminal career instead of reforming them.

Certified Industrial Schools

The thousands of poor children wandering or begging in the streets in the nineteenth century caused great concern to the authorities and reformers, especially since crime levels seemed to be rising. The children's extreme poverty made it likely that they would steal just to stay alive.

Industrial schools were natural successors to ragged schools (Chapter 4). Workhouses were reluctant to take in children with previous criminal convictions, so charities and voluntary groups set up industrial schools for destitute children. These schools should not be confused with the workhouse industrial schools run by Poor Law authorities, although both sets of institutions trained children so that they could earn their own living.

In industrial schools, which were residential, children received an education similar to that in elementary schools, plus woodwork or metalwork classes. Industrial schools had farms or gardens attached, and the children were set digging.

Juvenile courts dealt with 'neglected' children, or those abused by a parent or guardian, as well as those who had offended. Magistrates could commit children at risk to the care of a relative or 'fit person', or to an industrial school.

Critics pointed out that children who had not committed any offence were being treated the same way as young offenders, but the Home Office felt that in practice 'there is little to choose between the circumstances of the two classes of children' because offenders were often neglected children, too.

If a parent did not want their child to go to a reformatory or industrial school, they could apply to the Home Office. Conversely, parents could ask for their children to be sent to a reformatory or industrial school if they could not cope with their behaviour, but they had to guarantee to pay the child's school fees, or part of them.

Impoverished children were given detention orders and sent to industrial schools if they were beggars, or 'found wandering'; if their parents were in prison, or if a parent was criminal or drunken. A girl whose father had committed a sexual offence against her or a sister could be sent to an industrial school. Children up to 14 years old were given detention orders if they committed an offence, or were 'refractory paupers', or failed to obey a school attendance order (played truant).

Children stayed at industrial schools until they were 15 (later 16), and up to age 19 for reformatories, but school managers could allow them out on licence after eighteen months. The schools usually held an annual camp, and children could go home for a little while during the school's holiday.

Children under the age of 8 who were committed by magistrates to industrial schools were sometimes boarded out with foster parents instead by some local authorities, such as London County Council.

In 1916, 10,897 boys and 3,052 girls went to industrial schools; and 883 boys and 410 girls were committed to 'day industrial schools' (*2nd Report of the Children's Branch* (HMSO, 1924)).

Day industrial schools were for children who were neglected and needed feeding. These children were given meals, industrial training and education, but not lodging. The need for these schools reduced when ordinary elementary schools began providing meals.

Most industrial schools were Protestant, but there were establishments for

Roman Catholic or Jewish children. In some places such as Liverpool, London and Sheffield, special industrial schools for truants were set up by school boards and local authorities after 1876.

Concerns about child prostitution, which was carried on openly in the middle of large cities, gave rise to a change to the Industrial Schools Act. The age of consent was only 12 years of age until 1875, when it was raised to 13 years. Prostitution was not illegal, but the superintendents of industrial schools and reformatories often refused to accept girl prostitutes.

To tackle the problem of child prostitution (partly because if these girls had babies they were a charge on the poor rates), the Industrial School Amendment Act of 1880 was passed. If a child was found living in a brothel, even if its parents owned it, or if the child was found in the company of prostitutes, magistrates could commit her to an industrial school.

The age of consent was later raised to 16 years in 1885 (the Criminal Law Amendment Act) following a sensational campaign by William Stead and Josephine Butler.

Certified schools and reformatories were subject to inspection by HMI and kept official records such as registers of admissions and discharges, general conduct books, punishment books, medical officer's books and cash books showing receipts for the work done by the children, e.g. on the institution's farm. Industrial school records may also include inmates' birth certificates. Governors' minute books may have details of individual youngsters.

Case Study

Following the Industrial Schools Act of 1861, Boughton Ragged School, Chester became a Certified Industrial School in 1863. The minutes for the Chester Ragged School Society Managing Committee dated 2 July 1880 include a report by the honorary secretary on two boys who had absconded. The 'boy Stevenson' was caught, and the committee decided to write to his father 'pointing out the penalty he had rendered himself liable to for encouraging the boy to abscond'.

The other boy, John (?) Clark was found to have, 'enlisted as a bugler in the 1st Battalion Rifle Brigade, North Camp, Aldershot'. Clark was reportedly 'doing well', so the committee decided he would benefit from being left there. It was decided to ask the Home Office if he could be discharged from the school (CALS DES/23/3).

As mentioned previously, ordinary schools sometimes underwent several name changes and moved premises during their existence, and this was true of reformatories and industrial schools, too.

Case Study

Bradwall Reformatory was founded in 1855 by G.W. Latham of Bradwall Hall, Sandbach. In 1908 its name changed to Bradwall Training School. The First World War saw an upsurge in young people's bad behaviour (because fathers were away at the trenches), and extra accommodation was needed. The School took over the Cheshire Agricultural and Horticultural College at Holmes Chapel as an annexe for two years, and senior boys were accommodated there; the juniors stayed at Bradwall. In 1920, after new buildings were constructed, the whole school moved to Holmes Chapel. The school's name changed to Saltersford School five years later (*Saltersford School, Holmes Chapel: A Short History*, CALS D4304/101).

If a child at an institution died suddenly, an inquest was held, and the circumstances of the death reported to the Home Office Inspector. The reformatory superintendent also sent returns of admissions and discharges, and quarterly lists of children under detention, to the Home Office.

In 1933 the Children and Young Persons Act reclassified reformatories and industrial schools as 'approved schools'. Industrial and reformatory school records may be archived in county council education department files, and some councils kept registers of young offenders committed to these institutions, with details of where the youngster was sent. TNA has several series with information on reformatories, industrial and approved schools (Section A1).

Directories of reformatories and industrial schools were published (1914 onwards) by the government; the directories include 'special schools' for children with a mental disability.

The Society of Superintendents of Certified Reformatories and Industrial Schools printed a journal, the *Certified Schools Gazette*, founded *c*. 1908 (later the *Approved Schools Gazette*), with news stories relating to these institutions. For example, the July 1921 issue of the *Gazette* has photographs of a sports day and prize-winners at Somerset Boys' Home, Prior Park (CALS D4304/84).

See Pamela Horn, *Young Offenders: Juvenile Delinquency 1700–2000* (Amberley Publishing, 2010) and Jeannie Duckworth, *Fagin's Children: Criminal Children in Victorian England* (Hambledon & London, 2002).

Stephen Wade, *Tracing Your Criminal Ancestors* (Pen & Sword, 2009) and David Hawking, *Criminal Ancestors* (History Press, 2009) discuss techniques for researching relatives with a shady past. Ruth Paley and Simon Fowler's *Family Skeletons: Exploring the Lives of Our Disreputable Ancestors* (TNA, 2005) has a chapter on child murderers.

Outlawing Child Cruelty

An Englishman's home was his castle and his family was considered inviolable by the State and society at large. John Stuart Mill commented on the 'misapplied notions of liberty' which stopped the State from interfering in people's home lives: 'One would almost think that a man's children were supposed to be literally, and not metaphorically, a part of himself, so jealous is opinion of the smallest interference in law with his absolute and exclusive control over them' (*On Liberty*, 1859).

A certain amount of physical correction by parents was deemed necessary by society; exactly how hard a beating was 'reasonable' was rather more difficult to decide. How could children be protected in their own homes?

One shocking case was the death of Ellen (Helen) Barratt, aged 17, of Apsley Guise, near Woburn. In 1856 her parents Samuel and Susannah, and Ellen's older sister Elizabeth were charged with causing her death by neglect, starvation and cruelty. Samuel Barratt was a shepherd, seemingly respectable, who lived in a well-furnished cottage. Susannah and Elizabeth kept the four youngest girls – Ellen, Charlotte, Julia and Susannah – at work for 14 hours each day making hand-made pillow lace.

Charlotte, Julia and young Susannah were witnesses for the prosecution at their parents' and sister Elizabeth's trial. The girls subsisted on a meagre diet of gruel, bread and dripping – if they did not complete 5ft feet of lace each day, they had no supper, were whipped and endured other disgusting cruelties. Ellen had nothing to eat at all for the last two or three days before she died. (It was the physical cruelty that was unusual in this case; long working hours were common for pillow-lace workers.)

At the dead child's inquest it was found that Ellen's stomach was only as large as a that of a 5-year-old. All the younger Barratt girls were small for their age, and wasting away. After the inquest they were taken into the workhouse, and quickly gained weight (the workhouse could be a blessing for those in real need).

At Bedford Assizes in July 1856, Samuel, mother Susannah and Elizabeth were found guilty of manslaughter. Samuel was imprisoned for a year, but Susannah and Elizabeth, whom the jury considered most culpable as they 'cared' for the children whilst he was at work, were sentenced for four years' penal servitude (*The Times*, 28 May, 16 July 1856).

Local communities greatly disapproved of the ill-treatment of children like Ellen Barratt. The problem was that by the time cases like Ellen's reached the courts, it was often too late to save a child. It was not until the 1880s that the first steps were taken to protect children at risk of abuse or cruelty at home.

In England the first society for the prevention of cruelty to children was formed at Liverpool in 1883. The London Society for the Prevention of Cruelty to Children (1884) worked hard to publicise cases of cruelty towards children. Through its official newspaper, the *Child's Guardian* (1882 onwards), it highlighted some horrific cases.

The Society and its campaigning leader, the Revd Benjamin Waugh (1839–1908), brought prosecutions against cruel parents like Alice Clay, and showed that child abuse was not confined to the lower classes.

The London Society's prosecution of Alice Clay was successful even though it was three years since she had injured her child. On 4 January 1888 Clay, the wife of a veterinary surgeon at Cromford, was found guilty at Derbyshire quarter sessions of inflicting grievous bodily harm on her 6-year-old daughter with a red-hot poker. Clay was sentenced to six months' hard labour (*The Times*, 5 January 1888).

In 1889, the London Society was re-named the National Society for the Prevention of Cruelty to Children (NSPCC). That same year, Parliament passed the landmark Prevention of Cruelty to Children Act, popularly known as the 'Children's Charter'.

Cruelty cases, fortunately, were rare compared with the total population. In 1900, 4,106 people were tried for cruelty and other offences against children, and by 1923 this number had fallen to 1,586 cases (*2nd Report of the Children's Branch* (HMSO, 1924)).

The NSPCC's archive is not currently accessible to researchers, but you can write to the records manager at Weston House for advice on sources (Section B). Local record offices and reference libraries may have branch records such as minute books. Records for the Liverpool Society for the Prevention of Cruelty to Children, including a register of prosecutions, are held at Liverpool Record Office.

Chapter 6

HELPING HANDS

During the eighteenth century, philanthropists such as Thomas Coram and Jonas Hanway were horrified by the hundreds of babies and children abandoned by their parents each year. The bodies of newborn babies were thrown on rubbish heaps, or left in the street.

Women who gave birth to an illegitimate child faced great social stigma. They may have been too ashamed or frightened to ask the parish authorities for help. As we have seen, babies in eighteenth-century poorhouses had little chance of survival before Hanway's Acts became law.

The Foundling Hospital

The Foundling Hospital was the most famous charity for unwanted and abandoned infants. It was founded in 1741 by Captain Thomas Coram. The first premises used by the hospital were some houses in Hatton Garden; later a grand new building was erected near Gray's Inn.

Mothers left a small token with their baby as a means of identification if they wanted to reclaim their child. A silk purse, a coin and even a lottery ticket were some of the items deposited (John Brownlow, *Memoranda, or Chronicles of the Foundling Hospital* (Sampson Low, 1847)). After 1760 the Hospital issued a receipt when a mother left her child. Only a tiny number of children were reclaimed each year.

Each child was allotted a number, and baptised with a new name. Not all the infants abandoned were illegitimate; a baby may not have been wanted because it was an extra mouth to feed in an already crowded household.

After a child was admitted, it was boarded out in the country for a couple of years; its nurse was paid weekly, and received an extra payment if the child was successfully raised. When they were about 3 years old, the children went back to the Hospital to be educated. The children were also inoculated against smallpox. The nurses reportedly got very attached to their charges, and were very distressed when they left; it must have been traumatic for the children, too.

The Foundling Hospital. *Old and New London Vol. V* (Cassell, Petter & Galpin, *c.* 1895).

The Foundling Hospital apprenticed out its children when they were about 15 years old. It kept detailed records, most of which are held by LMA (A/FH): general registers, petitions from mothers (a child was not always accepted), baptism registers, inspection books, nursery books and apprenticeship registers. Once you have discovered the foundling's number, you may discover quite a lot of information about the child (there's a guide on the LMA website). The records include schools and nurseries run by the Hospital. Records are closed for 110 years.

When civil registration was introduced, children from the Foundling Hospital did not receive a birth certificate from the GRO: the Hospital issued its own certificates. The GRO holds the Thomas Coram Register 1853–1948.

However, readers wishing to enquire about a foundling or order a birth certificate for a foundling should first contact Coram (the charity's modern name). Coram will order a certificate from the GRO, but these certificates are only the 'short' version, and do not include parents' names.

Another well-known charity was the Female Orphan Asylum at Lambeth, founded by John Fielding in 1758. The asylum took girls from 8 to

10 years old, and cared for them until they were 14, when they were apprenticed out as domestic servants (Sampson Low Jr, *The Charities of London* (Sampson Low, 1850)). The Asylum later became the Royal Female Orphanage, and moved to Beddington in 1866; records from the 1870s are held by Sutton Local Studies and Archive Centre.

By 1850 the London area alone had fifteen charity orphanages, plus sixteen asylums for needy children. Other large cities such as Liverpool and Manchester had orphanages, too. Some children's homes were linked to occupations, e.g. they were for the children of sailors or clergymen. An 'orphan' was not necessarily a child who had lost both parents; the term 'orphan' was also used for a child with one parent alive.

Case Study
The London Orphan Asylum (1813) at Clapton clothed and educated children aged 7 to 11 from all over the country, especially if their father had served in the armed forces. The asylum moved to Watford in the early 1870s. A search of the NRA index for 'London Orphan Asylum' shows that its records are held at the LMA and Surrey History Centre.

Homeless street-sweepers sleeping under a railway arch in London in the 1880s. *Cassell's Family Magazine* (Cassell & Co. Ltd, 1883).

Mud-larks on the Thames trying to earn a living by scavenging. *Old and New London Vol. III* (Cassell, Petter & Galpin, *c.* 1878).

As we saw previously, in the nineteenth century there was increasing disquiet about the thousands of destitute children in London and other big cities. They slept where they could: under railway arches, on the streets, under hedges. Abandoned by their parents, or kicked out of doors when they were old enough to toddle, they survived by begging, stealing, sweeping the streets or scavenging rubbish to sell. 'Incorrigible and irrepressible . . . they turn up at every corner – as fusee-vendors [match-sellers], or very small acrobats, performing cartwheels, or throwing wild somersaults . . . or standing on their head against a wall' to coax a few pence from passers-by (Harold King, 'A Boys' Home', *Once A Week*, 25 August 1866).

How could these children be saved from their poverty, ignorance, and a potential life of crime? Putting them in prison meant that they mixed with bad company, and were likely to re-offend. Well-meaning individuals such as Dr Barnardo spent many years rescuing impoverished children.

Dr Thomas Barnardo opened his first children's home, for boys, in

Postcard of the Babies' Castle, Hawkhurst, Kent, a Dr Barnardo home, postmarked 1911.

Stepney in 1870. Three years later, a home for girls was founded at Barkingside. Dr Barnardo (1845–1905) took in children with disabilities and social handicaps such as illegitimacy at a time when some other charities imposed restrictions on admission.

In 1884 Barnardo opened a 'Babies Castle' at Hawkhurst, but later boarded out the infants, not only because it was cheaper than keeping them in an institution, but also because the children were healthier (Mrs Barnardo and J. Marchant, *Memoirs of Dr Barnardo* (Hodder & Stoughton, 1907)).

Another famous organisation was the Church of England Society for Waifs and Strays (1881), later the Church of England Children's Society (1946). It is now the Children's Society (Section A2). A virtual archive, 'Hidden Lives Revealed', is dedicated to children cared for by the charity.

The National Refuges for Homeless and Destitute Children, founded by William Williams and Lord Shaftesbury, cared for nearly 1,000 boys and girls in 1894. The organisation ran several children's homes including the Farm School at Bisley, Girls' Homes at Sudbury and Ealing, and two training ships on the Thames, the *Arethusa* and *Chichester*. In 1904 the society was renamed Shaftesbury Homes and Arethusa Training Ship; it is now

Shaftesbury Young People. See Marion Bailey, *The Chance of a Lifetime: the Shaftesbury Homes and Arethusa – 150 Years* (Dianthus Publishing, 1996). Surviving records are at LMA.

The Save the Children Fund was founded in 1919 by sisters Eglantyne Jebb and Dorothy Buxton at Fairfield House. During the Second World War, the charity set up residential nurseries for evacuees, day nurseries for the children of working parents, play groups in air-raid shelters and play centres.

The Save the Children archive (University of Birmingham Special Collections) includes records for its children's homes; see the online catalogue. Records of local branches of Save the Children may be held locally.

Once a child was in the care of a charitable institution, it was not always easy for their family to get them back again. In 1860, the older sister of 14-year-old Elizabeth Daley successfully obtained a writ of habeas corpus against the matron and secretary of the Refuge for Houseless and Destitute Children, Broad Street, Bloomsbury.

The Daley family were Roman Catholics; Elizabeth's older sister cared for her and two other siblings after their parents' deaths. When Elizabeth was about 13 the little family got into financial difficulties and she was admitted to St Margaret's Workhouse, Westminster, as a temporary expedient. Elizabeth's older sister promised to come back for her as soon as she could. Shortly afterwards, Elizabeth was transferred to Marylebone Workhouse.

When Elizabeth's sister tried to retrieve her, she discovered Elizabeth had been transferred to a school on Marylebone Road attached to the Refuge for Houseless and Destitute Children, and was about to emigrate to Tasmania; she thought her family had forgotten her.

As soon as Elizabeth saw her big sister, she wanted to stay, and said that she had been forced to attend Anglican Church services in spite of being a Catholic. Elizabeth asked to leave the Refuge with her big sister, but permission was refused. When a judge heard all the evidence, he ordered the Refuge to return Elizabeth to her family.

Records for Children's Homes

Typical records for orphanages, asylums and refuges include minute books, logbooks, admission and discharge registers, correspondence, lists of children sent abroad, lists of children helped outside the orphanage, photographs, etc. Census returns should have lists of children living in the orphanage.

> **Case Study**
> ### Webb Orphanage, Crewe
> This orphanage was founded under the will of F.W. Webb, a London and North Western Railway locomotive engineer, for the children of deceased employees of the LNWR. The minute book commences on 10 November 1911. It contains a list of the first children accepted for admission (twelve boys and five girls) that year, with their ages, including 'J. E.' age 8, from Liverpool, and 'M. R.' age 9 years and 3 months, from Manchester (full names are given in the book).
>
> Later entries in the minute book note the names of new arrivals. Sometimes brief details of new children's deceased parents are included (CALS D7286).

> **Case Study**
> ### National Children's Home and Orphanage, Frodsham Branch
> The National Children's Home (NCH) and Orphanage at Frodsham had a school attached (later the Kingsley & Newton Temporary Council School). The school logbook mentions events such as school trips and the outbreak of illnesses. An entry dated 13 September 1920 notes the funeral of a pupil, James Howard from Class III, who died in Chester Infirmary on 10 September (CALS SL 319/1).

Records for children's charities will not necessarily all be held at one location or archive; if a charity had local branches, then check the relevant record office, too.

In addition to the NRA database, the DANGO website is a useful finding aid for charities and other non-governmental organisations, including over sixty bodies concerned with child health or welfare.

DANGO covers organisations and pressure groups from 1945 onwards, but includes charities founded much earlier such as Coram and the NSPCC. The database has contact details and locations for archives relating to the organisations listed, sometimes with links to online catalogues (some information may be out of date), www.dango.bham.ac.uk/index.htm.

For example, the University of Liverpool Special Collections and Archives (Section A4) holds some records for Barnardo's charity. The DANGO website has an online information sheet cataloguing Liverpool University's social work archives, with details on access restrictions, and a useful bibliography, www.dango.bham.ac.uk/catalogues/C54Barnardo.doc.

The Barnardo's archive has records dating from the 1870s. Barnardo's also holds records for the Children's Aid Society, Macpherson Homes, Marchmont Homes, Liverpool Sheltering Home and Sharman's Home and can search these records if requested. Barnardo's has a family history research service for relatives of children cared for by them.

Section A2 lists some archives for children's charities; see Section B for addresses of more charities. Charity Commission reports (Chapter 4) have information on children's charities.

Tip

In 1942, seven charities banded together to form The Constituent Societies of the National Council of Associated Children's Homes. Its founder members were: Dr Barnardo's Homes, Catholic Child Welfare Council, Church of England Children's Society, National Children's Home, Jewish Board of Guardians, Shaftesbury Homes and *Arethusa* Training Ship and the Children's Aid Society.

This constituent organisation, which acquired new members over the years, and still includes some founder members, became the National Council of Voluntary Child Care Organisations (NCVCCO) in 1965. In 2008 it was re-named Children England.

The Charity Organisation Society

The 'Charity Organisation Society' (COS) or the Society for Organising Charitable Relief and Repressing Mendicity, founded by Octavia Hill and others in London in 1869, co-ordinated relief work.

This tough-minded, influential society was keen to ensure that charities focused their energies on the 'deserving poor'. Precious resources should not be wasted on 'indiscriminate charity'. The COS believed that open-handed relief discouraged independence, encouraged pauperism and lowered wages. It strongly disapproved of State aid, even for those in need. For example, the Society argued that giving free school meals to poor children might encourage their mothers to be 'lazy' and stop cooking proper meals for them.

The COS later became the Family Welfare Association (FWA), currently Family Action. LMA holds a collection of records for the FWA, including case files, correspondence, financial accounts and other records for several children's charities, missions and homes such as the Stainer Homes for Deaf and Dumb Children. The collection is closed for sixty years, except annual reports and other publications; researchers wishing to consult the records must first write to the Director of Family Action for permission.

The Senate House Library, University of London holds the FWA Library, a large collection of books and pamphlets on poverty, society and charities, including COS publications such as the *Charities Digest and Register*.

See Charles Loch Mowat, *The Charity Organisation Society 1869–1913: Its Ideas and Work* (Methuen, 1961), Madeline Rooff, *A Hundred Years of Family Welfare* (Michael Joseph, 1972) and Robert Humphries, *Poor Relief and Charity 1860–1945: the London Charity Organisation Society* (Palgrave Macmillan, 2001).

Emigration Schemes

Emigration was seen as a 'cure-all' for child deprivation; children could start afresh far away from the bad influences of street life.

The Children's Friend Society (1830) was one of the earliest charities to send children abroad. Founder Captain Brenton set up an asylum for boys at Hackney Wick and the Victoria Female Asylum at Chiswick: poor children were trained so that they could emigrate to Australia, Canada or South Africa. 'I would gladly see ten thousand boys properly prepared and sent out there, rather than see them starving and naked in our streets, or pining in Cold-bath Fields or Newgate [prisons]' (Sir J. Brenton, *Memoir of Capt. Edward Pelham Brenton* (London, 1842)). Some children in his asylums had previously spent time in prison.

The asylum at Hackney Wick offered industrial training and an education. Boys got up at 5.45 am. They were taught the 3 'Rs' and given religious instruction until about 8 am. After breakfast they did character-building work with a spade or pickaxe on the land until lunchtime. When the meal was over the boys went to the refuge's library or playground. At 2 pm they did more agricultural work until suppertime. The boys had more lessons until 8 pm, when they went to sleep in their hammocks.

The girls at Chiswick learnt domestic skills such as laundry work and cookery. No corporal punishment was used; punishments were solitary confinement and less food. The children emigrated when they were 15 or 16 (Charles Forss, *Practical Remarks on the Education of the Working Classes . . . at the Brenton Asylum* (Hackney Wick, 1835)).

Anthony Ashley Cooper, seventh Earl of Shaftesbury was a great believer in child emigration. Shaftesbury was chairman of the Ragged School Union, and the charity raised enough funds to send several batches of children to Australia (Chapter 4).

The shoe-black brigades were part of the ragged school movement. Boys were lent shoe-blacking materials (they had to repay the cost over

Shoe-black boy. *Illustrated London News*, 24 May 1851.

time) and part of their earnings was put in a savings bank to enable them to emigrate.

In the late 1860s philanthropists such as Maria Rye and Annie Macpherson sent hundreds of children overseas and apprenticed them as farm labourers and domestic servants. Poor Law authorities in cities such as Liverpool and London sent children abroad from their workhouses under the auspices of Miss Rye, but this practice was temporarily paused from 1875 to 1884 following a critical report by government inspector Andrew Doyle on the child migrants' living and working conditions in Canada.

Meanwhile, Dr Barnardo had rescued so many children that he was struggling to find work for them once they were old enough to leave his homes. He began a programme of emigration.

Barnardo and others were convinced that poor children had much better prospects in life once separated from their feckless, unworthy or impoverished parents. He did not scruple to practically kidnap them to get them off the streets or away from their parents, and even sent children overseas without their relatives' consent. Barnardo's methods were controversial, and he was involved in over eighty court cases.

Following one court case, the Prevention of Cruelty to Children Act of 1889 permitted children to be taken away from their parents if they had been tried for neglect. The Custody of Children Act (1891) further curtailed parents' rights. A later Act (1894) permitted children whose parents had lost custody to be sent overseas if the Home Secretary gave permission.

The Barnardo emigration programme continued after his death; the Barnardo's archive has records for children who emigrated to Australia and Canada with the charity's help.

Children's charities and religious organisations such as the Waif and Strays Society, Fairbridge Society, the Roman Catholic 'Crusade of Rescue', Salvation Army and the National Children's Home (now Action for Children) also sent children abroad as migrants.

Time and again, child migrants were told by the institution caring for them that they were orphans when this was not, in fact, true. Often they were sent abroad without the knowledge or permission of any surviving relatives.

Sometimes children volunteered to go, after being told tales of the wonders of Canada and Australia. Others were shipped overseas without being asked for their consent. Some children were treated very kindly in their new homes, but others endured physical and sexual abuse at the hands of their 'carers'. Child migration schemes continued well into the twentieth century. Child criminals transported abroad are discussed in Chapter 5.

Migration Records

Section C has a list of websites related to child migrants. For child migrants to Canada, see Joy Parr, *Labouring Children, British Immigrant Apprentices to Canada, 1869–1924* (University of Toronto Press, 1994). Andrew Morrison's e-thesis *Thy Children Own Their Own Birth* has interviews with descendants of 'Home Children' sent to Canada, with a comprehensive bibliography, http://etheses.nottingham.ac.uk/276/1/Thy_Children_Own_Their_Birth.pdf.

The Child Migrants Trust, a charity set up in 1987 by Margaret Humphreys, helps former child migrants obtain information about their origins and provides a counselling service. It has branches in the UK and Australia. The Trust's website has information about tracing records and the history of child migration, www.childmigrantstrust.com.

See Roger Kershaw and Janet Sacks, *New Lives for Old: The Story of Britain's Child Migrants* (TNA, 2008), which has a guide to child migrants' records, and Roger Kershaw, *Migration Records: A Guide for Family Historians* (TNA, 2009).

You may find the Child Migrant Central Information Index mentioned on some websites. It was formerly held by the NCVCCO; the Department of Health took over responsibility for it in 2002. The Department of Health's current advice is that the Index cannot be accessed by members of the public. It suggests that readers seeking information on child migrant relatives should contact the sending agency (if known) first.

Special Schools for Special Children

There was no State provision for children with disabilities until late in the nineteenth century. Children who were blind, deaf and dumb, or had other handicaps were reliant on charities or the Poor Law authorities.

In England, the first school for the blind was founded in Liverpool in 1791 by Edward Rushton, a blind poet; it moved from Commutation Row to Hotham Street in 1800. Another school opened at Bristol two years later.

Following the success of the Liverpool school, a School for the Indigent Blind was founded at St George's Fields, Southwark in 1799. At first the school only accommodated 15 pupils, but later moved to larger premises at St George's Fields and by 1851 it had 150 students. The pupils, aged 12 upwards, were taught to read using raised type, and writing using a special apparatus; they learnt arithmetic, history, geography and so on.

Postcard of children at the Royal School for Deaf and Dumb Children, *c.* 1910.

Boys learned practical skills such as basket-making, rug-making and shoe-making. Girls learnt basket-making, knitting and rope-making. The idea was that children could earn some money when they left school. The School for the Indigent Blind (later the Royal Blind School) moved to Blackfriars Road in 1810, and in 1902 it moved again to Leatherhead.

Thomas Henshaw founded an Asylum for the Blind at Manchester in 1837. At Norwich, a Hospital and School for the Indigent Blind was founded at Magdalen Street (1805) by Thomas Tawell. At first the Hospital was only for local children, but Thomas Henshaw offered the institution 500 guineas if it opened its doors to blind children from all over the UK. Pupils entered the school when they were 12 years old, and stayed for five years. They learnt industrial skills, too.

Several schools for the blind had adult pupils as well as children. Often institutions for the blind pooled their resources with those for deaf and dumb children. In 1845 the Poor Law Amendment Act allowed Poor Law guardians to contribute towards asylums for the blind, and in 1868 a law was passed permitting them to send blind children to uncertified as well as certified schools.

Following the 1870 Education Act, school boards like Leeds and London began to provide specialist help but it was not compulsory for school boards to educate blind or deaf children until the Elementary Education Act of 1893.

Records for schools for blind, deaf or deaf and dumb children can be found in local record offices. For example, Birmingham Archives and Heritage Service holds records for the Royal School for Deaf Children, Birmingham, including registers of children.

The Royal National Institute for the Blind (RNIB) has its own archive and library. The University College London (UCL) Ear Institute Library has collections relating to the treatment of deaf people. The Royal National Institute for the Deaf (RNID) Library Institutional Collection holds archives of organisations for the deaf, including records relating to education such as schools' annual reports and school magazines. (RNID is now Action for Hearing Loss). There's an online catalogue of schools and organisations represented in the RNID collection, www.ucl.ac.uk/ls/sites/rnid/rnid_list-of-institutions.pdf.

An Act of 1899 gave school boards powers to make the parents of children who had a mental disability send them to a special school. Many children committed to reformatories and industrial schools were found to be suffering from a physical or mental disability, and they could be transferred to special schools.

Following the Mental Deficiency Acts of 1913 and 1914, more special schools were set up by LEAs for 'mentally defective' children (as they were called). For example, London County Council ran a Residential School for Mentally Defective Boys at Acre Lane, Brixton. The school had room for thirty-six scholars, but 'only educable mental defectives' were admitted (*Directory of Schools Certified by the Secretary of State under the Children Act, 1908* (HMSO, 1924) (CALS D4304/92)).

The historical background to the provision of special educational needs was included in the Warnock Report of 1978. You can read it on the Education in England website, www.educationengland.org.uk/documents/warnock/warnock02.html.

Local authority social services, children's services, education department and school board records may have lists of children who were mentally or physically 'defective'. Hospital records (see below) may include records of disabled children.

Records relating to children's homes and hospitals, including those for poorly or special children, may be archived with local authority files (Poor

Law authorities, public assistance committees or county councils), depending on the date. However, personal case files may have been destroyed (see Chapter 2).

Any surviving records for charities that cared for children with a mental disability, such as homes or residential schools, are most likely to be held locally.

Children's Hospitals, Maternity Hospitals and Medical Records

Medical care was expensive. Poor families relied on workhouse infirmaries or charities if they were sick or injured.

Until very recent times, most babies were born at home. However, several large towns had lying-in hospitals funded by charities where poor married women could have their babies. Some charities gave help to poor women who had their babies at home: extra linen, baby clothes and food.

Case Study

Records for lying-in hospitals can be extremely detailed. For example, the register for births for the British Lying-In Hospital, Brownlow Street, Holborn (RG 8 at TNA and bmdregisters.co.uk) gives the mother's age and the father's occupation as well as the child's date of birth.

This Hospital was for the wives of industrious local people. Sarah Berry (age 27), wife of William Berry, a shoe-maker, of the parish of St Andrew, Holborn, was admitted to the British Lying-In Hospital on 2 July 1758. Sarah was given an admission order for the hospital by the Revd Harry Hankey. Her child George was born on 4 July and baptised on 9 July. Sarah was discharged from hospital on 22 July (RG 8/54/folio10, copyright TNA and courtesy TheGenealogist.co. uk).

Unmarried mothers faced great prejudice and even hostility from their own families. Organisations like the Salvation Army ran maternity hospitals for those in need. The Salvation Army International Heritage Centre holds surviving records for these hospitals (Section A2). The Heritage Centre website has more information about the Salvation Army's work with unmarried mothers and the types of information available, www.salvationarmy.org.uk/uki/heritage.

Hospitals for the sick and injured were privately run (patients paid for treatment), or were organised by charities, voluntary societies or Poor Law institutions. Treatment at a charitable institution usually depended on the patient being given a ticket or letter of admission from a subscriber.

The first hospital specialising in children's diseases in the UK was the Great Ormond Street Hospital founded by Charles West in 1852. At first the hospital struggled for funding, but writers like Charles Dickens and later J.M. Barrie lent a hand. Children were treated as inpatients and outpatients. The hospital had over thirty beds. During its first 5 years it treated over 50,000 children; it also trained specialist paediatric nurses. It had a convalescent home, Cromwell House, at Highgate, where children recovered from their illnesses.

Following the abolition of Poor Law boards of guardians, workhouse infirmaries and hospitals became part of local authority services. When the National Health Service Act took effect in 1948, all hospitals became part of the Ministry of Health, and were managed by regional hospital boards. The vast majority of hospitals became part of the National Health Service, except for a couple of charities that opted out.

Great Ormond Street Hospital for Sick Children. *Old and New London Vol. IV* (Cassell, Petter & Galpin, *c.* 1895).

Nurse and children at Cromwell House, Great Ormond Street Hospital's convalescent home. *Old and New London Vol. V* (Cassell, Petter & Galpin, *c.* 1895).

Local authorities no longer supervised hospitals, but took over public services such as child welfare and maternity services, district and health nursing services, and vaccination.

Public health department, maternity, child welfare, health clinics, council-run nurseries and local authority children's home records may include registers of children with dates and locations when they were immunised and/or inoculated against diseases such as diphtheria, tuberculosis, tetanus, polio, measles and rubella. (School records may also include medical inspection records, or immunisation registers.)

Hospital records comprise admission and discharge registers, creed registers, registers of births and deaths, mortuary registers, case files, post-mortem books and so on. Patients' personal information such as case notes may be closed to researchers.

Hospital or institution records may be kept in the institution's own archive (e.g. such as the Great Ormond Street Hospital Archive), local record offices, or academic repositories. Some specialist hospital archives such as St Bartholomew's Hospital Archives and the Royal London Hospital Archives hold collections for several hospitals including some dedicated to children.

Record offices such as LMA have produced guides to their hospital collections, and some online databases are available to help you track down patient records.

Hospital Records Database

This joint project between TNA and the Wellcome Trust includes maternity and lying-in hospitals, and over 130 specialist children's hospitals. The database, which can be searched online, gives administrative details for the hospitals listed, their status or type (private, voluntary, NHS) including name changes, the location of administrative and clinical records and the dates covered. The database mentions any lists, catalogues or other finding aids available, and has weblinks to some online hospital catalogues, www.nationalarchives.gov.uk/hospitalrecords.

For example, a search for 'Birmingham' on the database elicits sixteen results including the Birmingham Children's Hospital and the Birmingham Maternity Hospital.

Historic Hospital Admission Records Project (HHARP)

This website has databases for over 120,000 children's hospital admission records from the 1850s to the First World War. Currently the project covers

Postcard of the Children's Hospital, Birmingham, *c.* 1906. (Nigel Wilkes Collection)

four children's hospitals: Great Ormond Street Hospital for Children (now an NHS Trust); the Evelina Hospital (now part of Guy's and St Thomas's NHS Trust), whose records are held at LMA; the Alexandra Hospital for Children with Hip Disease (records held at the Museum and Archive Department of St Bartholomew's and the London NHS Trust) and the Royal Hospital for Sick Children, Glasgow.

The amount of information available for each patient varies from hospital to hospital, e.g. the Evelina Hospital transcripts include brief details for cause of admission, treatment and post-mortem reports. You must register (free) to view details of patients on the databases. The website includes articles about the hospitals' histories, and stories of some child patients, http://hharp.org.

The Wellcome Trust Medical Archives and Manuscripts Survey is a database of medical records from 1600–1945. There's more information on the survey (not updated since 2000), which includes a list of the institutions covered, on the Wellcome Library website, http://wellcomelibrary.org/about-us/about-the-collections/archives-and-manuscripts/finding-medical-archives-elsewhere/.

Chapter 7

CHILDREN IN WARTIME

Children have served their country from a surprisingly early age, by modern standards, and many young sailors, soldiers and marines made the ultimate sacrifice for their coutnry.

The Army

The army has always attracted boys with an adventurous streak. Traditionally, boys joined up as drummers, bandsmen or fife boys.

During the Napoleonic Wars, fears of a French invasion ran high, and the army faced a manpower shortage. In 1797 regiments of feet were permitted to recruit boys as young as 13. Three regiments of foot (the 22nd, 34th and 65th) were allowed to increase their complements to 1,000 rank and file each by enlisting pauper boys from parishes; the boys were given a guinea and a half (31s 6d) when they joined up. A regulation of 1804 permitted each battalion to recruit 100 boys under the age of 16.

Historian Richard Holmes has discovered that James Wade was only 7 years old when he joined the 9th Foot in 1800, but this is exceptional. Suffolk lad John Shipp (c. 1784–1834) enlisted in 1797, when he was about 13. John's mother had died and his father was serving as a soldier abroad. Shipp and his older brother were consigned to the Saxmundham poorhouse. After Shipp's big brother was press-ganged onto a man-o'-war, John was apprenticed out to a local farmer as an agricultural labourer. He was treated very cruelly.

Shipp had always longed to be a soldier, and was overjoyed when the parish overseer told him that the 22nd (Cheshire) Regiment was recruiting at Colchester. He asked John if he wanted to enlist. Shipp was given new clothes and shoes, and taken by coach to the town. His hair was cut, and his clothes exchanged for a uniform: 'red jacket, red waistcoat, red pantaloons, and red foraging-cap' (John Shipp and H. Manners Chichester (eds), *Memoirs of the Extraordinary Military Career of John Shipp* (T. Fisher Unwin, 1890)). Shipp joined the regimental band, where he learned to play the flute and the fife. In 1800 the Cheshire Regiment embarked for South Africa, where Shipp saw his first active service.

The minimum army recruitment age was fixed at 18 years in 1882, but no proof of age such as a birth certificate was required until after the First World War. This meant that in practice it was common for underage recruits to join the ranks. In the Second World War, some recruiting sergeants showed a distinct lack of interest about checking young lads' identity cards, and 14-year-old lads successfully volunteered for military service.

Some youngsters were awarded this country's highest honours for their bravery. Medals for gallantry and promotions were published in the *London Gazette*, which you can search online, www.london-gazette.co.uk.

Army Records

To find an army ancestor's records at TNA, you need to know the name of their regiment or corps, plus approximate dates of service. For soldiers who were not discharged to pension (most of them) TNA has army service records from the 1730s to the late 1890s including muster rolls, pay lists and description books (with physical information about each soldier). Each regiment regularly compiled a roll of serving soldiers: a muster roll. Some soldiers' records include date and place of birth. TNA army muster rolls and pay lists 1730–1898 can be accessed at www.nationalarchives.gov.uk/records/research-guides/army-muster-1730-1898.htm.

For British army soldiers who were discharged to pension (before 1913), pension records at TNA are searchable by name. See TNA Guide to soldiers' discharge and pension records, www.nationalarchives.gov.uk/records/research-guides/british-army-soldiers-discharge-and-pension-records.htm.

Digitised service records for both world wars for the army, royal navy and merchant navy are available from TNA website, ww.nationalarchives.gov.uk/records/our-online-records.htm.

Dozens of books and websites are devoted to the world wars and military history: several websites are listed in Section E. Some servicemen's records and 'rolls of honour' are available on genealogy subscription websites.

See Michael Watts and Christopher T. Watts, *My Ancestor was in the British Army* (Society of Genealogists, 2009), Simon Fowler, *Tracing Your Army Ancestors* (Pen & Sword, 2006) and William Spencer, *Army Records: A Guide for Family Historians* (TNA, 2008).

The Militia

The militia was a forerunner of today's Territorial Army. Its role was to act as a standby force in case the country was invaded. Generally militiamen enlisted at 18, but boys as young as 14 could serve in the London militia in

1813 (54 Georgii III C.38). The militia's ranks were filled by ballot (organised by the parish authorities), and service was not popular because it was compulsory.

Every parish drew up lists of men who were eligible to serve in the militia, and these lists include information on a recruit's family, such as the number of children under 14. This was important because a militiaman's wife and children might become chargeable to the parish whilst he served (Chapter 2).

When a French invasion seemed imminent (Napoleonic Wars and the late 1850s), many volunteer regiments were formed in counties such as Cheshire and Lancashire. Volunteers were exempt from the compulsory ballot.

When a militiaman or soldier was recruited, he signed an 'attestation paper', and TNA holds these (WO 96 for militiamen). Attestation papers dating from 1806–1915 have been digitised and are available from Findmypast, and militia attestation papers from 1860–1915 have been indexed on Origins.Net. TNA guide to militia records is at www.national archives.gov.uk/records/research-guides/armed-forces-1522-1914.htm. Findmypast's Military Collection (army and militia) is at www.findmy past.co.uk/MilitaryXdbStartSearch.jsp. Origins.Net's collection is at www.origins.net/ help/aboutbo-militia.aspx.

County archives hold local militia lists and muster rolls (e.g. Lancashire Archives has put a catalogue of its holdings online), and the Ancestry website has some militia records.

Some militia lists have been published. See Jeremy Gibson and Meryvn Medlycott, *Militia Lists and Musters 1767–1876*, 4th edn (Family History Partnership, 2000).

Army Education

Sandhurst must be one of the most famous military colleges in the world, although it was not the first in the UK. The Royal Military Academy at Woolwich (1741) took 'gentleman cadets' between the age of 14 and 16 to train as officers.

In 1802 a military college was founded at Great Marlow. It had 100 cadets, aged 13 to 15, and some places (for officers' orphans) were free. The cadets learnt subjects such as mathematics, fortification, gunnery and artillery. The college moved to Sandhurst in 1812. The Royal Military College (later Academy) at Sandhurst trained boys as officers from age 16. They were destined for the 'Cavalry, the Guards and the Line' (*First Report . . . into the Present State of Military Education* (1869)).

The Woolwich and Sandhurst establishments merged in 1947. The

Woolwich and Sandhurst cadet registers kept at the Royal Military Academy Sandhurst (not TNA) can be searched online. Records include a cadet's name, age, date of admission, date when commissioned and corps or regiment joined. The Royal Military Academy Woolwich registers cover 1790–3, 1799–1805 and 1820–1939. Registers for the Royal Military Academy Sandhurst cover 1800–1946. A fee is payable to download an image of the original record, http://archive.sandhurstcollection.org.uk.

The East India Company had its own armed force; initially some cadets trained at Woolwich and Great Marlow. The Company founded a military seminary in 1809 at Addiscombe Place, near Croydon, for cadets aged 14 and up. The British Library's Asian and African Studies collections include cadet papers (application forms and birth or baptism certificates) and cadet registers for the seminary.

Schools like Eton, Harrow and Wellington College prepared their pupils for the entrance examinations to Woolwich and Sandhurst.

The earliest army schools educated adult soldiers; later in the nineteenth century, these schools taught soldiers' children, too. Regimental schools were inspected by the War Office, not HMI; in the 1860s the Royal Military Council for Education became the supervisory body.

Soldiers' wives often accompanied them on military service. When soldiers changed their posting, their families either went with them, or sent their children back to the UK to be educated. Army children might attend the Royal Military Asylum or a private boarding school.

The Duke of York founded the Royal Military Asylum at Chelsea in 1803 for the children of soldiers serving in the regular army; this 'handsome, spacious edifice' was a boarding school. 'The establishment is conducted according to a strict system of military discipline' (Daniel Lysons, *The Environs of London* (London, 1811)).

In 1808 the Asylum had accommodation for 792 boys and 348 girls. Children who were soldiers' orphans were given first preference; next, those whose father had died on active service. Children with a father away on foreign service, or whose parents had several children to maintain, could also attend.

The pupils were taught tailoring or shoe-making (girls learnt domestic skills) so that they could be apprenticed out. Boys joined the army if they preferred. Children entered the school from the age of 5 and left at age 14. By 1816, the Asylum had an infant school or nursery on the Isle of Wight, which took army children from birth (*Report from the Select Committee into the Education of the Lower Orders in the Metropolis* (1816)).

The Asylum was renamed the Duke of York's Royal Military School in 1892, and stopped admitting girl pupils; it moved to Dover in 1909. Records for the Royal Military School and its predecessors, including admission and discharge registers, apprenticeship records and offences books, are at TNA, WO 143. Indexes of admissions are available.

Wives and children of soldiers living in married quarters (after 1868) may be recorded in 'marriage rolls' in the muster rolls (WO 10) at TNA. For registers of baptisms, marriages and burials in UK and overseas garrisons (1808–2007), see WO 156. Ministry of Pensions records at TNA include allowances paid to children of army officers killed during the First World War, PMG 46.

The GRO indexes include births, marriages and deaths recorded overseas. For British army regiments, records of births or baptisms, marriages and some deaths are available for 1761–1924. Army chaplains also recorded births, marriages and deaths, 1761–1880. The indexes include births and deaths of children born to British army personnel or their families, 1881–1965. For marine vessels, births and deaths recorded at sea are available from 1837 onwards; for British aircraft, births and deaths from 1947 onwards. A full listing of events recorded overseas can be found on the government website, http://bit.ly/YQ6Sg6.

The Army Children's Archive website has information on schooling, charities and living conditions, with stories and memories of former 'barrack rats', www.archhistory.co.uk.

The Royal Navy

The Royal Navy has kept Britain's shores safe and guarded its interests worldwide for centuries. A career in the navy was an exciting prospect for young lads, despite the dangers, and provided a route to fame and fortune if all went well.

Boys serving on Royal Navy ships shared the same dangers as the men on board. Over 100 lads under 18 died when HMS *Royal Oak* was torpedoed by a German submarine in Scapa Flow in 1939.

One of our country's youngest heroes was John Travers Cornwell (1900–16), who died of his wounds on 2 June 1916 following the Battle of Jutland. 'Jack', as he was known, joined the Royal Navy when he was 15 years old. He served on HMS *Chester* as a sight-setter for naval guns, and was ranked as a Boy seaman, First Class. During the battle Jack stayed resolutely at his post whilst all his shipmates were killed around him.

Jack was actually buried twice. He was originally interred in a communal

Jack Cornwell's second funeral in 1916. Central News photograph from Harry Golding (ed.), *The Wonder Book of Ships*, 11th edn, Ward, Lock & Co., *c.* 1920. (Nigel Wilkes Collection)

grave (his family only had modest means) in Manor Park Cemetery, but when the story of his courage was publicised by the newspapers, the authorities gave him a lavish funeral. Jack was exhumed and re-buried in Manor Park on 29 July 1916 with full military honours. On 15 September 1916, the *London Gazette* reported that Jack had been posthumously awarded the Victoria Cross for his bravery.

Royal Navy Records

Trafalgar Ancestors Database
Over 18,000 people took part in the Battle of Trafalgar on 21 October 1805, in which Lord Nelson was killed, and their names are listed in a database on TNA website. Some participants were only children. The youngest boy on

the database appears to be 8-year-old Thomas Wilcott from Gosport in Hampshire, serving on HMS *Neptune*.

The database was compiled using ships' muster rolls. You can search the database by surname, and an advanced search facility, by first name, age on 21 October 1805, birthplace, ship's name, rating and rank. If you find an ancestor on the database, follow the online links to order a copy of the original record, www.nationalarchives.gov.uk/trafalgarancestors.

Service records for royal naval ratings after 1923 are held by the Ministry of Defence, not TNA, and cannot be viewed by the general public. Relatives of deceased servicemen, or persons who served in the Home Guard, can apply for a copy of their records, https://www.gov.uk/requests-for-personal-data-and-service-records.

You can search the Discovery catalogue on TNA website for service records for Royal Navy ratings, commissioned or warrant officers before 1923. For ratings, the two main series are continuous service engagement books from 1853–72 (ADM 139) and registers of seamen's service 1873–1923 (ADM 188). (A 'rating' was anyone below officer class.)

When a boy joined the Royal Navy, he signed a form to say that he would serve for ten years after he became 18 years old. The TNA guide for ratings 1853–1923 has an example of a boy's certificate (which boys signed when joining the service). The records give date or year of birth, place of birth, names of ships served on, dates of joining and discharge from each ship, length of time in service and the person's service number. TNA guides are at www.nationalarchives. gov.uk/records/royal-naval-seamen.htm,www.national archives.gov.uk/records/looking-forperson/commissionedofficerroyalnavy.htm and www.nationalarchives. gov.uk/records/looking-for-person/warrantofficer royalnavy.htm.

The Fleet Air Arm Museum holds a large collection of Royal Navy service record cards and engagement ledgers. There's a detailed list on the website, www.fleetairarm.com/royal-navy-royal-marines-services-documents.aspx.

See Simon Fowler, *Tracing Your Naval Ancestors* (Pen & Sword, 2011) and Bruno Pappalardo, *Tracing Your Naval Ancestors* (Public Record Office, 2003).

Officer Training

Middle and upper-class boys who wished to train as officers traditionally joined a ship under the captain's patronage. It was a popular career choice for a family's younger sons, as it was cheaper than paying for university fees or an army commission.

Boys got their first taste of the sea when they were about 10 or 12 years old. Horatio Nelson (1758–1805) was 12 when he joined HMS *Raisonnable*, commanded by his uncle, Captain Maurice Suckling. Everyone who served on a Royal Navy ship had their name entered in the muster book or roll.

In Nelson's day, boys under 15 were usually classed as a boy (sometimes volunteer) third class, progressing to second class as they grew older. The ratings above them were: land-man, ordinary seaman, able seaman then the petty officers. After 1794 captain's servants training as midshipmen were rated as 'volunteers first class'.

Alternatively, lads like novelist Jane Austen's brothers Francis and Charles trained at the Royal Naval Academy, Portsmouth, founded in 1729. After 1773 some government-subsidised places became available for officers' sons. In 1806 the Academy was re-named the Royal Naval College, Portsmouth, and the number of scholars increased from forty to seventy.

Some ships had a schoolmaster on board to help boys continue their education, and in the 1820s, when the number of schoolmasters had increased, the College at Portsmouth closed.

Naval cadets learning woodwork. Photo by Stephen Cribb, *c.* 1920 from Percival A. Hislam, *The Navy Shown to the Children* (T.C. and E.C. Jack, *c.* 1920). (Nigel Wilkes Collection)

In the mid-nineteenth century the Admiralty decided that 'cadets', as trainee officers were now known, should begin their naval education in a ship (moored) before they went to sea.

The first Admiralty training ship, the *Illustrious*, was stationed in Portsmouth Harbour in 1857. Only boys under 15 could be admitted (the age requirement varied over time).

In 1863 the navy founded the Brittania Royal Naval College at Dartmouth; it had room for over 300 pupils. Boys had to pass an entrance exam to train as an officer on *Brittania*, and several preparatory schools specialised in 'cramming' boys to get them through. Life on the *Brittania* was harsh and discipline was strict; cadets trained for two years. This was a fee-paying school.

The training ship at Dartmouth was replaced by a splendid building early in the twentieth century. Whilst it was under construction, young naval cadets began their training at the Royal Naval College, Osborne on the Isle of Wight before moving up to the Britannia Royal Naval College (there's a museum in one of the cadet gun-rooms) (Section F). The Admiralty set up five other specialist schools in England from the 1870s onwards.

Few records appear to have survived for the Royal Naval Colleges; see the National Maritime Museum listing (Section A3). See also Randolph Cock and N.A.M. Rodger (eds), *Guide to the Naval Records in The National Archives of the UK* (Institute of Historical Research, 2006).

Royal Navy Schools

The Royal Greenwich Hospital for naval veterans had schools for seamen's children. The Royal Hospital Schools, Greenwich were known as the 'cradle of the navy'. The schools were founded in 1715, but it was not until 1783 that a special schoolroom and dormitories for 200 children were built within the Hospital walls.

In 1821 the Royal Hospital Schools merged with the Royal Naval Asylum for naval seamen's orphans (founded in Paddington in 1798). The schoolboys in the Hospital moved to the Queen's House at Greenwich (where the Asylum had moved in 1818).

The 'Upper School' at Greenwich had a 'first class' of 100 boys for sons of commissioned and ward room officers in the Royal Navy or Royal Marines. The 'second class' of 300 boys was for the sons of officers or those of 'inferior rank', and the sons of seamen and officers of the merchant navy. Boys were admitted from age 11, and received three years' training before they went to sea.

Royal Naval Schools, Greenwich: 'the cradle of the navy'. *Old and New London Vol. VI* (Cassell, Petter & Galpin, *c.* 1895).

The 'Lower School' had 400 boys and 400 girls, either seamen's orphans, children of seamen injured in service or children with no mother whose father was away at sea. 'These children are admitted from nine to twelve years of age, and quit the institution at fourteen, the boys being sent to sea, and the girls put to trades or domestic service' (E. Miles and Lieutenant Lawford Miles, *An Epitome, Historical and Statistical, of the Royal Naval Service of England* (London, 1841)). The girls' school closed in 1841.

Boys from the school did not necessarily join the navy after they finished their training. At the end of midsummer term in 1850 a total of 198 boys left the upper and lower schools, from which 126 went to sea. Of these boys, 96 joined the Royal Navy and 30 went to the merchant navy. Boys from the Hospital Schools also trained to enter Royal Marine bands.

Each year, four boys who showed great promise in practical mechanics

A boy training at Watt's Naval School, North Elmham, Norfolk, 1920s. Photograph from *Cassell's Book of Knowledge Vol. V* (Waverley Book Co., c. 1920). (Nigel Wilkes Collection)

were apprenticed to the steam-factories in HM dockyards. There were also sixteen pupil-teachers in the school. They were apprenticed to the schoolmaster for six years from the age of 15 (*Copy of the Annual Report on Greenwich Hospital Schools, made to the Admiralty by Her Majesty's Inspector of Schools* (446) (1851)).

The Royal Hospital Schools moved to Holbrook, Ipswich in 1933. TNA holds detailed admission papers and school registers for the Royal Hospital Schools.

The records of the Royal Greenwich Hospital (also at TNA) may prove useful for nautical ancestors because it provided pensions for seamen, payments to seamen's widows and orphans, and sometimes paid orphanages to provide places for seamen's children.

After Greenwich Hospital closed, the navy set up an officer training establishment there, the Royal Naval College (1873), for the sons of officers killed or injured whilst on active service.

The Royal Naval Benevolent Society was a charity that cared for the widows, children and orphans of deceased officers, and the families of officers who had fallen on hard times. Its records are held at the Royal Naval Museum at Portsmouth. The Museum does not have any personnel service records or ships' logbooks in its collections.

Poor Law boards trained lads for the sea service. For example, the Metropolitan Asylums Board ran a training ship, the *Exmouth*; boys from several Poor Law authorities were admitted. In 1880 there were 860 boys training on the *Exmouth*; that year 259 boys left, of which 177 joined the Royal Navy and the merchant navy, and 17 boys joined military bands.

The Navy League (Chapter 8) ran nautical schools, and Dr Barnardo's managed several including Watts Naval Training School at North Elmham (1903–49).

Royal Marines

As late as the Second World War, boys as young as 14, like volunteer Len Chester, served in the Royal Marines as boy buglers and saw active service. They signed on for twelve years. Schools were attached to the barracks at Woolwich, Chatham, Portsmouth and Plymouth. They were attended by the marines and their children.

The history of the Royal Marines, particularly its administration, is complicated and many different records are available at TNA. There's a guide for tracing non-commissioned ranks of the Royal Marines, www.national archives.gov.uk/records/looking-for-person/royalmarines.htm.

The archive at the Fleet Air Arm Museum includes a large collection of records for the Royal Marines and the Royal Naval School of Music, including attestation papers and service certificates, from the 1850s to 1925.

See Richard Brooks and Matthew Little, *Tracing Your Royal Marine Ancestors: A Guide for Family Historians Published in Association With The Royal Marines Museum* (Pen & Sword, 2008).

The Royal Marines Museum website has tips for researching the history and family history of Royal Marines, www.royalmarinesmuseum.co.uk/category/researching-family-and-royal-marine-history.

National Registration

A type of 'census' – a National Registration scheme – was in force during both world wars, although it differed slightly in its scope and use for each conflict.

In the First World War, the government needed to find out how many men were available for active service, and how many people needed to be fed if rationing was introduced (compulsory rationing was not introduced until early 1918).

The National Registration Act 1915 required that on 15 August, every person aged 15 to 65 must fill out a form disclosing their name, age, address, if married, number of dependents, nationality (for non-British) and employment details. People living in workhouses or hospitals, mental hospital patients and prisoners did not have to register. People already serving in the armed forces were not included.

Changes of address had to be notified and new arrivals recorded in each area. Most records for the 1915 National Register, which were held locally, were destroyed in 1919, but a few county record offices hold these registers.

At the beginning of the Second World War the government faced similar problems to those of the First World War, but this time children living far from the war front were under threat from the enemy's bombs and shells.

The government needed to plan for conscription, rationing and the evacuation of civilians, and in 1939 a National Registration Act was passed. On the night of 29 September 1939 details of every man, woman and child in the UK were recorded, except for those in the armed services who were away on duty, and merchant seamen.

Registration was conducted in a similar fashion to the national censuses: enumerators collected completed forms from each householder. Each person was issued with an identity card showing their National Registration number, address, name, sex, marital status and occupation. Every person, including babies and children, was given a ration book for food (which showed a person's date of birth). Clothing was also rationed. Identity cards were updated whenever a person changed address.

Unlike the 1915 registration, a central register of the information was kept in 1939. The National Registration scheme ended in 1952, but the identity card numbers were used as National Health Service numbers when the system was introduced that year.

You can request a search of the 1939 register from the Health and Social Care Information Centre (Section B). The Health and Social Care Information Centre only provides information for deceased individuals. There's more detailed information and a request form on the website, http://www. ic.nhs.uk/register-service.

National Registration cards, certificates and ration books from both world wars can be found in local record offices. You may also discover enumerators' schedules or notes for the 1939 National Registration with names of householders.

Child Evacuees

When the Second World War broke out, the authorities in Australia, Canada, the other Dominions and the USA offered to care for children from the UK, including war orphans. Children would be looked after in private homes. Thousands of well-off parents sent their children overseas by private arrangements using agencies such as the American Committee for the Evacuation of British Children (records at the Borthwick Institute).

In 1940 the British government set up the Children's Overseas Reception Board (CORB) to send more children abroad. There was a deluge of applications from parents anxious to get their children to safety. Only children aged 5 to 16 were eligible; parents paid towards their travel expenses. LEAs helped organise the arrangements.

Over 2,600 children had already been evacuated overseas when the scheme was put in jeopardy by enemy action. Over 300 children had a lucky escape when the SS *Volendam* was torpedoed by a German U-boat in August 1940.

The government's evacuation of children overseas was halted in October 1940 following the horrific loss of the SS *City of Benares* on 17 September 1940. A U-boat torpedoed the ship, which was carrying ninety child evacuees. Michael Brooker and Patricia Allen, two children who died, had previously survived the torpedoing of the *Volendam* a fortnight earlier.

Shortly afterwards a British warship rescued thirteen child passengers, including seven evacuces, from the *Benares*. Another seven children, and forty adults, survived the sinking: Kenneth John Sparks (13) of Wembley was one of the lucky few spotted by a passing plane eight days later after enduring freezing conditions in an open boat in the mid-Atlantic (*The Times*, Friday 27 September 1940).

The records of CORB from 1940–59 are kept at TNA, DO 131. Each child had a CORB 'official number'. The catalogue can be searched online by name for children's case histories: information given includes date of birth, child's address before evacuation, destination and the piece reference of the record. Use the piece reference to order a copy, www.nationalarchives. gov.uk/records/looking-for-person/emigrants.htm.

The Board of Trade outward passenger lists (BT 27 at TNA), digitised by Findmypast, have details of child migrants who left the UK from 1890–1960, including children sent by charities' emigration programmes; www. ancestorsonboard.com.

Prior to the abortive CORB scheme, in September 1939 Britain witnessed its first mass civilian evacuation – 'Operation Pied Piper' – from towns and cities at high risk from enemy bombs. For three days, railway stations and trains were jammed with children, pregnant women and mothers with crying babes in arms. The children carried their gas masks and had labels with their name on pinned to their coats. There were further large-scale evacuations when bombing intensified.

The evacuation caused a massive social and cultural shock as children from poor areas, such as the East End of London, went to stay with middle or upper-class families. Brothers and sisters were split up if their 'billet' did not want more than one child. Some receiving families were appalled to find that the child they had taken in was dirty, had nits or wet the bed. Many children from the slums were poorly clothed. Conversely, children from comfortable homes were dismayed to find themselves in houses with no running water. Some children later returned home.

Thousands of children's schooling was inevitably disrupted; several schools closed during the war, and some schools were evacuated wholesale.

To trace a child evacuee, ideally you need the name of the school they attended before they went away, the date and preferably the place where they were sent. If not, your search will not be easy as over 800,000 children were evacuated to safety during the first phase of evacuation.

Some families stayed with, or sent their children to, relatives or friends during the bombing; children's names may crop up in school attendance registers. Seemingly, not many local authority registers for these children have survived.

Local archives and libraries may have records of child evacuees; a search of the A2A index online for 'evacuees' elicits over 1,000 possible sources, although some are general policy documents rather than lists of names.

County or district council archives may include records of the Second World War Government Evacuation Scheme in civil defence records, emergency planning or Air Raid Precautions (ARP). Check the records of the local authority that sent children to safety, and the local authority that received them.

Look for registers of unaccompanied children, registers of billeting forms, records of home visits by welfare officers, board and lodging records and requests for re-billeting (change of family looking after an evacuee).

Registers of evacuees regarding billeting arrangements were usually compiled by street name rather than family name and should include the name of the householder looking after a child, the child(ren)'s name, date of arrival and any changes of address. Families that took in evacuees received payments for items such as clothing or blankets. Local authorities also made lists of households and families who needed to be taken to safety.

Records of a sensitive nature, e.g. appeals to tribunals concerning the billeting of evacuees, complaints about 'difficult' child evacuees or requests by families or children for a change of billet are likely to be closed for seventy-five years or more.

Case Study

For example, LA holds a register for 'Unaccompanied Children Returned Home' for one party of children returned to London from Lancaster (first part of the volume) and another party of children returned to Salford from Lancaster (second part). The register is in alphabetical order of surname.

Each record notes the child's name, date of birth, national identity registration number, name and address of parent or guardian (noting if a parent was deceased), date when evacuated, whether as part of a school party or privately, name and address of the billet in the reception area, name and address of schools attended in the evacuation area and reception area, name of evacuation authority, billeting authority, recovery authority and date and place where the child was returned (if not the original address)

'M.D.', born in 1928, attended Pendleton High School for Girls, Eccles Old Road, Salford prior to evacuation. Her father, 'Mr H.D.', lived on Great Cheetham Street East, Higher Broughton in Salford. 'M.D.' was evacuated to Lancaster on 2 January 1941 by Salford Education Authority and attended Lancaster Grammar School; the child stayed with a lady in Torrisholme Road. 'M.D.' returned home on 19 October 1941 (full date of birth, names and addresses are given) (LA DDX 2744/1/1).

LEA correspondence or financial records relating to evacuees may include lists of children, with school names, home addresses, date of first attendance at the billeting authority's school, length of stay, etc.

Education committee records may have details of schools where evacuees were sent, or records of teachers responsible for teaching evacuee children. School records may include evacuation registers and temporary logbooks compiled during the evacuation period, e.g. the admission registers for Church Minshull County Primary School, Cheshire include a register for children evacuated from Eldon Street RC School, Liverpool. You may find letters written home by evacuees to parents to let them know how they were getting on.

Some councils set up wartime nurseries and temporary schools for evacuees, and their admission registers or logbooks may still exist. Pregnant women and poorly evacuees may be listed in hospital or infirmary records.

When the evacuation scheme ended, some children had no homes to return to because they had been destroyed by enemy action, and registers of these children may have survived in local authority records, too.

TNA does not hold individual records for evacuees; its collections have information on government policy and administration relating to civilian evacuation such as railway transport arrangements (AN 2). More sources for evacuation policy and CORB are listed in Section A1.

The Imperial War Museum website has images of children during both world wars including Girl Guides and Scouts 'doing their bit' for the war effort, wartime nurseries and child evacuees (search by keyword such as 'children', 'evacuees' or 'home front'), www.iwm.org.uk/collections.

For the London area, R. Samways, *We Think You Ought To Go* (Greater London Record Office, 1995) covers the role played by the London City Council in 'Operation Pied Paper' and lists sources in LMA. LMA's information sheet on child evacuees is online, http://goo.gl/CHGV0.

The Evacuees Reunion Association publishes a bi-monthly newsletter, *The Evacuee*, which has a 'Lost Touch' section where people can make contact with old friends, www.evacuees.org.uk.

Chapter 8

TEAM SPIRIT

Between the Crimean War and the First World War, great emphasis was placed on the need to train the country's future citizens. It was feared that the UK was falling behind Continental powers like Germany, and that the Empire would not have enough future soldiers to protect its interests. There was a great flowering of uniformed voluntary organisations offering 'pre-training' for the armed forces.

Army Cadets

Today's Army Cadet Force dates its origins back to 1859, when there were fears of an invasion from England's traditional enemy, France. The War Office appealed for the formation of Rifle Volunteer Battalions for home service. Several public schools like Rossall and Eton set up cadet units. More schools such as Charterhouse followed suit in the following decades. Robert Baden-Powell was a school cadet.

In the 1860s a Royal Commission into the condition of volunteer forces in the UK found that 'numerous corps have been formed in connection with volunteer corps, public and other schools'. It appears few records of these early cadet corps have survived, although school archives may include muster rolls.

In 1908 the army was reformed and changes made to cadet training. Volunteer regiments were united to form the Territorial Army, and the War Office supervised a newly formed Army Cadet Force; later Territorial Army Associations took over day-to-day running of cadet battalions.

Some public schools such as King Edward's School, Birmingham formed junior sections of the Officer Training Corps (later known as Junior Training Corps), which attracted youngsters like J.R.R. Tolkien, later a famous author.

Reformatories such at Saltersford Training School (formerly Bradwall Reformatory) had a cadet corps attached, and many old boys from institutions served in the world wars.

The horrific waste of so many young lives in the First World War led to a decline in popularity for cadet-type training. Government funding was withdrawn in 1930, and a charity, the British National Cadet Association (BNCA), was formed. The BNCA later supervised cadet training. The BNCA changed its name to the Army Cadet Force Association after the end of the Second World War.

Cadet membership increased with the outbreak of the Second World War. The War Office became the supervisory body once more, and the Army Cadet Force was formed; boys as young as 14 could enrol. By the winter of 1942 the Army Cadet Force had 170,000 members (Eric Macfarlane, *Education 16–19: In Transition* (Routledge, 1992)).

The Combined Cadet Force was formed in 1948 for boys over 17 years of age and 100 schools with Junior Training Corps joined this new, separate organisation for army, sea and air cadets.

There was no central register of cadets in the Army Cadet Force until 2007. Any surviving records for cadet corps such as enlistment and discharge details are most likely to be archived with the regimental archive, or county Territorial Army association records or the educational establishment they were associated with. For example, Norfolk Record Office holds a Cadet Corps nominal roll and logbook for Great Yarmouth Grammar School.

Sea Cadets and Air Cadets

The naval schools and colleges mentioned in the previous chapter were all boarding schools. In 1856 Naval Lads' Brigades were founded by ordinary seamen to encourage boys to train for the navy whilst living at home.

The Navy League, founded in 1893, campaigned for naval reform. It joined forces with the Naval Lads' Brigades, and when the First World War broke out, the Navy League was re-named the Navy League Sea Cadet Corps.

Sea cadet membership was extremely popular; writer George Orwell joined when he was 7 years old, and by the beginning of the Second World War there were 100 units with a total membership of 10,000 sea cadets. The Navy League had its own training ship, the *Bounty*.

The Navy League Sea Cadet Corps was re-named the Sea Cadet Association in 1976. Later, the Marine Society and Sea Cadet Association merged (2004) to form the Marine Society and Sea Cadets charity. For Marine Society history and archives, see Chapter 6.

Navy League archives are held at the Marine Society & Sea Cadet Association. Records for individual units such as minute books or photographs may be held locally; see the DANGO database. (Sea Scout groups belonged to the Scouts Association.)

The Air Training Corps was founded in 1941 for boys aged 13 and up, and local record offices may have air cadet archives such as photos, enrolment registers or lists of cadets. For example, Glamorgan Record Office holds some Air Training Corps (Welsh Division) records for the 1940s–50s including attendance registers (D455).

In the Second World War, girls who wanted to play their part in the war effort and train for the armed forces did not initially have as many opportunities as boys. This problem was addressed by the National Association of Girls' Training Corps (NAGTC), formed in 1942. The Association was the mother organisation for the Girls'Training Corps, Girls' Nautical Training Corps and the Women's Junior Air Corps.

Unlike the Air Training Corps and other boys' cadet corps which trained boys for the armed forces or civil defence, the NAGTC was supported by the Board of Education. Girls could join when they were 14 years old, but had to provide their own uniform. In 1980 the Girls Nautical Training Corps merged with the Sea Cadet Corps.

The DANGO database has details of archive locations for some local branches of the Marine Society and Sea Cadets, and Girls'Nautical Training Corps, http://bit.ly/11fYCeR and http://bit.ly/V6Yqb5.

Towards the end of the nineteenth century, several famous voluntary organisations grew up as a response to society's concerns about social problems such as intemperance and juvenile delinquency.

Temperance Organisations

The 'demon drink' was a particular worry for reformers because the lives of so many families were blighted by alcohol misuse. The temperance movement grew up in England in the early 1830s (it had already gained momentum in Scotland and Ireland). One of the first temperance groups was the Oak Street Temperance Society, formed in Manchester (1830). The society flourished, and five years later was renamed the Manchester and Salford Temperance Society. Members pledged to abstain from all intoxicating drinks. By the early 1840s this society and its affiliates had over 18,000 members.

The Independent Order of Rechabites (Salford Unity) promoted temperance but was also a friendly society. The Order was founded in Salford in 1835. The Independent Order of Rechabites (IOR) was named after a tent-dwelling tribe in the Bible that did not drink wine.

The IOR was a sickness and burial club and it greatly appealed to the working classes. Women had their own Independent Order of Female

Rechabites, which merged with the IOR in 1856. Juvenile tents (groups or branches) first appeared in 1840. At that date a widow and orphans' fund was added to the Order's financial services. The IOR's records, including certificates, registers listing juvenile tents, juvenile committee minute books, etc., are held at the Senate House Library, University of London. Local Rechabite tent records including registers of juvenile members may be held at local record offices.

The famous 'Band of Hope' was founded by Ann Jane Carlile and Jabez Tunnicliffe in 1855. The Band's clubs offered a ray of sunshine to many working class children. Members enjoyed fun activities such as magic lantern shows and competitions. By the late 1890s the Band of Hope had over 3 million child members: Henry Morton Stanley was one who 'took the pledge'. The Band of Hope changed its name to Hope UK in 1995 and is still involved with children's welfare.

Temperance societies, leagues, guilds, Band of Hope records such as account books, minute books, pledge registers, certificates, photographs can be found at local record offices (use the NRA index). Temperance or abstainers' registers may be archived with Sunday school records.

Joseph Livesey of Preston was perhaps the movement's greatest spokesman, and the University of Central Lancashire (UCLAN) holds a special collection on Livesey's work and temperance organisations such as the Band of Hope and the Rechabite Friendly Societies. Digital images of some items from this collection can be viewed on the UCLAN website, www.uclan.ac.uk/students/library/livesey_collection.php.

Boys' and Lads' Brigades

The Boys' Brigade, first founded in Glasgow in 1883 by William Alexander Smith, became immensely popular. Boys were given a uniform, taught good behaviour and learnt military style discipline. Brigades attracted many working-class boys who could not afford a Scout uniform. By the early 1930s, the Brigade had 97,000 members in the UK (Joanne Bourke, *Working-Class Cultures in Britain 1890–1960: Gender, Class and Ethnicity* (Taylor & Francis, 2009)).

The Boys' Brigade archive is held at its Hemel Hempstead office; some local record offices hold records such as minute books and correspondence for individual 'companies'.

Churches were particularly anxious to instil moral instruction in young people and the Anglican Church, Roman Catholics and Jews set up their own separate 'Brigades'. The Church Lads' Brigade was formed in 1891. Girls were not allowed to join, so the Church Nursing & Ambulance

Brigade for Young Women & Girls was formed in 1901. It was re-named the Church Girls' Brigade in 1923, and merged with the Church Lads' Brigade in 1978.

The Church Lads' and Church Girls' Brigade has its own archive; the records of some brigade regiments are held in local record offices, e.g. papers for the 1st Norwich Battalion of the Church Lads' Brigade are at Norfolk Record Office. Many former Church Lads and Boys' Brigade members were killed in the First World War, and are listed on rolls of honour.

The Jewish Lads' Brigade was founded in London in 1895 by Colonel Albert Goldsmid; he wanted Jewish boys to enjoy activities like those offered by the Boys' Brigade.

Salvation Army

The Salvation Army had 'junior soldiers' (age 7 and upwards); they worked for award schemes or played in the band. Youngsters aged 12 and over could become 'Corps Cadets', studying the Bible and training as future Officers (ministers) or Local Officers (senior lay members).

The Salvation Army Heritage Centre holds Junior Soldiers' rolls for several Corps (churches). The rolls, dating from the 1920s, include the names and addresses of Junior Soldiers, along with the dates they enrolled. The Centre also has copies of publications such as the *War Cry, Young Soldier* and *Salvation Army Year Book*, which may have photos of local Corps. The Society of Genealogists' Library also has some recent copies of the *Year Book*.

Youth Clubs

The organisers of some boys' clubs concentrated on providing a safe place where the rougher boys could enjoy games like billiards and football rather than military style drilling like the boys' brigades. The London Federation of Working Boys' Clubs had over thirty members by 1889 (LMA).

Some early youth clubs, such as the Adelphi Lads' Club at Salford, founded in 1888, were offshoots of ragged schools, and had a very large membership. Boys' clubs were also set up by employers such as collieries.

In the Second World War the National Association of Boys' Clubs (1925) was a major player in young people's lives. Clubs helped with the war effort by looking after child evacuees, for example.

The movement for girls' clubs began with efforts to help teenage girls who had left home, perhaps to work in a factory or as domestic servants, and to keep them safe from temptation. Mary Townsend founded the Girls' Friendly Society in 1875, and this was perhaps the first major organisation for women and girls. The Women's Library (London School of Economics) holds records for the Girls' Friendly Society.

Another pioneer was Maude Stanley (1833–1915), who began the Soho Club for Working Girls in 1880. The club provided lodgings and reasonably priced meals, and was aimed at respectable working-class girls. By 1889 the Soho Club had 230 members, of which 60 were aged 16 and under; 4 girls were only 13. The ethos of clubs like these, however, focused on nurturing the domesticity and femininity of girls rather than encouraging an adventurous streak. The National Association of Girls' Clubs was formed in 1911.

Wales had a separate youth movement. The Urdd Gobaith Cymru or Welsh League of Youth was founded by Sir Ifan ab Owen Edwards in 1922 following some unsuccessful attempts by his father, author O.M. Edwards (who was also Chief Inspector for Education in Wales), to found a similar movement. The Urdd encouraged the use of the Welsh language and fostered awareness of Welsh culture.

By the late 1920s the Urdd had eighty local branches, and in the 1930s it set up residential centres and camps for youngsters. The Urdd still organises the 'Eisteddfod Yr Urdd', or Youth Eisteddfod. The NLW holds records for the Urdd Gobaith Cymru.

Records for individual boys' and girls' clubs such as minutes, correspondence or photos may be held in local record offices. Records for girls' clubs are not as plentiful as those for boys (only eighteen are listed on the NRA index).

In 1941 the Board of Education asked all boys and girls aged 16 and 17 to register with their LEA (circular 1577: Registration of Boys and Girls Order). The idea was that youngsters should be compelled to join youth clubs, cadets or civil defence organisations, with the ultimate aim of preparing them for military service.

The element of compulsion was dropped, but teenagers were sometimes interviewed to assess their suitability, and encouraged to join cadet forces. Records relating to the 1941–5 'Service of Youth' order may be found in LEA files in record offices.

Scouts and Guides

Some thoughtful people were concerned by the militaristic nature of organisations like the Boys' Brigade. The Scouting movement was founded by Sir Robert Baden-Powell in 1908. Baden-Powell wanted to train boys to become self-reliant, good citizens. The Scouts' Association swiftly became a national and then an international movement. There were an estimated 350,000 boy scouts in the British Empire by the 1920s.

Girls were attracted to the Scout movement, too, and tried to set up their own troops. In 1910 Baden-Powell set up the Girl Guides Association, a separate body, and asked his sister Agnes Baden-Powell to lead it. A junior branch called 'Rosebuds' was formed four years later; the name was changed to 'Brownies' shortly afterwards.

Churches set up their own Scout and Wolf Cub troops, Brownie and Guide packs, and their records may be filed under parish records. Other faiths including Jews (and more recently Muslims) also ran Scout troops.

In the Second World War, Boy Scouts performed a huge variety of tasks to help the war effort. In 1938 the Scout Association launched a National Service badge for scouts over the age of 14 who had qualified as a second-class scout, and by September of that year 18,000 boys had earned their badges. They acted as messenger boys for ARP stations, police stations, hospitals and coastguard stations. They assembled and delivered gas masks to households, manned first-aid posts and dug trenches (*The Times*, 18 February, 1 September and 15 November 1939).

Scouts and Girl Guides acted as marshals to look after children when they were evacuated. Guides helped at hospitals and nursery schools, washing children and babies and helping at mealtimes.

The Scout Association and Girl Guiding Association each have their own archive, but records of regional groups are most likely to be held locally. For example, Glamorgan Archives holds records for local Scout Associations in East Glamorgan, Mid Glamorgan, Cardiff and the Welsh Scout Council: DCSO.

Scouting and Guiding records at local archives may include cash books, certificates, logbooks, minute books, subscription registers, patrol mark books, photograph albums and yearbooks, etc. Logbooks will help you explore the troop or pack's activities such as fundraising activities and may include photos.

Very few records are listed on the NRA index for individual wolf cub packs and Brownie packs; records for scout and guide groups are more plentiful. You may have to seek special permission from the depositor for access to these records.

The Scout Association Archive holds some warrant holder registers and cards, arranged by county, then surname, with addresses. The archive's website has searchable databases of rolls of honour for scouts and former scouts killed in both world wars. The website also has a searchable database of award (medal) cards for child scouts and adults from 1908–90s, some with photographs. A small fee is payable to download records, www.scouts records.org.

The archive at Girlguiding UK only holds personal information about adult members of the movement, not Brownies and Girl Guides in individual units. It does have general information about Guiding activities and the badges that girls worked for. Girl Guides could progress to Rangers and Sea Rangers after the age of 14.

Red Cross and St John Ambulance

Girls (and boys) could join the British Red Cross, which had a Juniors Section from 1924. Schools had Red Cross 'Links' (clubs) for children as young as 5 years old; some Links were affiliated to youth clubs (there were no independent Links). When junior members were 14 they could join a cadet unit linked to an adult Red Cross group or voluntary aid detachment (VAD), and wear a uniform.

Members of the Junior Red Cross earned proficiency badges and took examinations for certificates. In the Second World War a Junior Gallantry Medal was introduced for youngsters who displayed courage or quick-thinking in emergencies. In 1942 Red Cross Youth Groups were formed for youngsters aged 16 to 20 and thousands of them took training courses so that they could join adult detachments when old enough. The Red Cross had almost 38,000 junior members by early 1950 (David V. Glass and J.R. Hall, 'Education and Social Mobility', in David V. Glass (ed.), *Social Mobility in Britain* (Routledge and Kegan Paul, 1954)).

The Red Cross, which is no longer a membership organisation, has its own archive and museum in London; it holds branch records such as minute books. (Sadly the rolls listing junior badge holders have not survived.) The archive has registers of Links with details of the institutions (e.g. name of school) to which they were attached.

It also has copies of the *Junior Red Cross Journal* (1924–73); the magazine ran items on activities undertaken by Junior members, with competitions and news. Local record offices may also hold items relating to the Junior Red Cross.

Another well-known voluntary organisation, the St John Ambulance Brigade, was founded in 1887. After the First World War, many young people (aged 11–18) joined the Order of St John as cadets. During the Second World War, boy and girl cadets from the Red Cross and St John Ambulance were used as messengers. Family history enquiries should be directed to the Museum of the Order of St John in London. The Red Cross archive holds First World War VAD records for St John Ambulance personnel, too.

In addition to the voluntary organisations mentioned here, children joined sports clubs, bands, choirs, etc., and matches or performances may be reported in local newspapers. Local and county archives may hold records such as minute books, newspaper cuttings, photographs, etc. for football clubs (often associated with boys' brigades), school football associations, junior football leagues, hockey or netball clubs and so on.

Official Records

Education Department (ED) files at TNA include Youth Welfare Services. Series ED 124 (1939–74) has papers relating to youth clubs in England and Wales, youth welfare services, the youth registration scheme 1941–5, juvenile delinquency and industrial welfare. See ED 149 for HMI reports on Youth Welfare Services including youth clubs, day continuation classes and borstals.

National Fitness Council records at TNA include applications for grants for playing fields, gyms or community centres from voluntary organisations such as the Boys' Brigade, Church Lads' Brigade, Girls' Friendly Society, Girl Guides' Association, the National Association of Boys' Clubs, National Council of Girls' Clubs and the Welsh League of Youth, ED 113.

The online Encyclopaedia of Informal Education has detailed articles (with references) on the history of youth clubs: www.infed.org/index .htm.

Voluntary organisations may have changed name over time or merged with other charities. For example, the National Association of Boys' Clubs changed its name to NABC-Clubs for Young People when girls' clubs joined the association in 1992. In 1999 it became the National Association of Clubs for Young People, in 2005 its title was Clubs for Young People, and in 2012 the organisation changed name again to Ambition.

Conclusion

It has only been possible to give a brief survey in this book of the multitude of different sources that can help you explore your ancestors' childhood days.

Genealogy and family history magazines such as *Family Tree, BBC Who Do You Think You Are?, Your Family History* and *Your Family Tree* often include features on childhood records such as apprenticeship indentures, updates on new resources and Internet databases, and reviews of new books. Some magazine websites have free databases of records or 'downloads' of trade directories and other resources.

Thanks to the Internet and the growth of genealogy subscription services, many records have been indexed, transcribed or digitised and are available online. More records are being added all the time.

A great many titles have been published for genealogists on the information available on the Internet (and potential pitfalls) including Peter Christian, *The Genealogist's Internet*, 5th edn (Bloomsbury, 2012) and Chris Paton, *Tracing Your Family History on the Internet* (Pen & Sword, 2011).

If you are on a tight budget (and genealogy can be an expensive hobby), there are lots of free resources online: some are listed in Sections C, D and E of the Research Guide. If you are having problems tracing your family tree, try one of the online genealogy forums. Online mailing lists can be helpful if you seek information on a particular surname or are researching a particular place or institution.

If you do not have access to the Internet at home, your local library may offer free access to members for a set time per day, and members can usually access one of the subscription genealogy services via one of their computers. Libraries stock a good range of genealogy titles and books devoted to local studies.

If you are unable to visit an archive in person, the majority of archives offer a research service and/or photocopying services. Payment rates vary, but generally the longer a search takes, the more expensive it will be.

You may wish to consider joining one of the many family history societies, or local history and heritage groups. They sometimes have their own library; several societies have visiting speakers, and members are often extremely knowledgeable about local records.

Archives and museums may have oral histories that you can listen to, or transcripts of oral histories that you can read. Costumed interpreters and 'living history' days at museums give a real flavour of what life was like for your ancestors when they were children. A selection of heritage sites is listed in Section F.

Many people have published memoirs of their childhood; published diaries can provide a real window into the past, too.

Finally, you may wish to compile your own family archive of photographs or other memorabilia of your schooldays, or your children's schooldays. Note the names of the schools they attended, with dates, and if they were members of clubs or organisations. It's a good idea to make copies of important documents and store them separately in case of accidents. Write down your own childhood memories, and the recollections of other family members, so that future generations can one day re-live your childhood for themselves.

Part 2

RESEARCH GUIDE

A
ARCHIVES AND REPOSITORIES

For reasons of space, only a brief selection of records is included for each archive. Check the archive's catalogues for more details of their business, Church, judicial, Poor Law and school records. Collections may have moved, or archive contact details may have changed, since going to press. Remember to check if children's and young people's records are closed to public access before travelling to consult them in person. Use the NRA index to find records of people, businesses and organisations, www.nationalarchives.gov.uk/nra.

Access to Archives
http://nationalarchives.gov.uk/a2a.

ARCHON
Directory of repositories in the UK and abroad which have collections catalogued in the NRA index, www.nationalarchives.gov.uk/archon.

Archives Hub
Finding aid for specialist library and repository resources, http:/archives hub.ac.uk.

AIM25
Archives and sources database for over 100 repositories in London and the M25 area, www.aim25.ac.uk/index.stm.

Archives Network Wales
Electronic catalogue for archives in Wales. NB not all collections with Wales-related material are listed (e.g. TNA holdings not included). www. archivesnetworkwales.info.

List of Repositories in Wales
www.archiveswales.org.uk/anw/browse_repository.php.

A1: The National Archives, Kew

Readers are advised to explore TNA's vast collections using the online Discovery catalogue. Many research guides are available online.

Charity Commission: CHAR 2, CHAR 8.
Department of Education and Science and predecessors including Board of Education: ED.
Educational census of 1871: ED 2–3, ED 16. (Ecclesiastical census of 1851 includes some returns for 1851 educational census: HO 129.)
Committee of Privy Council on Education minutes and reports, including HMI reports: ED 17. LEA files re school attendance following the Elementary Education Act 1870; school leaving age; Second World War education problems: ED 18.
Public elementary school (grant-aided) files including changes of name or administrative area, HMI reports: 1857–1946: ED 21.
Educational charities: ED 21, ED 27, ED 37–40, ED 49.
Institution schools (under 1902 Education Act) including orphanages: ED 30.
Special schools' files 1894–1973 including inspections: ED 32.
Records relating to secondary education: ED 35. School Board Office and Pupil-Teacher Centre series 1884–1911: ED 57.
LEA maintenance grants to poor pupils (files arranged by county/county borough) 1919–55: ED 63. LEA nursery education files include wartime nurseries 1918–66 (only samples for some dates, counties): ED 66.
Welsh Department files relating to general, elementary and secondary education: ED 91–3, ED 111. Welsh Department records on special schools 1904–76: ED 224.
Administration papers and HMI reports, for boarding homes for maladjusted, educationally disabled and diabetic children 1932–70: ED 122. HMI reports on special schools 1947–92: ED 195.
Youth welfare services 1939–74: ED 124. HMI reports on youth welfare services: ED 149.
Lists of educational institutions 1826–1986: ED 270.

Royal Military Asylum (later Royal Military School) and Royal Hibernian Military School records 1801–1980: WO 143. Includes Royal Military Asylum registers of admissions and discharges 1803–1923, records of admissions to Royal Military School 1906–56 and index of admissions to Royal Hibernian Military School 1803–1919.

Admiralty service records including applicants for admission to Greenwich Hospital, records of Charity for Relief of Sea Officers' Widows, and nominations for naval cadetships 1673–1960: ADM 6. Indexes available for some records.

Royal Greenwich Hospital archive includes admission registers for Royal Hospital School: ADM 72–3, ADM 80, ADM 161. ADM 73 includes school admission papers 1728–1870 with baptismal or birth certificates of children, marriage certificates of parents and fathers' naval services; school registers 1728–1883; registers of claims and candidates, admissions, apprenticeship records, etc., of boys and girls. Admissions of boys to the school 1731–75; charity accounts 1737–1814; Naval Asylum 1801–21: ADM 67. Registers of applications to maintain orphans: ADM 162–4; for widows and children, see ADM 166.

List of cadets and staff at Royal Naval College, Portsmouth 1817–32: ADM 30/21.

Home Office Reformatory and Industrial Schools Department out-letters relating to care and employment of children, byelaws made under Employment of Children Act 1903 and emigration of children committed to custody of local authorities and voluntary organisations 1905–21: HO 167.

Records of reformatories, industrial schools, approved schools, etc., including registers of admissions, discharges and licences, diaries and logbooks, and returns of children detained under Industrial Schools Act (1866) 1855–1965: HO 349. See also HO Division 5.

Reformatories and industrial school records including registers of admissions, 1855–1965, HO 349; reports on approved schools HO 360; general files HO 361; and inspectors' reports HO 366.

Children's Department inspectors' reports on approved schools 1946–75: HO 360.

Inspectors' reports on children's homes 1941–72: HO 366.

Reviews by inspectors of LEA child-care arrangements and work of NSPCC, 1945–71: BN 61. Inspectors' visits to approved schools, remand and voluntary homes run by local authorities, voluntary bodies 1897–1990: BN 62.

Registrar-General: Nonconformist registers RG 4–6, RG 8, Fleet marriages and baptisms RG 7.

British Lying-In Hospital, Holborn registers of births and baptisms 1749–1868: RG 8/52–66.
Guide to Nonconformist and non-parochial registers: www.national archives.gov.uk/records/research-guides/nonconformists. htm.

Local Government Board and predecessors' correspondence with Poor Law unions and other local authorities (includes workhouse records, letters about parish apprentices) 1833–1909: MH 12.
Correspondence with Poor Law unions, some relating to Children Act 1908, and emigration to Canada, 1904–33: MH 68.
Poor Law schools: see MH 12, MH 27, MH 32 and ED 132. Children's Department files include industrial and approved schools: MH 102.

Children's Overseas Reception Board (CORB) files 1940–59: DO 131.

Guide to education inspectorate (HMI) reports:
www.nationalarchives.gov.uk/records/research-guides/education-inspectorate-reports.htm.
Guide to looking for records of a school:
www.nationalarchives.gov.uk/records/looking-for-place/school.htm.
Guide to records on elementary and primary schools:
www.nationalarchives.gov.uk/records/research-guides/elementary-education. htm.
Guide to records on secondary schools:
www.nationalarchives.gov.uk/records/research-guides/secondary-education .htm.
Guide to Special Services in education:
www.nationalarchives.gov.uk/records/research-guides/special-education. htm.
Discovery catalogue:
http://discovery.nationalarchives.gov.uk.
TNA Our Online Records:
www.nationalarchives.gov.uk/records/our-online-records.htm.
TNA Digital Microfilm:
www.nationalarchives.gov.uk/records/digital-microfilm.htm.

The National Archives, Kew, Richmond, Surrey, TW9 4DU; www.national archives.gov.uk; email contacts: www.nationalarchives. gov.uk/contact/ form; tel: 0208 876 3444.

A2: Archives for Children's Charities and Voluntary Organisations

Barnardo's Archive and Making Connections Service

See also the University of Liverpool listing in Section A4.

Barnardo's holds records for children brought up in Barnardo's homes. Family history service available. Photographic archive of 500,000 images. Research fee payable for children who lived in the UK, free initial search for children who emigrated to Australia and Canada.

www.barnardos.org.uk/family_history_service.

www.barnardos.org.uk/what_we_do/who_we_are/history/family_history_service/family_history_service_our_service.htm.

www.barnardos.org.uk/what_we_do/working_with_former_barnardos_children.htm.

Directory of former Barnardo's Homes:

www.barnardos.org.uk/what_we_do/who_we_are/history/barnardos_homes.htm.

Barnardo's Family History Service, Cottage 4, Tanners Lane, Barkingside, Essex, IG6 1QG; www.barnardos.org.uk; email: familyhistoryservice@barnardos.org.uk; tel: 0208 498 7536.

Boys' Brigade

Central and local records, including minutes, correspondence and annual reports 1883–twentieth century.

History of the Boys' Brigade: www.boys-brigade.org.uk/history.htm.

The Boys' Brigade, Felden Lodge, Hemel Hempstead, Hertfordshire, HP3 0BL; www.boys-brigade.org.uk; enquiries@boys-brigade.org.uk; tel: 0144 223 1681.

Catholic Children's Society, Westminster

The Society was previously known at the Crusade of Rescue.

Records relating to the Society's children's homes, child migrants and Catholic workhouse children. Descendants of deceased former residents, or child migrants, or former residents of children's homes run by the Society, or birth relatives seeking information on adopted adults, should contact the archive by post or via the online forms. A research fee is payable.

www.cathchild.org.uk/pages/post-adoption-and-care.html.

Adoption and After-care Team Leader, Catholic Children's Society, 73 St Charles Square, London, W10 6EJ; www.cathchild.org.uk; tel: 0208 969 5305.

Children's Society Records and Archive Centre

Formerly the Church of England Waifs and Strays Society, and Church of England Children's Society.

Records of the Society from 1890–1970. Some branch records may be held locally. Case files of children held at the archive usually include date when the child entered care and reason for admission, where the child was cared for, and date and nature of eventual discharge. Family historians wishing to access this information should contact the archive; normally the archivist will compile a summary of a child's early life from the case files.

History of the Society: www.childrenssociety.org.uk/about-us/our-history.

'Hidden Lives Revealed 1881–1981' virtual archive has 150 case files (anonymous) of children cared for by the Waifs and Strays Society. Photographs, information on the Society's children's homes, Society publications, learning resources and more. Online catalogues for case files of disabled children with records of the Children's Union; records relating to St Nicholas' and St Martin's Homes, Tooting, Surbiton and Pyrford; St Chad's Home, Far Headingley; St Agnes' Home, Croydon; Bradstock Lockett Home, Southport; Halliwick School, Winchmore Hill; St Agnes' Home, Pevensey Bay; St Monica's Home, Kingsdown and Corfield House Home, Rustington:

www.hiddenlives.org.uk/including_the_excluded/completed_catalogues.html.

Archivist Ian Wakeling, Children's Society Records and Archive Centre, Block A, Floor 2, Tower Bridge Business Complex, 100 Clement's Road, London, SE16 4DG; www.hiddenlives.org.uk; email: Hidden-Lives-Revealed@childrens society.org.uk; tel: 0207 232 2966.

Church Lads and Church Girls' Brigade Archive (CLCGB)

The archive includes Royal Reviews of the Brigade: documents, reports, letters, photographs, parade orders, programmes, certificates. Annual reports of Church Lads' Brigade and the Church Lads' and Church Girls' Brigade, 1891–2002.

Brigade Lists (Annual Directory) 1895–1918. Correspondence, photographs, minutes, local company histories (a detailed catalogue is on A2A). The archive is open by appointment only.

The CLCGB Historical Group produces a magazine, The Brigader. www.clcgb.org.uk/historical-group.
Historical Group Factsheets are online: www.clcgb.org.uk/documents/cat_view/5-historical-group.

National Headquarters, 2 Barnsley Road, Wath-upon-Dearne, Rotherham, S63 6PY; www.clcgb.org.uk; email Historical Group contact Mr Robin Bolton: rob.bolton@talk21.com; tel: 0170 987 6535.

Girlguiding UK
17–19 Buckingham Palace Road, London, SW1W 0PT; www.girlguiding. org.uk/home.aspx; email: archives@girlguiding.org.uk; tel: 0207 834 6242, ext. 3001.

London City Mission (LCM) Archive
LCM Magazine (1836 onwards) including material from missionaries' daily journals and annual reports may include ragged schools set up by the mission. LCM Annual Reports (1835 onwards). Minutes of LCM Committee (weekly from 1835). Unpublished annual reports of individual missionaries, autobiographical accounts, etc. Photos. Researchers wishing to enquire about archival items should use the online form or contact the archives by post.

Archives, London City Mission, 175 Tower Bridge Road, London, SE1 2AH; www.lcm.org.uk/Groups/9369/London_City_Mission/Features/Archives/A rchives.aspx.

Marine Society & Sea Cadet Association
Navy League records, 1895–1975.
www.ms-sc.org.uk/history.
An appointment is needed to visit the library. See also the National Maritime Museum listing in Section A3.

202 Lambeth Road, London, SE1 7JW; www.marine-society.org/research; email: info@ms-sc.org; tel: 0207 654 7008.

Norwood Archives
Records relating to the Norwood Home for Jewish Children (The Jewish

Orphanage), now merged with Ravenswood.
See the University of Southampton listing in Section A4.
History of Norwood 1795–1995:
www.norwood.org.uk/Page/A-History-of-Norwood.
Norwood Old Scholars Association:
www.norwood.org.uk//Page/The-Norwood-Old-Scholars-Association.

Norwood's Archive Department, Norwood, Broadway House, 80–2 The
Broadway, Stanmore, Middlesex, HA7 4HB; www.norwood.org.uk//Page/
History-and-Archives; email: info@norwood. org.uk; tel: 0208 809 8809.

Royal National Institute for the Blind (RNIB)
School records *c*. 1920–90.

RNIB Heritage Services, 105 Judd Street, London, WC1H 9NE;
www.rnib.org.uk/ABOUTUS/RESEARCH/HERITAGE/ARCHIVE/Pages/arc
hive.aspx; email: heritageservices@rnib.org.uk; tel: 0207 391 2052.

Planned Environment Therapy Trust (PETT) Archive and Study Centre
Audio, oral and video histories relating to therapeutic work with children,
young people and adults, 1930–80. Over 800 oral history recordings. You
must make an appointment to visit the archive and research library.

Planned Environment Therapy Trust, Church Lane, Toddington, Cheltenham,
Gloucestershire, GL54 5DQ; www.pettrust.org.uk/about/ archive-and-study-
centre and www.archive.pettrust.org.uk; tel: 0124 262 1200.

Red Cross Museum and Archives
An appointment is necessary to access the archives.

British Red Cross Museum and Archives, 44 Moorfields, London, EC2Y
9AL; www.redcross.org.uk/About-us/Who-we-are/Museum-and-archives;
email: enquiry@redcross.org.uk; tel: 0207 877 7058.

Salvation Army International Heritage Centre
Museum, library and archive. Social service records include 'Girls' Statement
Books' from the Salvation Army's Women's Social Work Headquarters,
including details for most women in Salvation Army maternity homes in
Britain 1886–1993.

Records for maternity homes (dates are for records held, not dates the home was open): Ivy House, Hackney (1890–1910); Thorndale, Belfast (1905–83); Brent House, Hackney (1913–25); Elmswood, Liverpool (1914–70); Clement Park House/Florence Booth House, Dundee (1932–90s); Northlands, Cardiff (1933–89); Hopedene, Newcastle-upon-Tyne (1941–94); Fraser of Allander, Glasgow (1947–84).

Registers of dedications for some Corps from 1899 onwards; some dedication certificates.

Some 'Junior Soldiers' Rolls' from various Corps with names, addresses and dates of enrolment, 1920s onwards.

Contact the archive first before travelling to check if records have survived; seventy-five-year closure for records.

An appointment is needed to view items from the library or archive. The archivist will answer an initial family history query free; further in-depth research is charged at £20 per hour.

Salvation Army International Heritage Centre, William Booth College, Champion Park, London, SE5 8BQ; www.salvationarmy.org.uk/uki/heritage; email: heritage@salvationarmy.org.uk; tel: 0207 326 7800.

Scout Association Archive

Records of scout groups, awards to individuals and much more. Photographic and film collections. Online databases for individuals including award cards (some with photographs) and online catalogues for collections.

The Scout Association, Archive and Heritage Deptartment, Gilwell Park, London, E4 7QW; www.scoutsrecords.org; tel: 0208 433 7195.

Museum of the Order of St John

An appointment is needed to visit the Library; order rolls and membership forms can only be accessed by museum staff. Family history enquiries can be sent by post or email; a £10 donation is suggested to cover administration costs.

Key records at Library:
www.sja.org.uk/sja/about-us/our-library/researching-sja.aspx.

The Museum of the Order of St John, St John's Gate, St John's Lane, London, EC1M 4DA; www.museumstjohn.org.uk; email: museum@nhq.sja.org.uk; tel: 0207 324 4005.

A3: Local and Specialist Archives and Repositories

Aviva Archives

Records for over 650 insurance companies: statutory records, minute books, annual reports, share registers, financial records, journals, ledgers, cash books, policies, photographs, staff records and more. No burial club payment records.

An appointment is necessary to visit the archive. Customer records under 100 years old are closed to researchers; contact the helplines below if you think your ancestor had a recent policy.

Anna Stone, Group Archivist, Aviva Group Archive, 8 Surrey Street, Norwich, NR1 3NG; www.aviva.com/about-us/heritage/heritage-contacts; email: anna.stone@aviva.com; tel: 0160 368 2645; general enquiries email: here-to-help@aviva.co.uk; life & pensions helpline: 0800 068 6800; general insurance policies helpline: 0800 068 5670.

Birmingham Archives and Heritage Centre

Middlemore Homes minutes, financial records, correspondence, case studies, 1871–2000: MS 517. Admission registers for Middlemore Homes 1872–1949: MS 517 additional.

Royal School for Deaf Children records 1814–1934, and registers of children 1949–80: MS 1060.

Princess Alice Orphanage records include minute books, logbooks, registers of children, photographs, press cuttings and magazines 1878–1980: MS 1249.

The Birmingham Archives and Heritage Centre is now closed and re-opens September 2013 in the Library of Birmingham, Centenary Square, Birmingham. http:// libraryofbirmingham.com/; email: library.of.birmingham @birmingham.gov.uk.

Bristol Record Office

Royal Blind Asylum records. Red Lodge Reformatory registers: 5137 (see also Mary Carpenter records: 12693). Kingswood Schools: 28776.

Society of Merchant Venturers ships' muster rolls, registers of apprentices and indentures 1653–1930: SMV.

Records of National Nautical School, Portishead and Clifton Certified Industrial School 1869–1972 (seventy-year access restriction) include admission registers (NS/A8), registers of boys (NS/A7), punishment book, etc. (NS/A11): 38087.

(NB Researchers wishing to consult records for the National Nautical School less than seventy years old should contact: Secretary, The Portishead Nautical Trust, 108 High Street, Portishead, Bristol, BS20 9AJ.)

Bristol Record Office, 'B' Bond Warehouse, Smeaton Road, Bristol, BS1 6XN; www.bristol.gov.uk/page/records-and-archives-0; email: bro@bristol.gov. uk; tel: 0117 922 4224.

British Library, Boston Spa

Archives of Shaftesbury Society, Parts1–3, on microfilm and microfiche. Part 1: minutes of Ragged School Union and Shaftesbury Society 1844–1944. Part 2: Ragged School Union Magazine 1849–75. Part 3: Ragged School Union Magazine 1876–1907, Shelfmarks MFR 3106, MFE 197. Hard copy indexes available.

Archives of COS 1869–1938 on microfilm, including the Charity Organisation Reporter 1872–84, Charity Organisation Review 1885–1921 and Charity Organisation Quarterly 1921–38, Shelfmark MFR 6124.

The British Library, Boston Spa, Wetherby, West Yorkshire, LS23 7BQ; www.bl.uk/aboutus/quickinfo/loc/bsp/index.html; tel: 0193 754 6070.

British Library, St Pancras

India Office records are in the Asian and African Studies reading room at the British Library: IOR. Addiscombe Military Seminary records 1809–62: IOR/L/MIL/9/333–357.

Cadet Papers (1789–1860) and Cadet Registers (1775–1860): IOR/L/MIL/9/107–269. India Office family history search: http://india family.bl.uk/ui/Home.aspx.

The British Library, 96 Euston Road, London, NW1 2DB; www.bl.uk; tel: 0207 412 7676.

British Library Newspapers

British Library Newspapers, Colindale Avenue, London, NW9 5HE; www.bl.uk; tel: 0207 412 7353.

Cheshire Archives and Local Studies

Poor Law union records. School records include Saltersford School (formerly Bradwall Reformatory), Audlem Free Grammar, Bunbury Grammar, Frodsham Grammar, etc.

Church Minshull County Primary School logbooks and admission registers 1892–1982 (SL420) include children evacuated from Eldon Street RC School, Liverpool: SL420/2/3.

School admission registers normally subject to restricted access for ninety years (secondary schools) and ninety-five years (primary schools).

Cheshire Archives and Local Studies Service, Cheshire Record Office, Duke Street, Chester, Cheshire, CH1 1RL; http://archives.cheshire.gov.uk /default.aspx; email: RecordOffice@cheshiresharedservices.gov.uk; tel: 0124 497 2574.

Church of England Record Centre (CERC)

See also the listing for Lambeth Palace Library.

Archive of the National Society (search the collection by typing 'NS' into the order number box of the online catalogue).

CERC does not hold any National School admission registers or logbooks except for these Teacher Training institutions: Central Schools/ Westminster Training Institutions, St Mark's College and Battersea St John's College admission registers (11 volumes) 1812–51: NS/7/6 (some registers are missing). Guide on education sources: http://www.lambethpalacelibrary.org/content /education.

An appointment and a reader's ticket (photo ID required) are needed to consult the collections. Catalogue for Lambeth Palace Library and CERC archival holdings: http://archives.lambethpalacelibrary.org.uk/archives/.

Church of England Record Centre, 15 Galleywall Road, South Bermondsey, London, SE16 3PB; www.lambethpalacelibrary.org/content/cerccollections; email: archives@churchofengland.org (write 'CERC' in the subject line); tel: 0207 898 1030.

Cumbria Archive Centre, Kendal

Casterton (formerly the Clergy Daughters' School, Cowan Bridge) School entrance book 1824–33: WDS 38.

Cumbria Archive Centre, Kendal County Offices, Kendal, LA9 4RQ; www.cumbria.gov.uk/archives; email: kendal.archives@cumbria. gov.uk; tel: 0153 9713 540 or 9713 539.

Derbyshire Record Office
Databases of Poor Law removal orders.
The website has a free searchable database of prisoners, including children, held in the County Gaol and houses of correction 1729–1913. If you find a relative, note the reference number and contact the Record Office to order a copy of the original entry: www.derbyshire.gov.uk/resources/Prisoner Search/default.aspx.

Derbyshire Record Office, County Hall, New Street, Matlock, Derbyshire, DE4 3AG; www.derbyshire.gov.uk/recordoffice; email: record.office@ derbyshire.gov.uk; tel: 0162 953 8347.

Fleet Air Arm Museum
An appointment is needed to visit the Archive Search Room in the Centre for Naval Aviation Records & Research.
Guide to collections: www.fleetairarm.com/naval-aviation-research.aspx.
Guide to Royal Naval and Royal Marines Service Documents: www. fleetairarm.com/royal-navy-royal-marines-services-documents.aspx.

Fleet Air Arm Museum, RNAS Yeovilton, Ilchester, Somerset, BA22 8HT; www.fleetairarm.com; email: research@fleetairarm.com; tel: 0193 584 2608.

Glamorgan Archives
Quarter sessions and petty sessions records. Juvenile court registers and convictions.
Poor Law union records include settlement papers. Public Assistance Committee records. Ships' crew agreements (includes apprentices) and official logbooks 1863–1913: DPROCA/C.
Records for children's homes, social services.
Air Training Corps (Welsh Division) records for the 1940s–50s including membership lists, attendance registers and lists of cadets: D455.
Online catalogue: http://calmview.cardiff.gov.uk/CalmView.

Glamorgan Archives, Clos Parc Morgannwg, Leckwith, Cardiff, CF11 8AW; www.glamarchives.gov.uk; email: glamro@cardiff.gov.uk; tel: 0292 087 2200.

Great Ormond Street Hospital Archives
Open by prior appointment only.

Museum & Archives Service, Great Ormond Street Hospital, Great Ormond Street, London, WC1N 3JH; www.gosh.nhs.uk/about-us/our-history/museum-and-archive-services; email archivist and curator Nicholas Baldwin: BaldwN@gosh.nhs.uk; tel: 0207 405 9200, ext. 5920.

Guildhall Library
City of London Livery Company archives including admission of freedom registers and apprentice bindings 1380–1998: COL/CP.
Online guide to freedom papers: http://goo.gl/Iq81t.
Guide to searching for members or those apprenticed to members of City of London livery companies: http://goo.gl/evDYI.
Worshipful Company of Merchant Taylors records, including school records are on microfilm: CLC/L/MD.
Company of Watermen and Lightermen records include apprenticeship indentures 1688–1971: CLC/L/WA. Online guide: http://goo.gl/dHxoU.
The Library formerly held the Christ's Hospital archive, now at LMA.
Historical directories.
A reader's ticket or Archives History Card is needed to consult these collections.
The Guildhall Library is now part of LMA; telephone and written enquiries for Library collections should be directed to LMA.

Guildhall Library, Aldermanbury, London, EC2V 7HH;
www.cityoflondon.gov.uk/things-to-do/archives-and-city-history/guildhall-library/Pages/default.aspx; email: guildhall.library@cityof london.gov.uk; LMA tel: 0207 332 3820.

Hull History Centre
Online information guides on the archive's collections of Trinity House muster rolls, apprenticeship records, fishing vessel crew lists 1884–1914, and maternity and children's homes records.

Hull History Centre, Worship Street, Hull, HU2 8BG; www.hullhistory centre.org.uk; email: hullhistorycentre@hullcc.gov.uk; tel: 0148 231 7500.

Lambeth Palace Library
Attendance lists for some Sunday schools.
Records for the Clergy Orphan Corporation 1808–1952: MSS.3018-3059.
A reader's ticket is needed to consult the collections (photo ID required).

The Library's online printed books catalogue lists many published sources on education.

Guide to Local History includes some endowed, charity and Sunday school sources for various counties held at Lambeth Palace Library: www.lambeth palacelibrary.org/files/Local_History.pdf.

Catalogue for Lambeth Palace Library and CERC archival holdings: http://archives.lambethpalacelibrary.org.uk/archives.

Lambeth Palace Library, London, SE1 7JU; www.lambethpalacelibrary.org; email: archives@churchofengland.org; tel: 0207 898 1400.

Lancashire Record Office

Many school records. Liverpool Juvenile Reformatory Association records 1855–1956 include Red Bank School, Girls' Reformatory, training ship *Akbar* (later Heswall Nautical School) and more: DDX 824.

Swinton Industrial Schools institution admission and discharge books 1846–8, 1850–1934; school admission and discharge books 1892–1926; indices 1848–1935; and a Master's journal 1922–9: PUG.

Online research guides include 'Handlist No. 29' (Second World War records) with a catalogue of records for evacuees from London, Manchester and Salford. Online district guides include catalogues of Poor Law records, court records, education and school records: http://bit.ly/qgAPJv.

Preston Guild Rolls online 1397–1992 list names of burgesses, their sons if added to the rolls, and apprentices: http://bit.ly/OKBCO2.

Photographs and criminal records of persons arrested 1866–92: PLA 16/1.

Lancashire Record Office, Bow Lane, Preston, Lancashire, PR1 2RE; www.lancashire.gov.uk; email: record.office@lancashire.gov.uk; tel: 0177 253 3039.

Record Office for Leicestershire, Leicester & Rutland

Long Street, Wigston Magna, Leicester, LE18 2AH; www.leics.gov.uk/ index/community/museums/record_office.htm; email: recordoffice@leics. gov.uk; tel: 0116 257 1080.

Liverpool Record Office

Liverpool Society for the Prevention of Cruelty to Children records including minute books, register of prosecutions, newspaper cuttings (various dates) 1883–1957: 179 CRU. Liverpool Orphanage (formerly Female Orphan

Asylum, Boys Asylum and Infants Orphan Asylum) and Salisbury House School records (closed for 100 years) 1771–1977: 362 SAL.

Kirkdale Industrial School records include admission and discharge registers 1862–5, classification registers 1845–97, creed registers 1869–1904: 353 SEL.

Records of *Indefatigable* and National Sea Training School for Boys on microfilm: 387 IND.

Liverpool Catholic Reformatory Association records include rolls and registers of juvenile offenders: 364 CAT.

An index of school records is available.

Community archives include Merseyside Jewish community records.

Liverpool Record Office, Central Library, William Brown Street, Liverpool, L3 8EW; www.liverpool.gov.uk/libraries-and-archives/archives-local-and-family-history; tel: 0151 233 5817.

London Metropolitan Archives

Vast collections relating to schools, Poor Law records, children's homes, etc. Christ's Hospital (Blue Coat School) records (2013/00045) include minute and account books, estate papers, admission and discharge registers for children 1563–1911 (no girls after 1891), and registers for Royal Mathematical School 1673–1911. Incomplete series of Christ's Hospital presentation papers, containing petitions submitted by parents, guardians, etc., providing some personal and financial details of children's families, up to 1911 for boys, and up to 1890 for girls.

London Orphan Asylum creed register 1875–99, Acc B09/107, admission requests and assignments 1796–1866: O/174.

Jews' Free School records (LMA/4046, LMA/4290, LMA/4297) include minute books 1826–8 (with some pupil lists) and admission/discharge registers 1869–1939.

Westminster Jews' Free School records: LMA 4047 and LCC/EO.

Shaftesbury Young People archive includes registers for Training Ships *Arethusa* and *Chichester* (1872 onwards) and some records for Shaftesbury Homes.

Middlesex County Council Children's Department 1933–65 Adoption Index Cards: MCC/CH/A/IND.

London County Council Children's Department records (twentieth century) includes children's homes, places of detention, residential nurseries: LCC/CH.

London County Council Special Schools: LCC/SS.

FWA records (formerly the COS) 1843–1965: A/FWA. Guidelines are available for enquiries about adopted children or those in care.

Prison records include House of Correction, Cold Bath Fields and New Prison, Clerkenwell: MA/G. Middlesex Industrial School, Feltham registers of inmates 1859–70: MA/GS/010.

Metropolitan Asylums Board (MAB) records include registers of workhouse boys sent to the Training Ship *Exmouth* 1876–1947: MAB/2512. Case numbers for individual boys: MAB/2492–2499.

London Federation of Boys' Clubs (formerly Federation of London Working Boys' Clubs) archive includes minutes, annual reports, souvenir brochures, photos 1888–2000: LMA/4283.

Collections guides: http://goo.gl/M 3UCe

Sources for history of education at LMA: http://bit.ly/LuDeGF.

Education in London guide: http://bit.ly/WReE7D.

Foundling Hospital Records guide: http://goo.gl/Fz133..

Guide to hospital records: http://bit.ly/UV84MG.

Some LMA collections are available on Ancestry: http://landing. ancestry.co.uk/lma/default.aspx.

LMA catalogue: http://search.lma.gov.uk/opac_lma/index.htm.

London Metropolitan Archives, Head Archivist, Dr Deborah Jenkins, 40 Northampton Road, London, EC1R 0HB; www.cityoflondon.gov.uk/lma; email: ask.lma@cityoflondon.gov.uk; tel: 0207 332 3820.

Greater Manchester County Record Office with Manchester Archives
NB GMRCO with Manchester Archives will move to Archives+, Manchester Central Library in early 2014 (check the website for updates).

Parish registers, court records, Poor Law records. School records include Manchester Grammar: M516. Manchester Royal Residential Schools for the Deaf 1823–1984: M437. Swinton Industrial School: list of children sent to the school, 1846–65, M4/20/1, and a logbook (boys), March 1919–September 1927: M66/85/1/1/1. Styal Cottage Homes records include logbooks (restricted access). Salford Cottage Homes, Culcheth photographic archive DPA/1679.

Adelphi Lads' Club photos 1899–1955: DPA/1117. Charter Street Ragged School papers 1861–1971: G25. Jewish Lads' Brigade papers 1908–65: MS 130. Hulme Lads' Club: M716.

Greater Manchester Pastfinder catalogue: http://bit.ly/WAb0R1.

School collections: http://bit.ly/Sr1oKn.

Poor Law, workhouse and industrial school records: http://bit.ly/10Meln1.

Greater Manchester County Record Office, 56 Marshall Street, New Cross, Manchester, M4 5FU; www.manchester.gov.uk/libraries/arls; email: archiveslocalstudies@manchester.gov.uk; tel: 0161 832 5284.

Mercers' Company Archives

Records of Mercers' Company business, charities and properties from fourteenth century onwards. Register of Freemen and Apprentice Registers. St Paul's School admission registers contain details of pupils' names, date of admission, sometimes date of birth, age when admitted and the name and occupation of father, dates available 1748–73, 1773–1807, 1807–34 and 1860–76 (see also St Paul's School listing in Section D).

Family history enquiries should be submitted by post (allow three months for a reply): researchers should consult secondary sources such as Mercers' Company histories and other publications first (the Guildhall Library has copies).

Archivist and Records Manager, The Mercers' Company, Mercers' Hall, Ironmonger Lane, London, EC2V 8HE; www.mercers.co.uk/archive; email: archives@mercers.co.uk; tel: 0207 726 4991.

Merseyside Maritime Museum Archives and Library

Shipping records.

Lancashire and National Sea Training Homes records include minutes, subscription records, treasury books, sea registers, financial records 1896–1945: D/NL, online catalogue: bit.ly/SpoXBC.

Records of *Indefatigable* and National Sea Training School for Boys include minute books (1864–1984), registers (1865–1995), visitor report books (1865–1978), punishment books (1951–95), boys' discharge book (1953–86), series D/IND, online catalogue: bit.ly/PvMYnm.

Training ship HMS *Conway* records include muster rolls, wages books, registers of cadets 1857–2003: D/CON. Online catalogue for HMS *Conway*: bit.ly/NVkdmL.

Child emigration information sheet: bit.ly/SVVWMT.

Major collections: www.liverpoolmuseums.org.uk/maritime/archive/ collections /index.aspx.

Maritime Archives and Library, Merseyside Maritime Museum, Albert

Dock, Liverpool, L3 4AQ; www.liverpoolmuseums.org.uk/maritime/ archive; tel: 0151 478 4499.

National Maritime Museum, Greenwich, London

Merchant shipping collections include crew lists (see online guides for genealogists).

Marine Society and Sea Cadets Archive (MSY/L) and (MSY/M) includes minutes, registers and accounts of Marine Society 1756–1978. Boys admitted 1756–63, 1889–1958; boys received and discharged from the Marine Society's training ship 1786–1874; apprentices sent to merchant ships 1772–1950, with indices 1770–1838; girls apprenticed by Marine Society 1772–1957, and girls 'placed out' from the Hickes Fund 1926–78; awards of merit 1898–1954; members of TS *Warspite* Old Boys Association 1917–49: MSY.

Registers of Boys Entered as Servants in the King's Ships 1770–1873 with indices: MSY/O/1–15.

Records of cadets who served on HMS *Worcester* (Thames Nautical Training College) 1863–1968: WOR. Minute books: WOR/B.

Devitt & Moore archive includes records for Nautical College, Pangbourne; lists of ship's officers and cadets 1864–1916; registers of apprentices 1868–99, 1902–3, 1906–17; and registers of midshipmen, 1897–1917: DEM. P&O records include apprenticeships.

Greenwich Hospital School letter books and registers 1836–63 (some years missing): FIS.

Apprenticeship indentures.

Royal Naval College, Portsmouth account book 1795–1808: SOC.

Typewritten list of pupils attending training ship HMS *Brittania* in 1903: GOD/3.

A reader's ticket is required to access the collections.

Archive catalogue: http://collections.rmg.co.uk/archive.html#!asearch.

The Caird Library, National Maritime Museum, Greenwich, London, SE10 9NF; www.rmg.co.uk/researchers; email: manuscripts@rmg.co.uk; tel: 0208 312 6516.

Norfolk Record Office

Church Lads' Brigade 1st Norwich Battalion minutes, membership records, etc. 1897–1953: see SO 206. Great Yarmouth Grammar School records include Cadet Corps nominal roll and logbook 1920–45: D/ED 9/68.

Norfolk Record Office, The Archive Centre, Martineau Lane, Norwich, NR1 2DQ; http://archives.norfolk.gov.uk; email: norfrec@norfolk.gov.uk; tel: 0160 322 2599.

Parliamentary Archives
Parliamentary Archives, Houses of Parliament, London, SW1A 0PW; www.parliament.uk/business/publications/parliamentary-archives; email: archives@parliament.uk; tel: 0207 219 3074.

Royal London Hospital Archives
Collections include records for East End Maternity Hospital, East London Hospital for Children, London Jewish Hospital, Plaistow Maternity Hospital, Queen Elizabeth Hospital for Children, Queen Mary's Maternity Hospital and more.

9 Prescot Street, London, E1 8PR; www.bartsandthelondon.nhs.uk/about-us/museums-and-archives/the-royal-london-archives; email: rlharchives @bartsandthelondon.nhs.uk; tel: 0207 377 7608.

Royal Naval Museum
Photographic and oral history collections.
The museum library does not hold sea cadet records or naval service records.
Royal Naval Benevolent Society records: ledgers with entries of names and payments of membership and donations to the Benevolent Society 1791–1968.
Sea Your History website includes an image gallery and oral histories: www.seayourhistory.org.uk.
An appointment is necessary to visit the Reading Room in the Library.

Royal Naval Museum, HM Naval Base (PP66), Portsmouth, PO1 3NH; www.royalnavalmuseum.org/research.htm; email: library@nmrn.org.uk; tel: 0239 272 3795.

St Bartholomew's Hospital Archives and Museum
Collections include records of the Alexandra Hospital for Children with Hip Disease, and some records for the Mothers' Hospital of the Salvation Army including maternity registers (see also the Salvation Army International Heritage Centre listing in this section).
Free admission to the museum; appointment needed to visit the archive.

Archivist Katie Ormerod, Archives and Museum, North Wing, St Bartholomew's Hospital, West Smithfield, London, EC1A 7BE; www.bartsandthelondon.nhs.uk/about-us/museums-and-archives/st-bartholomew-s-archives; email: barts.archives@bartsandthelondon.nhs.uk; tel: 0203 465 5798.

Salford City Archive Centre
Adelphi Lads' Club papers include attendance registers, index of surnames, First World War roll of honour 1888–1990: U129. Adelphi Lads' Club Old Boys' Association 1920–54: U130.
Pendleton Ragged School papers 1864–1967: U69.

Salford City Archive Centre, Salford Museum and Art Gallery, Peel Park, The Crescent, Salford, M5 4WU; www.salford.communityleisure.co.uk/culture/salford-museum-and-art-gallery/local-history; archive email: roseanne.mclaughlin@salford.gov.uk; library email: local.history@scll.co.uk; archives tel: 0161 778 0814.

Surrey History Centre
Reed's School, Cobham (formerly the London Orphan Asylum) 1814–1988 administrative records: series ref: 3719. Royal Philanthropic Society 1788–1976: admission registers, photographs and more, series ref: 2271 (100 years' closure).
Guide to records and index of Registers of Admissions for Royal Philanthropic Society: http://bit.ly/zneEOL.
Many other schools and charitable institutions.
Albury Gypsy School, Hurtwood, Shere, newspaper cuttings and photos: 2570.
Princess Mary Village Homes pupils 1870–90: http://bit.ly/H7iSXa.
Index to deaths in Surrey County Gaol 1798–1878: http://bit.ly/xcnceC.

Surrey History Centre, 130 Goldsworth Road, Woking, Surrey, GU21 6ND; www.surreycc.gov.uk/recreation-heritage-and-culture/archives-and-history/surrey-history-centre; email: shs@surreycc.gov.uk; tel: 0148 351 8737.

Royal Military College Sandhurst
The Sandhurst Collection includes the archives of the academy and its predecessors, the Royal Military College Sandhurst 1799–1939 and the Royal Military Academy Woolwich 1741–1939. It also maintains the archive

of the current academy established in 1947. Photographic collection. Access by appointment only.

Sandhurst Collection, Royal Military Academy Sandhurst, Camberley, GU15 4PQ; www.sandhurstcollection.org.uk; tel: 0127 641 2489.

Tyne and Wear Archives

Charlotte Square Synagogue bris milah (circumcisions) 1877–81 (C.NC86). Sunderland Hebrew Congregation bris milah (circumcisions) 1850–89, birth register 1867–73 (C.SU74).

Online user guides available for coal industry, guild records including apprenticeship indentures (indexed), parish registers, Methodist registers, other denominations, Jewish community, maritime records including crew lists, Poor Law records, school records for Gateshead, Newcastle-upon-Tyne, North and South Tyneside, Sunderland, trade-union records, etc.: http://bit.ly/WRsmHy.

Tyne & Wear Archives, Discovery Museum, Blandford Square, Newcastle, NE1 4JA; www.twmuseums.org.uk/tyne-and-wear-archives.html; email: info@twarchives.org.uk; tel: 0191 277 2248.

National Library of Wales

Baptism, marriage and burial registers, BTs, marriage bonds, Nonconformist records, wills and probate records, quarter sessions, Poor Law and education records, etc. The South Reading Room has some logbooks and miscellaneous records for National Schools and documents relating to several Nonconformist academies and colleges, particularly for Welsh Calvinistic Methodist establishments. Sunday school registers. The National Screen and Sound Archive at the Library includes video and audio recordings of Welsh school choirs. Urdd Gobaith Cymru papers: URDD.

Online catalogue: http://wales.aquabrowser.com.

List of archives and manuscripts in the Library not yet included in online catalogue (e.g. try a search for 'school'): http://isys.llgc.org.uk/.

Welsh Journals Online (free) includes academic, antiquarian and historical publications relating to Wales: http://welshjournals.llgc.org.uk.

Blue Books of 1847 (An inquiry into the state of education in Wales): www.llgc.org.uk/index.php?id=thebluebooks.

Welsh school magazines and newspapers available at NLW: www.llgc.org.uk/index.php?id=welshschoolmagazines.

National Library of Wales, Aberystwyth, Ceredigion, Wales, SY23 3BU; www.llgc.org.uk; email: enquiry@llgc.org.uk; tel: 0197 063 2800.

City of Westminster Archives

Education and business records: www.westminster.gov.uk/services/ libraries/archives/family-history/school-records.

Parish and workhouse records: www.westminster.gov.uk/services/ libraries/ archives/family-history/parish-records.

Visitors must register (free) with Westminster Libraries and Archives to access the collections.

City of Westminster Archives Centre, 10 St Ann's Street, London, SW1P 2DE; www.westminster.gov.uk/services/libraries/archives; email: archives @westminster.gov.uk; tel: 0207 641 5180.

Wellcome Library

Records of societies, businesses or professional bodies concerned with child welfare, and personal papers of children's welfare professionals such as health visitors, MOHs and social workers.

MOH annual reports:

http://library.wellcome.ac.uk/using-the-library/subject-guides/public-health/MOH-reports.

Online catalogue of collections, including children and adolescents: http://library.wellcome.ac.uk/doc_WTL039897.html.

Wellcome Library, 183 Euston Road, London, NW1 2BE; http://library. wellcome.ac.uk; email: library@wellcome.ac.uk; tel: 0207 611 8722.

West Yorkshire Archives Service

School records are held by all five WYAS offices for their local area.

Ackworth school records: C678. See also C951, and printed sources which include registers of pupils 1779–1978 (3 vols) and an index to apprenticeships 1800–43.

Guide to schools collections: http://bit.ly/Xthhgt.

Parish registers guide: http://bit.ly/VkoXmP.

Health records guide includes maternity and children's hospitals: http://bit.ly/XRw6LZ.

West Yorkshire Archive Service, Registry of Deeds, Newstead Road,

Wakefield, WF1 2DE; www.archives.wyjs.org.uk; email: wakefield@wyjs.org.uk; tel: 0192 430 5980.

Dr Williams's Library

Congregationalist collections are in the Congregationalist Library in the same premises as Dr Williams's Library.
Collections: www.dwlib.co.uk/congregational/collections/union.html.

Dr Williams's Library, 14 Gordon Square, London, WC1H 0AR; www.dwlib.co.uk/dwlib/contact.html; email: enquiries@dwlib.co.uk; tel: 0207 387 3727.

A4: Special Collections at Universities

University of Birmingham

Special Collections include records of Christian and youth organisations, Christian education and training, and special education. Church Missionary Society archives: CMS.

Save the Children Fund collection: minutes, publications, administration records, Nursery Schools Committee, personal papers of fieldworkers, photographs 1919–2006: SCF (partially closed; contact the archivist first, giving at least ten working days' notice for an appointment). Some Save the Children Fund collections are catalogued on A2A.

Preliminary list (February 2012) of Save the Children collections: http://goo.gl/s0MS6.

UK Youth collections 1909–2002 (mostly from 1950s) includes predecessor organisations such as National Organisation of Girls' Clubs (various dates): MS227.

Local Christian Education Councils and Sunday School Unions' minutes and annual reports: LCEC.

Preliminary hand-list (2008) for LCEC archive: http://calmview.bham.ac.uk/GetDocument.ashx?db=Catalog&fname=LCEC.pdf.

National Christian Education Council (formerly National Sunday School Union) and related organisations: NCEC.

Preliminary hand-list (2009) for NCEC archive: http://calmview.bham.ac.uk/GetDocument.ashx?db=Catalog&fname=NCEC.pdf.

Alphabetical lists of organisations in collections: www.birmingham.ac.uk/facilities/cadbury/archives/organisations/index.aspx.

The Cadbury Research Library is on the lower ground floor of the Muirhead Tower, Edgbaston campus. A reader's ticket is needed.

Cadbury Research Library, University of Birmingham, Edgbaston, Birmingham, B15 2TU; www.birmingham.ac.uk/facilities/cadbury/index. aspx; email: special-collections@bham.ac.uk; tel: 0121 414 5839.

Borthwick Institute, University of York

Records of American Committee for the Evacuation of British Children 1940–69 (includes lists of children): EVAC.

Probate records and wills for the PCY, Dean and Chapter of York and Exchequer Court of York from 1359–1858.

Guide to probate courts and jurisdictions:

www.york.ac.uk/library/borthwick/research-support/probate-courts.

Borthwick Institute for Archives, University of York, Heslington, York, YO10 5DD; www.york.ac.uk/library/borthwick; email: bihr500@york.ac.uk; tel: 0190 432 1166.

Brunel University Archives

BFSS archive includes minute books (financial), schools correspondence, school inspection returns, etc., 1814–twentieth century.

Home and Colonial Infant School Society annual reports: dates 1836, 1870–1, 1903/4–10/11. Published works on infant education by Samuel Wilderspin.

An appointment is needed to visit the archive at the Old School House, 1 Hillingdon Hill, near Brunel University campus.

Archive catalogues: www.bfss.org.uk/archive/archive-contents.

Postal address: Phaedra Casey, Archivist, Brunel University Archives, Kingston Lane, Uxbridge, Middlesex, UB8 3PH; www.bfss.org.uk/archive; email: phaedra.casey@brunel.ac.uk; tel: 0189 526 7095.

University of Cambridge Library

SPCK Archives, dating from 1698, held at the Manuscripts Department include minute books, correspondence and charity school records. The Rare Books department holds SPCK publications.

Rare Books tel: 0122 333 3122/3123; Rare Books email: rarebooks@lib.cam. ac.uk; Department of Manuscripts and University Archives, Cambridge

University Library, West Road, Cambridge, CB3 9DR; library website: www.lib.cam.ac.uk; email: library@lib.cam.ac.uk; Manuscripts Department email: mss@lib.cam.ac.uk; library tel: 0122 333 3000; Manuscripts Department tel: 0122 333 3143.

University of Central Lancashire
Temperance collections includes the Joseph Livesey collection: www.uclan.ac.uk/students/library/livesey_collection.php.

University of Central Lancashire, Preston, Lancashire, PR1 2HE; www.uclan.ac.uk/students/library/using_special_collections.php; email: clok@uclan.ac.uk; tel: 0177 220 1201.

Institute of Education Library and Archives, University of London
Papers of David Hylton Thomas (1910–99) on the industrial schools movement: TH.
Archives include Girls' Public Day Schools Trust 1843–2006: DC/GDS.
British Families Education Service (1947–2001): DC/BFE.
Visits to the archives by appointment only.
Family history guide on education sources: www.ioe.ac.uk/services/documents/SG8_family_history_(March_2009).pdf.

Newsam Library and Archives, Institute of Education, 20 Bedford Way, London, WC1H 0AL; www.ioe.ac.uk/services/4389.html; archives email: arch.enquiries@ioe.ac.uk; library email: lib.enquiries@ioc.ac.uk; archives tel: 0207 612 6983; library tel: 0207 612 6080.

John Rylands University Library, Manchester
Special Collections include hundreds of records of companies, business associations, trade unions, charities, religious institutions, etc. Methodist Archives and Research Centre records include the Methodist Division of Education and Youth papers relating to youth organisations and Sunday schools: DDEy (much of this collection is closed).
Sunday School Union committee minutes 1874–97 include scholars' scripture examination results with names and addresses of candidates: DDEy/1/3/1-3.
Members of the public can visit the library once (photo ID needed), after which they must apply for external membership (fee payable).
Alphabetical list of special collections: www.library.manchester.ac.uk/searchresources/guidetospecialcollections/atoz.

Catalogue guide: www.library.manchester.ac.uk/searchresources/guideto specialcollections/atoz/catalogues.
ELGAR online catalogue: http://archives.li.man.ac.uk/ead/index.html.

John Rylands Library, 150 Deansgate, Manchester, M3 3EH; www.library. manchester.ac.uk; Special Collections email: jrul.special-collections@ manchester.ac.uk; tel: 0161 275 3764; Methodist archive enquiries email: peter.nockles@ manchester.ac.uk; tel: 0161 275 3755.

University of Liverpool Special Collections

Social Welfare Archives include records for Barnardo's, National Children's Home; Maria Rye's Emigration Home for Destitute Little Girls, Peckham; Fairbridge Society and other bodies. Watts Naval Training School (Barnardo's): photographs of staff and pupils: D.443.
Maria Rye papers including annual reports and correspondence: D630.
Liverpool Sheltering Homes minute books and annual reports: D715.
Finding aid for Maria Rye papers: http://bit.ly/OcnoTn.
Genealogists researching relatives from Barnardo's or Fairbridge homes are advised to try contacting those societies first (Sections A2, B).

Special Collections & Archives, Sydney Jones Library, The University of Liverpool, PO Box 123, L69 3DA; http://sca.lib.liv.ac.uk/collections; email: mwatry@ liv.ac.uk; tel: 0151 794 2696.

University College, London Ear Institute & RNID Libraries

UCL Ear Institute & RNID Libraries, at the RNTNE Hospital, 330–6 Grays Inn Road, London, WC1X 8EE; www.ucl.ac.uk/library/rnidlib.shtml; email: rnidlib@ucl.ac.uk; Ear Institute tel: 0203 456 5145; RNID Library tel and textphone: 0203 456 5145.

University of London, Senate House Library

Special collections include FWA Library of over 5,000 books and pamphlets: www.senatehouselibrary.ac.uk/our-collections/historic-collections/printed-special-collections/fwa/.
Independent Order of Rechabites collection: http://archives.ulrls.lon.ac. uk/resources/MS1158.pdf.
Papers of Samuel Wilderspin include materials related to infant schools: MS917, MS975.

Senate House Library, Malet Street, London WC1E 7HU; www.senatehouselibrary.ac.uk; email: shl.enquiries@london.ac.uk; tel: 0207 862 8500.

London School of Economics (LSE) Library

Youth Movement Archive includes Woodcraft Folk papers 1910–c. 85: YMA and YMA/WF.

The Women's Library @ LSE collections (formerly at Aldgate) include Girls' Friendly Society (GFS) records 1800–2001 including minute books, annual reports, journals and photographs: 5GFS.

Archives catalogue: http://archives.lse.ac.uk/Default.aspx?.

Archives Services Group, Library, 10 Portugal Street, London, WC2A 2HD; http://www2.lse.ac.uk/library/home.aspx; archives email: Document@lse. ac.uk; library email: library.enquiries@lse.ac.uk; archives tel: 0207 955 7223; library tel: 0207 955 7229.

Oxford University: Regent's Park College, Angus Library

Baptist history and heritage. Abingdon British School Society minutes 1824–97 and logbook (1863). Baptist Sunday School, Abingdon teachers' Quarterly Meeting Minutes 1859–86, 1887–1956. Sunday school registers 1870–1904 for Chipping Norton, minutes and accounts for Bluebell Hill Chapel (Kent). Young People's Society of Christian Endeavour 1894–1903, and registers for Gillingham 1824–1980s. Girls' Auxiliary papers (1903 onwards).

Regent's Park College, Pusey Street, Oxford, OX1 2LB; www.rpc.ox.ac.uk; email: angus.library@regents.ox.ac.uk; tel: 0186 528 8120.

University College Plymouth, St Mark and St John

Archives of two teacher-training colleges run by the National Society: St John's College, Battersea and St Mark's College, Chelsea. Student registers, committee minutes, photographs, etc.

Archivist, The Library, University College Plymouth St Mark and St John, Derriford Road, Plymouth, PL6 8BH; www.marjon.ac.uk/tudentlife/library/ libraryessentials/facilitiesandcollections/collections/archives; email: gfe wings@marjon.ac.uk; tel: 0175 263 6700, ext. 3086.

University of Southampton, Hartley Library

More than 850 collections of Anglo-Jewish archives, many with official correspondence and administration papers for institutions: several contain registers with names of individual children.

Archives of Jewish Care 1757–1989 includes Board of Guardians for Relief of the Jewish Poor, and Jewish Association for the Protection of Girls, Women and Children: MS 173. Norwood (Norwood Jewish Children's Society) archives, 1678–1951, includes predecessor organisations the Jews' Hospital and Jews' Orphan Asylum, with registers, logs, punishment books, apprentice records, etc.: MS 127. Jewish Deaf and Dumb Children's Home, London, papers 1865–1975: MS 218.

Jews' Free School minute book and papers 1831–84: MS 153. Hayes Certified Industrial School for Jewish Boys minute books 1898–1937: MS 181. Bayswater Jewish Schools papers 1881–1981: MS 211. Jewish Lads' and Girls' Brigade papers 1897–1991: MS 244. West Central Jewish Working Lads' Club papers 1887–1929 MS 152. Stepney Jewish Lads' Club papers 1924–63: MS 172.

Organisations that assisted Jewish refugees (often children): Chief Rabbi's Religious Emergency Council papers 1938–46: within MS 183, Papers of Rabbi Solomon Schonfeld. Polish Jewish Refugee Fund papers, *c.* 1940–7: MS 190.

Circumcision registers and papers: MS 159.

Survey of Jewish Archives: www.archives.soton.ac.uk/jewish.

(NB See also Norwood Archive, Section A2).

Online guide to collections: www.southampton.ac.uk/archives/catalogue databases/guideintro.html.

Collections database: www.archives.soton.ac.uk/guide.

An appointment must be made in writing <u>by post</u> (not telephone, fax or email) before visiting the archive.

The Archivist, Hartley Library, University of Southampton, Highfield, Southampton, SO17 1BJ; www.archives.soton.ac.uk; email: archives@ soton.ac.uk; tel: 0238 059 2721.

University of Warwick Modern Records Centre

University of Warwick Modern Records Centre, University Library, Coventry, CV4 7AL; www2.warwick.ac.uk/services/library/mrc/holdings/ main_archives; email: archives@warwick.ac.uk; tel: 0247 652 4219.

B
USEFUL ADDRESSES

Adoption Contact Register
Apply online or by post.
https://www.gov.uk/adoption-records/the-adoption-contact-register.

Adoptions Section, Room C202, General Register Office, Trafalgar Road, Southport, PR8 2HH; www.gov.uk/adoption-records; email: adoptions @ips.gsi.gov.uk; tel: 0300 123 1837.

General Register Office (England and Wales)
Birth, marriage and death certificates for England and Wales from 1 July 1837 onwards. Events recorded by GRO: http://bit.ly/YQ6Sg6.
Order a copy certificate: https://www.gov.uk/order-copy-birth-death-marriage-certificate.
Research your family history: https://www.gov.uk/research-family-history-general-register-office.
Search for a local register office: https://www.gov.uk/register-offices.

General Register Office Certificate Services Section, General Register Office, PO Box 2, Southport, PR8 2JD; www.gov.uk/general-register-office; email: certificate.services@ips.gsi.gov.uk; tel: 0300 123 1837.

Leeds District Probate Registry
Postal Searches and Copies Department, Leeds District Probate Registry, York House, York Place, Leeds, LS1 2BA; www.justice.gov.uk/courts/probate/probate-registries; email: LeedsDPRenquiries@hmcts.gsi.gov.uk; tel: 0113 389 6133.

Principal Registry of the Family Division (The Probate Service)
Find a probate registry: www.justice.gov.uk/courts/probate/probate-registries.
Guide to probate records in England and Wales: www.justice.gov.uk/courts/probate/family-history.

London Probate Department, PRFD, First Avenue House, 42–9 High Holborn, 7th Floor, Holborn, London, WC1V 6NP; www.justice. gov.uk/courts/ probate; general tel: 0207 947 6939; probate helpline and application forms requests tel: 0845 302 0900.

Beth Din (Ecclesiastical Court of the Chief Rabbi)
The London Beth Din, 305 Ballards Lane, North Finchley, London, N12 8GB; www.theus.org.uk/the_united_synagogue/the_london_beth_din/ about_us; email: info@bethdin.org.uk; tel: 0208 343 6270.

College of Arms
Official repository of the coats of arms and pedigrees of English, Welsh, Northern Irish and Commonwealth families and their descendants. Fee payable for record searches.

The College of Arms, Queen Victoria Street, London, EC4V 4BT; www.college-of-arms.gov.uk; tel: 0207 248 2762.

Family Search Record Centres
Search for a centre in your local area. Microfilms may need ordering in advance.
https://familysearch.org/locations.

Family History Societies
Federation of Family History Societies; online shop: www.ffhsservices.com.

Federation of Family History Societies, PO Box 8857, Lutterworth, LE17 9BJ; www.ffhs.org.uk; email: info@ffhs.co.uk; tel: 0145 520 3133.

Guild of One-Name Studies
Guild of One-Name Studies, Box G, 14 Charterhouse Buildings, Goswell Road, London, EC1M 7BA; www.one-name.org; email: guild@one-name.org; tel: 0800 011 2182.

Health and Social Care Information Centre
Health and Social Care Information Centre, The 1939 Register Team, Smedley Hydro, Room B108, Trafalgar Road, Southport, PR8 2HH; www.ic.nhs.uk/register-service; email: enquiries@ic.nhs.uk.

The Heraldry Society

Fee payable for record searches.
The Secretary, The Heraldry Society, PO Box 772, Guildford, Surrey GU3 3ZX, England; www.theheraldrysociety.com/home.htm; heraldry archive email: archive@theheraldrysociety.com; honorary librarian email: honlibrarian@theheraldrysociety.com; tel: 0148 323 7373.

Jewish Genealogical Society of Great Britain

Family history enquiries should be sent by post or email, not telephone.

Jewish Genealogical Society of Great Britain, 33 Seymour Place, London, W1H 5AU; www.jgsgb.org.uk; email: genealogy@jgsgb.org.uk; tel: 0207 724 4232 (ansaphone).

Quaker Family History Society

Enquiries should be sent by post (including a sae) or email.

Margaret Page, 39 Manor Avenue South, Kidderminster, Worcestershire, DY11 6DE; www.qfhs.co.uk; email: info@qfhs.co.uk.

Religious Society of Friends Library (Quakers)

Digests of births, marriages and burials. Indexes of some pupils at Quaker schools.
Hand-list of schools collections in the Library: www.quaker.org.uk/ schoolsdoc.
Researchers should contact the Library to register before visiting.

Library of the Religious Society of Friends in Britain, Friends House, 173–7 Euston Road, London, NW1 2BJ; www.quaker.org.uk/library; email: library@quaker.org.uk; tel: 0207 663 1135.

Society of Genealogists

National Library and Education Centre for Family History: www.sog.org.uk/library/intro.shtml.

Society of Genealogists, 14 Charterhouse Buildings, Goswell Road, London, EC1M 7BA; www.societyofgenealogists.com; email: membership @sog.org.uk; tel: 0207 251 8799.

Children's Societies and Charities
Action For Children
Formerly National Children's Home (NCH).

Action for Children, 3 The Boulevard, Ascot Road, Watford, WD18 8AG; www.actionforchildren.org.uk; email: ask.us@actionforchildren.org.uk; tel: 0300 123 2112.

Child Migrants Trust
Child Migrants Trust, 124 Musters Road, West Bridgford, Nottingham, NG2 7PW; www.childmigrantstrust.com; tel: 0115 982 2811.

Children England
Formerly the NCVCCO.

Children England, Unit 25, 1st Floor, Angel Gate, City Road, London, EC1V 2PT; www.childrenengland.org.uk; email: info@childrenengland.org.uk; tel: 0207 833 3319.

Coram
Formerly the Thomas Coram Foundation for Children. See also the University of Liverpool listing (Section A4) for Foundling Hospital records. Queries about children cared for by the Hospital, and requests for copy certificates of birth, should be addressed to Coram (not the GRO).

Coram, Coram Community Campus, 49 Mecklenburgh Square, London, WC1N 2QA; www.coram.org.uk; email: chances@coram.org.uk; tel: 0207 520 0300.

Evacuees Reunion Association
Evacuees Reunion Association, The Mill Business Centre, Mill Hill, Gringley on the Hill, DN10 4RA; www.evacuees.org.uk; email: era@evacuees. org.uk; tel: 0177 781 6166.

Fairbridge Society
See Prince's Trust listing (this section) and University of Liverpool listing (Section A4).

Family Action
Formerly the COS, and after 1944, the Family Welfare Association. See also the LMA listing (Section A3).

Family Action Central Office, 501–5 Kingsland Road, London, E8 4AU; www.family-action.org.uk; tel: 0207 254 6251.

Mencap
Mencap, 123 Golden Lane, London, EC1Y 0RT; www.mencap.org.uk; email: information@mencap.org.uk; tel: 0207 454 0454.

Middlemore Homes
This is now the Sir John Middlemore Charitable Trust.
See also Birmingham Archives and Heritage listing (Section A3).

55 Stevens Avenue, Birmingham, West Midlands, B32 3SD; http://middlemore. weebly.com/; email: admin@middlemore.org.uk; tel: 0121 427 2429.

National Society for the Prevention of Cruelty to Children
The NSPCC archive is not accessible to researchers. Former users of NSPCC services who wish to discover what information is held about them may write to the Data Protection Officer with details of their name, with their signature, and date of birth.

Data Protection Officer, NSPCC Legal Department, Weston House, 42 Curtain Road, London, EC2A 3NH; www.nspcc.org.uk; email: data protectionofficer@NSPCC.org.uk; tel: 0207 825 2856 and 0207 825 2971.

Nugent Care Society
To access a deceased relative's records, you must provide proof of death and evidence of relationship; fee payable for administration and copying costs. www.nugentcare.org/about-us/access-to-records.

The PMU Team Manager, Nugent Care, 99 Edge Lane, Liverpool, L7 2PE; www.nugentcare.org; email: info@nugentcare.org; tel: 0151 261 2000.

Prince's Trust
The Fairbridge Society is now part of the Prince's Trust.

The Prince's Trust, 18 Park Square East, London, NW1 4LH; www.princes-trust.org.uk; email: webinfops@princes-trust.org.uk; tel: 0207 543 1234.

C
USEFUL WEBSITES

Adoption, Child Welfare and Children's Homes
Adoption Search Reunion
For adoptions prior to 30 December 2005. 'Locating Adoption Records' database, research guidance and more: www.adoptionsearchreunion. org.uk/default.htm.
Locating adoption records database: www.adoptionsearchreunion.org.uk/ search/adoptionrecords.

Ambition
Formerly the National Association of Boys' Clubs.
www.ambitionuk.org/about-us/our-history.

Birmingham Children's Lives Blog
http://birminghamchildrenslives.wordpress.com.

Birmingham Children's Lives Project
www.connectinghistories.org.uk/childrenslivesinfo.asp.

Care Leavers Reunited
Social networking site for former residents of care homes, people who had foster carers, and relatives or friends of people formerly in care.
www.careleavers.com/clreunited.

Child Care History Network
Information relating to history of organisations and individuals involved in child care.
www.cchn.org.uk.

Children's Cottage Homes
www.childrenscottagehomes.org.uk.

Connected Histories
Searchable database with links to digital resources online (some free, some

subscription only), includes sources on the history of motherhood. www.connectedhistories.org/Default.aspx.

Cyndi's List
Orphans: www.cyndislist.com/orphans.

Fegan's Home for Boys, Stony Stratford
http://clutch.open.ac.uk /schools/watlingway99/DailyLife.html.

The Goldonian
Website dedicated to Goldings (William Baker Memorial Technical School), with memories and photos of Goldings and other Dr Barnardo's Homes, also sea cadets, Wimbledon ball boys, message board and more: www. goldonian.org/.
www.goldonian.org/photos/photo_archive_homes/old_homes_eng.htm.

Hidden Lives Revealed
Children's homes, ragged schools, reformatories, etc. Case studies and photographs of children in care.
www.hiddenlives.org.uk.

Quarriers Homes
Family history: www.quarriers.org.uk/resource/trace-your-history/genealogy -service.
Resources: www.quarriers.org.uk/resource.

Sailors' Children's Society, Hull
Formerly the Port of Hull Society. History of the Society: www. sailorschildren.org.uk/history/details.asp.

Shaftesbury Young People
History of the charity.
www.shaftesbury.org.uk/index.php/about-us/our-history.

St George's House, Northern Police Orphanage, Harrogate
Historical information and images. List of children admitted to orphanage 1898–1956.
www.stgeorgesharrogate.org/index.htm.
www.stgeorgesharrogate.org/stg23list.htm.

Their History
Philip J. Howard's website tells the story of his upbringing in a National Children's Home and has a timeline of NCH History. www.theirhistory.co.uk.

Together Trust
Formerly Manchester and Salford Boys' and Girls' Refuges and Homes. The Trust has an archive relating to children who were in its care. The website has a list of children's homes run by the charity: www.togethertrust. org.uk/about/history.
Archive blog: www.togethertrustarchive.blogspot.com.
Contact the archivist for family history enquiries: www.togethertrust. org.uk/contact/new.

Voluntary Action History Society Blog
Articles on the history of charities and voluntary societies including children's charities.
www.vahs.org.uk/blog.

Apprenticeship Records
Ancestry
Register of Duties Paid for Apprentices' Indentures (free to search and view) 1710–1811 (IR 1).
bit.ly/qrudUU.

Findmypast
Apprentices (IR1) 1710–74. Dorset parish apprentices 1605–1799. Lincolnshire parish apprenticeship indentures 1618–1925. Manchester apprentices 1700–1849 (some parish, some private apprenticeships). Somerset parish apprentices 1575–1800.
www.findmypast.co.uk.

Guildhall Library Apprenticeship Records Guide
http://bit.ly/Pt54GP.

Hertfordshire Apprentices Index (1599–1903)
www.hertsdirect.org/services/leisculture/heritage1/hals/indexes/indexes/ap prentice/.

Hull History Centre

Apprenticeship records for persons bound to freemen indexed by name (C BRG).
Guide to apprenticeship records: www.hullhistorycentre.org.uk/discover/ hull_history_centre/our_collections/sourceguides/apprenticeship.aspx.

London Lives

Overview of apprentice and parish apprentice records, with details of those for which indexes are available:
www.londonlives.org/static/Apprentices.jsp.
www.londonlives.org/static/IA.jsp.
www.londonlives.org/static/PA.jsp.

London's Livery Companies Online (ROLLCO)

www.londonroll.org.

Origins.Net

Database for Livery Companies of London (NB about 70 per cent of 'London' apprentices came from outside the metropolis). London Apprenticeship Abstracts index 1442–1850 includes over ½ million names (apprentices, their parents and masters).
www.origins.net/help/aboutbo-lonapps.aspx.
www.origins.net/help/aboutbo-lonapps-lcs.aspx.

Preston Guild Rolls

Preston Guild Rolls 1397–1992 have been transcribed and databases of transcripts are available on the Lancashire Archives website: http://bit.ly/OKBCO2.

Sheffield Records Online

Hallamshire Cutlers' Apprentices Index: www.sheffieldrecordsonline. org.uk/index_cutlers.html.

Genealogy Websites

1911 Census: www.1911census.co.uk
Ancestry: www.ancestry.co.uk
Ancestry Aid: www.ancestryaid.co.uk
Cyndi's List: www.cyndislist.com/uk
Family Relatives: www.familyrelatives.com

FamilySearch (Latter-Day Saints): https://familysearch.org/
Findmypast: www.findmypast.com
Free Reg (parish and Nonconformist registers): www.freereg.org.uk
Free UK Census: www.freecen.org.uk
Free UK BMDs: www.freebmd.org.uk
Free UKGEN http://freeukgen.rootsweb.com
TheGenealogist: www.thegenealogist.co.uk
Genes Reunited: www.genesreunited.co.uk
Irish Genealogy: www.irishgenealogy.ie
Lost Cousins: http://lostcousins.com
Mocavo: www.mocavo.co.uk
National Archives of Ireland: www.nationalarchives.ie
Origins Network: www.origins.net
Public Record Office of Northern Ireland: www.proni.gov.uk
Roots Chat: www.rootschat.com
Roots Ireland: www.rootsireland.ie
Roots UK: www.rootsuk.com/
ScotlandsPeople: www.scotlandspeople.gov.uk
UK Census Online 1841–1911: www.ukcensusonline.com

General
Baptist Historical Society
www.baptisthistory.org.uk.

Black Sheep Ancestors
Links to free databases and information on prisoners in the UK.
http://blacksheepancestors.com/uk/prisons.shtml.

British Newspaper Archive
www.britishnewspaperarchive.co.uk.

Charity Commission
www.charitycommission.gov.uk/index.aspx.
Register of Charities: www.charitycommission.gov.uk/showcharity/
registerofcharities/registerhomepage.aspx.
Access to Charity Commission records: www.charity-commission.gov.uk/
About_us/About_the_Commission/ccrecords.aspx.

Charles Booth Online Archive
Booth surveyed London lives, schools, work and poverty. Digital London poverty map. Search the online database to see if your family or the street where they lived was investigated. If so, you can request photocopies of the survey notebooks relating to the investigation, or contact the Archives Division of the British Library of Political and Economic Science to consult them in person.
http://booth.lse.ac.uk.
http://booth.lse.ac.uk/static/d/index.html#iii.

Currency Converter
Convert pre-decimal money to 2005 prices.
www.nationalarchives.gov.uk/currency.

DANGO
www.dango.bham.ac.uk/index.htm.

Deceased Online
Database for UK burials and cremations.
www.deceasedonline.com.

FamilySearch
Parish registers include births and christenings for England 1538–1975. Welsh parish registers. Nonconformist register indexes (RG 4–8). Cheshire workhouse records 1848 onwards. Kent workhouse records 1777–1911. Norfolk Poor Law union records 1796–1900. Indexes to Cheshire school registers 1796–1950, and some other school registers. Digital edition of published Harrow registers 1801–1900. Merchant Navy seamen record indexes 1835–1941. Free images available for some records.
https://familysearch.org.

Hope UK
Formerly the UK Band of Hope Union.
www.hopeuk.org.

Internet Archive
www.archive.org.

Jewish Communities and Congregations in England
www.jewishgen.org/JCR-UK/england_geographic.htm.

Jewish Communities and Congregations in Wales
www.jewishgen.org/jcr-uk/Wales.htm.

Jewish Surname Search
www.avotaynu.com.

Local History Online
www.local-history.co.uk/index.html.

Manchester and Stockport Certified Industrial Schools
Gerald Lodge's website has lots of interesting information on the schools' daily life, with links to images where available.
www.manchester-family-history-research.co.uk/new_page_2.htm.

Metropolitan and City Police Orphanage
Gallery of images.
www.met-cityorphans.org.uk/history/gallery.php.

Missing Ancestors
Mary Wall's website has information, including some surname indexes, on industrial and reformatory schools, emigration, children migrants to Canada and Australia, prisoners, boarded out children and more.
www.missing-ancestors.com/index.htm.

National Registration 1939
The 1911 census website has information on identity cards.
www.1911 census.org.uk/1939.htm.

NGOs (Non-Governmental Organisations) in Britain, 1945–97
www.ngo.bham.ac.uk.

Nonconformist and Non-Parochial Registers
RG 4–RG 8. RG 4 includes Royal Hospital Chelsea 1682 onwards and Greenwich Hospital 1694 onwards. RG 8 includes birth, baptism and death registers of the British Lying-in Hospital, St Giles in the Fields, Holborn, 1749–1868.
The website has detailed listings for each series and information on the indexes available.
Free search, pay to view.
www.bmdregisters.co.uk.

Nottinghamshire Youth Organisations
Catalogue of organisations at Nottinghamshire Archives includes Scouts, Girl Guides and Boys' Brigade.
http://cms.nottinghamshire.gov.uk/clubsandsocietiesyouthorganisations.pdf
.

Old Bailey Online
Proceedings of the Old Bailey 1674–1913. Search the proceedings of 197,745 criminal trials; detailed online instructions. Search the Ordinary of Newgate's Accounts 1676–1772.
www.oldbaileyonline.org.

Port Cities London
Social history, images and much more.
www.portcities.org.uk/london/.

Royal Philanthropic Society, Redhill
Alan Moore's website has info on the Society's history, the Redhill farm and staff, some class photos and photos of the graveyard.
www.redhill-reigate-history.co.uk/philanth.htm.

Salford Lads' Club, Ordsall
History of the club and photos.
http://salfordladsclub.org.uk.

Scouting Milestones: Jack Cornwell
Colin Walker's website tells the story of John (Jack) Travers Cornwell, his VC and the Scout badge named in his honour.
http://scoutguidehistoricalsociety.com/cornwell.htm.

Second World War Experience Centre
Stories of child evacuees.
www.war-experience.org/education/evacuation/evacuees.asp.

Sheffield Indexers
Searchable databases for burials, institutions, parish registers, schools and more.
www.sheffieldindexers.com.

Society for Promoting Christian Knowledge
www.spck.org.uk/about-spck/archives/.

Swing Riots and Rioters
Jill Chambers' very interesting website on the 'Captain Swing' rioters includes information on juveniles on the *Bellerophon* and *Euryalus* hulks: bit.ly/RhHgnp.
Prison hulks in Bermuda: bit.ly/OLNEoV.
www.swingriotsriotersblacksheepsearch.com.

Tyne and Wear Criminals, 1871–3
Tyne and Wear Archives and Museums' online images (Flickr and Pinterest) of prisoners at Newcastle City Gaol and House of Correction include child convicts. The Pinterest images include details of the children's crimes and sentences.
http://bit.ly/mDbgth.
http://pinterest.com/twmuseums/criminal-faces-1871-1873.

Urdd Gobaith Cymru (Welsh League of Youth)
www.urdd.org.

Victorian Crime and Punishment
Case studies of prisoners including under-18s.
http://vcp.e2bn.org.

Victorian London List of Charities
www.victorianlondon.org/dickens/dickens-charities.htm.

Virtual Museum of Childhood
www.museum-of-childhood.com.

Wandsworth Prison Photograph Albums, 1872–4
www.nationalarchives.gov.uk/records/victorian-prisoners-photographs.htm.

Welsh Children's Lives During the Second World War
Social history and photos (from the Geoff Charles collection) of Welsh children, schooldays and wartime evacuees.

http://bit.ly/Q26r3N.
http://bit.ly/RpcuOl.
http://bit.ly/UapDrV.
www.myglyw.org.uk.

Woodcraft Folk Heritage
Digital archive.
http://heritage.woodcraft.org.uk/archive.

Immigration and Migration
Ancestors On Board
TNA's Outward Passenger Lists (BT 27) for long-distance voyages leaving the UK, 1890–1960.
www.ancestorsonboard.com.

Ancestry
Australian Convict collection (some free indexes).
http://bit.ly/Uwl666.

British Home Children Canada
Database of over 57,000 child migrants sent to Canada by British child-care organisations from 1870–1957.
http://freepages.genealogy.rootsweb.ancestry.com/~britishhomechildren.

British Home Children Mailing List
http://lists.rootsweb.ancestry.com/index/intl/CAN/BRITISHHOMECHILD REN. html.

British Home Children Stories
www.pier21.ca/research/collections/online-story-collection/british-home-children.

British Isles Family History Society of Greater Ottowa
Middlemore Homes Index of Home Children. www.bifhsgo.ca/cstm_ home Children.php.

Canadian Centre for Home Children
www.canadianhomechildren.ca/index.php.

Convicts to Australia
Guide to researching your convict ancestors.
www.convictcentral.com/index.html.

Convict Transportation Registers Database
Details of over 123,000 convicts transported to Australia 1787–1867: names, term of years, transport ships and more.
www.slq.qld.gov.au/info/fh/convicts.

Cyndi's List
Home Children and Child Migrants: www.cyndislist.com/orphans/home-children.

Findmypast
Transcripts of prison hulk registers (HO 9) for the *Bellerophon*, *Euryalus*, *Hardy* and *Antelope*, and some records for Parkhurst prison, 1811–43.
www.findmypast.co.uk/search/military/hulk-registers/indexes.

Free Settler or Felon?
Jen Willett's website has searchable databases, and information on convict ships that sailed to Australia.
www.jenwilletts.com.

Genes Reunited
Prison hulk registers 1811–43 (free index).
www.genesreunited.co.uk/ search/index/military.

Home Children Canada (Pacific)
www3.telus.net/Home_Children_ Canada.

Library and Archives Canada
Home Children Database 1869–1930.
www.collectionscanada.gc.ca/databases/home-children/index-e.html.

Middlemore Atlantic Society, Canada
British Home Children's stories.
www.middlemoreatlanticsociety.com.

National Archives of Australia
Child migration fact sheet.
www.naa.gov.au/collection/fact-sheets/fs124.aspx.

Old Fairbridgians Association
Website for former children of Fairbridge Farm School, Molong, who migrated from Britain to Australia, 1938–74.
http://oldfairbridgians.org.

Ontario Genealogical Society
Information about British Home Children.
www.ogs.on.ca/services/bhc.php.

On Their Own: Britain's Child Migrants
http://otoweb.cloudapp.net.

Promise of Home
Rose McCormick Brandon's stories and photos of British Home Children.
http://littleimmigrants.wordpress.com/.

Miss Rye's Peckham Homes: Lists of Children, 1881
www.rootsweb. ancestry.com/~ote/orphans/miss-rye-peckham.htm.

Young Immigrants to Canada
Marjorie P. Kohli's website includes useful sources and lists of children.
http://jubilation.uwaterloo.ca/~marj/genealogy/homeadd.html.

Poor Law Records
Bedfordshire Archives Poor Law Records
www.bedfordshire.gov.uk/CommunityAndLiving/ArchivesAndRecordOffi
ce/GuidesToCollections/PoorLawUnionRecordsConspectus.aspx.

Cambridgeshire Archives Board of Guardians Guide
www.cambridgeshire.gov.uk/leisure/archives/catalogue/holdings/a_c/boar
dsofguardians.htm.

Llanfyllin Workhouse, Powys
Information on Llanfyllin Poor Law Union,Workhouse and School.
www.the-workhouse.org.uk/history.

Mold Poor Law Records
Includes 'bastard' children.
http://bit.ly/PTxGMT.

Nottinghamshire Poor Law Records
Apprenticeships, workhouses, lists of boarded out children and vaccination registers at Nottinghamshire Archives.
http://cms.nottinghamshire.gov.uk/poorlawrecords.pdf.

Sheffield Poor Law and Workhouse Records
Poor Law records at Sheffield Archives.
https://www.sheffield.gov.uk/libraries/archives-and-local-studies/collections/poor-law-records.html.

Wigan Archives Service
Vaccination registers for Wigan Poor Law Union (including Wigan Workhouse) 1899–1909: www.wlct.org/heritage-services/gwi155.pdf.
Leigh Union Minute books 1899–1914 include orphans, workhouse children, children's homes and boys sent to training ships: bit.ly/SBqmaq.

West Sussex Poor Law Database
Records of settlement and removal 1662–1835, bastard children, parish apprentices and more.
www.sussexrecordsociety.org.uk/plhome.asp.

Workhouses
Workhouses, schools, children's living conditions, details of Poor Law records and lots more: www.workhouses.org.uk/records/archives.shtml.
www.workhouses.org.uk.

D
SCHOOLS AND EDUCATION SOURCES

More school records can be found under individual archive listings in Section A3.

Ackworth School
Minute books, administrative records, photographs 1779–1999.

Ackworth, Pontefract, WF7 7LT; www.ackworthschool.com; email: admissions@ackworthschool.com; tel: 0197 761 1401.

Charterhouse School Archive
School records from 1872 onwards; some registers from earlier in the nineteenth century. See also the LMA listing in Section A3.

The Archivist, Catherine Smith, Charterhouse, Godalming, Surrey, GU7 2DX; www.charterhouse.org.uk/archives; email: archive@charterhouse.org. uk; tel: 0148 329 1604.

Christ's Hospital (Blue Coat School)
Records of boys admitted after 1911, and of girls after 1890. For further information write to the Clerk (access by arrangement only). See also the LMA listing in Section A3.

Clerk of Christ's Hospital, The Counting House, Christ's Hospital, Horsham, West Sussex, RH13 7YP; www.christs-hospital.org.uk/contact-christs-hospital-boarding-school.php; email: enquiries@christs-hospital. org.uk; tel: 0140 325 2547.

Eton College Archives
The Archives can be consulted in College Library by appointment only (forty-year closure on boys' records). Complete records for scholars available from 1791 onwards (incomplete for earlier years). Photographic archive.

The Archivist, Mrs Penny Hatfield, Eton College, Windsor, Berkshire, SL4 6DW; www.etoncollege.com/CollegeArchives.aspx; archivist email: p.

hatfield@etoncollege.org.uk; archives and library email: collections@eton
college.org.uk; photographic archives email: r.fisher@etoncollege.org.uk;
archives tel: 0175 367 1269; library tel: 0175 367 1221.

Harrow School Archives
School lists from 1770, including Bill Books. Personal papers from former
pupils and staff. Photographs of pupils, teams, house groups, school
buildings (more information on the archive's collections on the website).
Access to the archives by appointment only at the archivist's discretion.

Harrow School Archive, 5 High Street, Harrow on the Hill, Middlesex, HA1
3HP; www.harrowschool.org.uk/1843/public-facilities-and-holiday-courses
/the-harrow-school-archive; email: meredithac@harrowschool.org.uk; tel:
0208 872 8370.

Manchester High School for Girls Archive
Archive catalogue: www.mhsgarchive.org/catalogue.php.

Dr Christine A. Joy, School Archivist, Manchester High School for Girls,
Grangethorpe Road, Rusholme, Manchester, M14 6HS; www.mhsgarchive.
org; email: cjoy@mhsg.manchester.sch.uk; tel: 0161 249 2267.

Royal Hospital School
See TNA listing (Section A1). The school plans to open a museum, archive
and searchable digital archive with past issues of the school magazine from
1907. www.rhscommunity.co.uk.

The Royal Hospital School, Holbrook, Ipswich, Suffolk, IP9 2RX;
www.royalhospitalschool.org; tel: 0147 332 6200.

Rugby School
NRA catalogue of the school's archives: http://bit.ly/RmVIkT.

The Archivist, Temple Reading Room, Rugby School, Rugby, Warwickshire,
CV22 5EH; www.rugbyschool.net; email: counter@rugbyschool.net; tel:
0178 855 6227.

Shrewsbury School Library
Records 1552–1900s include minute books, admission registers from 1562
(some missing 1734–98), legal papers, etc.

Shrewsbury School, The Schools, Shrewsbury, SY3 7BA; www.shrewsbury
.org.uk/page/ancient-library; email Dr Mike Morrogh, Archivist: mmm@
shrewsbury.org.uk; tel: 0174 328 0595.

St Paul's School, London

See also the Mercers Company Archives listing (Section A3).

Records include governors' minutes 1749–1973. Some admission registers
have been published (see the Internet Archive): Registers of St Paul's
School 1509–1748 (1977); and Robert Barlow Gardiner (ed.), *Admission
Registers of St Paul's School, from 1748–1876* (1884) and *1876–1905* (1906).

St Paul's School, Lonsdale Road, London, SW13 9JT; www.stpaulsschool.
org.uk; archivist email: ama@stpaulsschool.org.uk; tel: 0208 748 9162.

Wellington College

Digital archive comprising past Year Books, Wellingtonians and other
documents is planned.

The Old Wellingtonian Society maintains a register of all former members
of the school: www.wellingtoncollege.org.uk/old-wellingtonians.

Wellington College, Crowthorne, Berkshire, RG45 7PU; http://intranet.
wellingtoncollege.org.uk/archives; email archivist: bpl@wellington college.
org.uk; general tel: 0134 444 4000.

Westminster School Archives

School records mostly date from 1868. (Earlier records are at Westminster
Abbey Muniment Room and Library: www.westminster-abbey.org/library-
research.)

Archivist Elizabeth Wells, Westminster School, Little Dean's Yard,
Westminster, London, SW1P 3PF; www.westminster.org.uk/about-us/the-
archives-collection.html; email: archives@westminster.org.uk; tel: 0207 963
1000.

Winchester College Archives

Collections include register of Scholars from 1394, College foundation records,
court books and court rolls of College manors, registers of leases granted by
College, annual bursars' accounts from 1394, registers of Commoners from

1836, title deeds and estate accounts for College estates, schoolboy letters and diaries from late nineteenth and early twentieth centuries.
An appointment is needed to visit the archive.

Archivist Suzanne Foster, Winchester College, Winchester, SO23 9NA; www.winchestercollege.org/archives; email: sf@wincoll.ac.uk; tel: 0196 262 1217.

Online Sources
Ancestry
Schools collection (free search, pay per view or subscription) includes London schools admission and discharge registers 1840–1911 for over 800 schools: http://search.ancestry.co.uk/search/db.aspx?dbid=1938. www.ancestry.co.uk.

Anguiline Research Archives
School and college registers, including Eton and Harrow, available on CD-ROM (some as digital downloads).
http://anguline.co.uk/schl.html.

Bristol Schools
www.bristolinformation.co.uk/schools.

Cambridgeshire Archives Service Handlist of School Records
http://bit.ly/RpfaKr.

Cheshire School Records, 1796–1950
www.familysearch.org/learn/wiki/en/England_Cheshire_School_Records_ (FamilySearch_Historical_Records).

Clutch Club
Children's stories and memories (including wartime) of some schools in Buckinghamshire, Bedfordshire and South Northamptonshire.
http://clutch.open.ac.uk.

Conwy School Records (Archives Network Wales)
bit.ly/OlWc9P.

Devon Record Office School Records
Includes industrial schools and reformatories.
www.devon.gov.uk/print/school_records.

Education for Deaf People
This blog on the UCL website has information and images relating to education for deaf children.
http://blogs.ucl.ac.uk/library-rnid.
Education in Wales: Powys Digital History Project http://history. powys.org.uk/history/common/edstart.html.

Familyrelatives
School registers search.
www.familyrelatives.com/search/search_school_indexes.php.

Fernhurst, West Sussex
Edwardian schooldays.
www.fernhurstsociety.org.uk/edwardian1.html.

Findmypast
Education records (free search, pay per view or subscription): Glamorgan School Admission Registers 1768–1911, Manchester Industrial School Registers 1866–1912, Manchester School Registers 1870–1924:
www.findmypast.co.uk/content/search-menu/education-and-work.
www.findmypast.co.uk/content/manchester-collection/school-registers. html.

TheGenealogist
School, university and college registers for nearly thirty counties (subscription website).
www.thegenealogist.co.uk.

Herefordshire Record Office School Records
www.herefordshire.gov.uk/docs/School_records(1).pdf.

History of Education in Britain
Full texts of some official reports and Acts of Parliament.
www.educationengland.org.uk.

Liverpool Schools
Liverpool schools, their history and teachers. Databases of pupils for some schools, e.g. Clarence St Pupil-Teacher College.
www.liverpool-schools.co.uk/index.html.

Manchester Libraries and Archives School Records Collections
www.manchester.gov.uk/info/1062/archive_collections/4670/archive_and_
local_collections/20.
Manchester Libraries and Archives Jewish Schools Collections.
www.manchester.gov.uk/info/448/archives_and_local_studies/462/family_
history_in_manchester/13.

Merseyside Jewish Community Archives: Education
Information on Liverpool Record Office's Jewish school holdings and
related organisations.
http://goo.gl/UA81V

My Home Town Schools
Searchable website with photos of schools.
www.myhometown-schools.co.uk.

Sedbergh School Archives
www.sedberghschoolarchives.org.

Sheffield Archives School Records
https://www.sheffield.gov.uk/libraries/archives-and-local-studies
/collections/school-records.html.

Somerset Record Office
School records.
http://www1.somerset.gov.uk/archives/Leaflets/SchoolRecords.pdf.

UK Genealogy Archives
Free school, college and university databases including Rugby School
(limited selection currently).
www.uk-genealogy.org.uk/school-registers.html.

Victorian School
www.victorianschool.co.uk.

Wirral Archives: Schools
User guide to school records.
www.wirral.gov.uk/my-services/leisure-and-culture/wirral-archives-service/
user-guides.

E
MARITIME AND MILITARY WEBSITES

Maritime
British Maritime History
Len Barnett's website has guides for genealogists seeking ancestors in the merchant and Royal navies.
www.barnettmaritime.co.uk/index.htm.

British Merchant Navy Cadet Training Ships
History of 'sea schools' from the 1650s, and training vessels from 1945–70s. Prospectuses (with photos) for training ships such as HMS *Conway*, and downloads about training policy. Information on shipping companies that operated cadet training ships. Useful weblinks and online forum for former cadets, and information requests. www.rakaia.co.uk.

British Merchant Navy Old Friends
Photos, memories and online forum.
www.merchant-navy.net.

Crew List Index Project
Tips on how to find merchant seafarers on British-registered ships 1861–1913. Weblinks to other useful sites and relevant archives. The crew names index is available at www.findmypast.co.uk.
www.crewlist.org.uk/index.html.

Maritime History Archive, Newfoundland
1881 crew lists database (ongoing); Crew Lists Index.
www.mun.ca/mha.

Naval Biographical Database
www.navylist.org.

Navy Records Society
www.navyrecords.org.uk/pages/home.

Old Pangbournians Society

Website has births/marriages online archive and obituaries of former pupils at the Nautical College, Pangbourne.

www.oldpangbournian.co.uk.

Royal Marines Band Service

Historical factsheets on the service's history and boy buglers.

www.royalmarinesbands.co.uk/reference/index.htm.

Royal Navy Research Archive

Articles and information on Royal Navy ships and crew, mostly from the Second World War onwards.

www.royalnavyresearcharchive.org.uk/.

Society for Nautical Research

www.snr.org.uk.

Training Ships on the Thames

bit.ly/QkjIiR.

Military

Army Ancestors

The Army Museums Ogilby Trust website has tips on researching military ancestors.

www.armymuseums.org.uk/ancestor.htm.

Army Cadet History

http://armycadets.com/about-us/our-history.

The Army Children Archive

www.archhistory.co.uk.

Army Records Society

www.armyrecordssociety.org.uk.

First World War

Includes memoirs and diaries.

www.firstworldwar.com/index.htm.

Forces Reunited

British armed forces community forum.

www.forcesreunited.org.uk.

Forces War Records
Military records and digital library of books, magazines and newspapers (subscription site).
www.forces-war-records.co.uk.

Genes Reunited
Military records 1656–2005.
www.genesreunited.co.uk/static/militaryrecords.

Junior Leaders' Regiment, Royal Armoured Corps Old Boys' Association
www.jlrrac.co.uk/history.php.

Militia Musters, 1781 and 1782
Information on muster rolls, etc. for Durham, Lancashire, Staffordshire, Warwickshire, Worcestershire and Yorkshire.
www.ramsdale.org/militia.htm#Other.

MOD Reunited
www.modreunited.com/.

Royal Military Asylum History
A.W. Cockerill's website has histories of the Asylum at Chelsea, Royal Hibernian Military School, information on military history and useful weblinks.
www.achart.ca.

Service Children Support Network
www.servicechildrensupportnetwork.com.

Veterans UK
www.veterans-uk.info.

Wartime Memories Project
Memories, photographs and stories of those who served in both world wars. Alphabetical indexes of people (if name submitted by families), regiments, ships, etc., including a list of those who sailed on the *City of Benares*:
www.wartimememories.co.uk.
www.wartimememories.co.uk/ships/cityofbenares.html.

F
PLACES TO VISIT

In addition to the heritage sites listed below, various museums in England and Wales have Edwardian, Victorian or wartime schoolrooms open to the public. Several are listed on the Victorian School website (some are only open for school group visits, so check before travelling): www.victorian school.co.uk/other_schools.html.

The Apprentice House, Styal
'Home' for the parish apprentices who worked at the Greg family's cotton mill. Tours of the Apprentice House are available for mill visitors during the summer.

Quarry Bank Mill, Quarry Bank Road, Styal, Wilmslow, Cheshire, SK9 4LA; www.quarrybankmill.org.uk; email: quarrybankmill@nationaltrust.org.uk; tel: 0162 552 7468.

British Schools Museum
First Lancasterian (monitorial) school in Hertfordshire. Furnished classrooms show the history of elementary education from the nineteenth century to late 1960s. The Museum Room has copies of the school's admission registers. (The school's address, in the same location, was formerly Dead Street.)

British Schools Museum, 41/42 Queen Street, Hitchin, SG4 9TS; www.britishschoolsmuseum.co.uk; email: admin@hitchinbritishschools. org.uk; tel: 0146 242 0144.

Brittania Museum, Brittania Royal Naval College
Midshipmen's journals and punishment records from HMS *Britannia*. The museum can only be visited by a pre-booked tour.

Britannia Royal Naval College, College Way, Dartmouth, TQ6 0HJ; www. devonmuseums.net/Britannia-Museum,-Britannia-Royal-Naval-College/

Devon-Museums; email: britanniamuseum@hotmail.co.uk; tel: 0180 367 7233.

Foundling Museum
The Foundling Museum, 40 Brunswick Square, London, WC1N 1AZ; www.foundlingmuseum.org.uk; tel: 0207 841 3600.

Museum of Childhood, Judge's Lodgings, Lancaster
Toys and games from the 1700s onwards. Edwardian schoolroom.

Judge's Lodgings, Church Street, Lancaster, LA1 1YS; http://bit.ly/HNcSjL; email: judgeslodgings@lancashire.gov.uk; tel: 0152 432 808.

National Memorial Arboretum
The Arboretum has memorials to the armed forces and many civilian organisations which have served society: apprentices, the Boys' Brigade, cadets, Church Lads' and Church Girls' Brigade, children, etc.

National Memorial Arboretum, Croxall Road, Alrewas, Staffordshire, DE13 7AR; www.thenma.org.uk; email: info@thenma.org.uk; tel: 0128 379 2333.

National Trust Museum of Childhood
Sudbury Hall and the National Trust Museum of Childhood, Sudbury, Ashbourne, DE6 5HT;
www.nationaltrust.org.uk/sudburyhall; email: sudburyhall@nationaltrust .org.uk; tel: 0128 358 5337.

Ragged School Museum
Ragged School Museum, 46–50 Copperfield Road, London, E3 4RR; www.raggedschoolmuseum.org.uk; email: museumraggeschoolmuseum .org.uk; tel: 0208 980 6405.

Red Lodge Museum, Bristol
The Museum has a room dedicated to Mary Carpenter and the Red Lodge Girls' Reform School.

The Red Lodge Museum, Park Row, Bristol, BS1 5LJ; www.bristol. gov.uk/ page/leisure-and-culture/red-lodge-museum; email: general.museum@ bristol. gov.uk; tel: 0117 921 1360.

Victoria & Albert Museum of Childhood

The Victoria & Albert Museum's collection of childhood-related objects from the 1600s to modern times.

V&A Museum of Childhood, Cambridge Heath Road, London, E2 9PA; www.museumofchildhood.org.uk; tel: 0208 983 5200.

Weaver Hall Museum and Workhouse

Weaver Hall Museum and Workhouse, 162 London Road, Northwich, CW9 8AB; www.weaverhallmuseum.org.uk; email: cheshiremuseums@cheshire westandchester.gov.uk; tel: 0160 627 1640.

West Wales Museum of Childhood

West Wales Museum of Childhood, Pen-ffynnon, Llangeler, Carmarthenshire, SA44 5EY; www.toymuseumwales.co.uk; email: info@ toymuseumwales.co.uk; tel: 0155 937 0428.

Workhouse Museum and Garden, Ripon

The Workhouse Museum, Sharow View, Allhallowgate, Ripon, HG4 1LE; http://riponmuseums.co.uk/museums/workhouse_museum_gardens; info@riponmuseums.co.uk; tel: 0176 569 0799.

The Workhouse, Southwell

The museum has 'Living History' days with costumed interpreters of pauper life.

Upton Road, Southwell, NG25 0PT; www.nationaltrust.org.uk/workhouse-southwell; email: theworkhouse@nationaltrust.org.uk; tel: 0163 681 7260.

SELECT BIBLIOGRAPHY

Manuscript Sources
26th Blackpool Holy Cross Girl Guides Company logbook 1930 LA PR3202/14/7
Altrincham Poor Law Union Register of Orphan Children Boarded Out 1869–1923 CALS LGB 17
Apprenticeship indenture 2 June 1802 LA DDHE/104/38
Bastardy Order 8 April 1800 CALS PC 19/6/6
Bradwall Reformatory School, Sandbach managers'minute book 1887–1890 CALS D4304/1
Bradwall Reformatory School rules and regulations 1871 CALS D4304/40
Calendars of Prisoners Tried At Chester Assizes 1828–1842 CALS D7734/1
Certified School Gazette, August 1919, July 1921 CALS D4304/84
Chester Chronicle, 4 September 1818 CALS
Chester Ragged School Society Annual Reports 1866–1876 CALS DES/23/6
Chester Ragged School Society Managing Committee minute book 1851–1862 CALS DES/23/1
Chester Ragged School Society Managing Committee minute book 1879–1889 CALS DES/23/3
Chester Workhouse Creed Register 1860–1880 CALS ZTRU/18
Chorley Union Workhouse Punishment Book 1872 LA PUX/7
Darnhall School attendance register 1770 CALS D4720/17
Educational Authority financial claims (evacuees) LA DDX 1525/2/8
Hambleton Board School logbook 1880–1927 LA CC/EXTF/11/1
Heswall Nautical School (*Akbar*) Log Book 1909 LA DDX 824/3/1
Home Office: 2nd Report of the Children's Branch, HMSO, 1924 CALS D4304/90
Knowle Green British School admission register 1882–1961: LA SMRB/1/4
Knowle Green British School logbook 1872–1895 LA SMRB/ 1/1
Lancashire Constabulary photographs and criminal records of persons arrested 1866–1892 LA PLA 16/1
Nantwich Urban District Council MOH register of births 1909–1916 CALS LUN 52
NCH Children's Home and Orphanage at Frodsham logbook CALS SL 319/1
Pupil-teacher apprenticeship indenture 1860 CALS P6/14/70
Reformatory and Industrial Schools Directory, HMSO, 1920 CALS D4304/02
Register of births for Great Boughton workhouse 1866–1914 CALS ZHC/7
Register of deaths for Great Boughton workhouse 1866–1913 CALS ZHC/9
Register of unaccompanied children returned home 1939–1944 LA DDX 2744/1/1
Ribchester National School evening school logbook 1899–1926 LA SMRB/2/8
Runcorn Rural Sanitary Authority: Annual Report (1882) of the Medical Officer of Health, Runcorn, 1883 CALS LRR/19/1
Saltersford School, Holmes Chapel: A Short History CALS D4304/101
Settlement examination of Mary Ellen Jones, notice and order of removal LA QSP 3190/26, QSP3196/35
Swinton Industrial Schools boys' school admission and discharge register LA PUG 2/1
Vaccination register for Frodsham District July 1875–January 1877 CALS LG3/3
Webb Orphanage, Crewe minute book CALS D7286

Contemporary Works
Parliamentary Papers
7th Annual Report of the Poor Law Commissioners, with Appendices, 1841
10th Annual Report of the Local Government Board 1880–1881, 1881
13th Annual Report of the Poor Law Commissioners, with Appendices, 1847
Children's Employment Commission (1862), Fourth Report of the Commissioners, with Appendix (3), 1865
Children's Employment Commission (1862), Third Report of the Commissioners, with Appendix (3), 1864

Copy of the Annual Report on Greenwich Hospital Schools, made to the Admiralty by Her Majesty's Inspector of Schools (446), 1851

Copy of Circular Letters to the Commissioners to Boards of Guardians dated 15 February 1841 respecting Relief of Vagrants . . ., XXI (149), 1841

Correspondence between the Poor Law Board and Guardians relative to the transference of Pauper Children to the Factory Districts (259), 1861

Correspondence . . . relative to the Emigration of Pauper Children to Bermuda (243), 1851

Directory of Schools Certified by the Secretary of State under the Children Act, 1908, HMSO, 1924 (held at CALS D4304/92)

First Report . . . into the Present State of Military Education, XXII (4221),1869

Minutes of the Committee of Council on Education 1853–4 Vol. 1, 1854

Report of the Commissioners Appointed to Inquire into the Condition of the Volunteer Force (3053), XXVII, 1862

Report from His Majesty's Commissioners into the Administration and Practical Operation of the Poor Laws, 1834

Report from the Select Committee on the Education of Destitute Children (460), 1861

Report from the Select Committee on Friendly Societies (531), 1852

Report relative to the System of Prison Discipline by the Inspectors of Prisons, XXV–XXVI, 1843

Report on the State of Small Pox and Vaccination in England and Wales and Other Countries, and on Compulsory Vaccination (434), 1853

Reports of the Assistant Commissioners . . . into the State of Popular Education in England, Vol. III, 1861

Reports of the Commissioners . . . into the State of Popular Education in England, Vol. I, 1861

Reports of Special Assistant Poor Law Commissioners on the Employment of Women and Children in Agriculture, XII, 1843

School Enquiry Commission: Special Reports of Assistant Commissioners and Digests of Information Received, North Midland Division, Vol. XVI, 1869

Second Report of the Children's Employment Commission: Trades and Manufactures XIII, 1843

Second Report of the Children's Employment Commission 1862: Lace, Hosiery &c. (3414), XXII, 1864

Second Report on the Employment of Children in Factories (519), XXI, 1833

Sixth Report of the Inspectors Appointed . . . To Visit the Different Prisons of Great Britain, XXX, 1841

Third Report of the Inspectors Appointed . . . To Visit the Different Prisons of Great Britain: I: Home District, 1838

Two Reports of John Henry Capper, Esq., Superintendent of Ships and Vessels Employed for the Confinement of Offenders Under Sentence of Transportation, Vol. 162, 1824

Books, Magazines and Newspapers

5th Annual Report of the Ragged School Union, Ragged School Magazine Vol. 1, London, 1849

An Account of the Hospital and School for the Indigent Blind at Norwich, Norwich, 1845

An Account of the Nature and Present State of the Philanthropic Society, London, 1816

An Address to the Public from the Philanthropic Society, London, 1792

Annual Register, Vol. 91, 1850

The Byelaws and Regulations of the Marine Society, 6th edn, 1820

The Christian Reformer No. LIV, June 1849

The Christian Reformer, or Unitarian Magazine and Review, New Series Volume V, January to December 1849, London, 1849

A Day in a Pauper Palace, 13 July 1850

Dickens, Charles (ed.), *Household Words*, Vol. 1, London, 1850

Gentleman's Magazine, June 1784

Gentleman's Magazine, February 1827, Vol. XCVII Part 1, 1827

Gentleman's Magazine, February 1849

How to Make a Will: A Familiar Exposition of the Statute 1st Victoria, Cap. XXVI, Henry Kent Causton, 1849

The Official Year Book of the Church of England, SPCK, 1884

The Official Year Book of the Church of England, SPCK, 1897

The Philanthropic Society's Farm School for the Reform of Criminal Boys, Redhill, Reigate, Surrey: 1858, London, 1858

Report of the Committee for the Society for the Improvement of Prison Discipline and the Reformation of Juvenile Offenders, London, 1818

Scholastic Register and Educational Advertiser, Dean & Son, 1869

The Times, 13 January, 20 January 1849

Adshead, Joseph, *Prisons and Prisoners*, Longman, Brown, Green & Longman, 1845

Brownlow, John, *Memoranda, or Chronicles of the Foundling Hospital*, Sampson Low, 1847

Brenton, Sir Jahleel, *Memoir of Capt. Edward Pelham Brenton*, London, 1842

Carpenter, Mary, *Reformatory Schools for the Children of the Perishing and Dangerous Classes, and for Juvenile Offenders*, London, 1851

Cornwallis, Caroline Francis, *The Philosophy of Ragged Schools*, London, 1851

Couling, Samuel, *History of the Temperance Movement in Great Britain and Ireland*, London, 1862

De Fonblanque, Edward Barrington, *Treatise on the Administration and Organisation of the Army*, Longman, Brown, Green & Roberts, 1858

Foster, Joseph (ed.), *Alumni Oxonienses, The Members of the University of Oxford 1715–1886*, Later Series A–D, Parker & Co., 1888

Foster, T. Campbell and Finlason, W.F., *Reports of Cases decided at Nisi Prius and at the Crown Side on Circuit*, Vol. II, London, 1862

Fowle, T.W., *The Poor Law*, 2nd edn, Macmillan & Co., 1898

Gregory, Alfred, *Robert Raikes, Journalist and Philanthropist*, Hodder & Stoughton, 1880

Hanway, Jonas, *An Earnest Appeal for Mercy to the Children of the Poor*, London, 1766

Hill, Octavia, 'The Importance of Aiding the Poor without Almsgiving', *Transactions of the National Association for the Promotion of Social Science*, Longmans, Green & Co., 1870

Hughes-Hughes, W.O. (ed.), *The Register of Tonbridge School from 1820 to 1886*, Tonbridge, 1886

Jewitt, L., *The Wedgwoods*, London, 1865

King, Harold, 'A Boys' Home', *Once A Week*, 25 August 1866

Knight, Charles (ed.), *London*, Vol. III, London, 1851

Knipe, William, *Criminal Chronology of York Castle*, Simpkin, Marshall & Co., 1867

Lamb, Charles, *The Works of Charles Lamb Vol. III*, W.J. Widdleton, 1866

Loch, C.S. (ed.), *Charities Register and Digest*, Longmans, Green & Co., 1890

Love, B., *The Handbook of Manchester*, Manchester, 1842

Low Jr, Sampson, *The Charities of London*, Sampson Low, 1850

Lysons, Daniel, *The Environs of London (2nd ed.): The County of Middlesex*, Vol. II, Part 1, London, 1811

Mann, Horace, *Census of Great Britain, 1851: Education in Great Britain*, London, 1854

Mayhew, Henry, *London Labour and the London Poor*, Vol. 2, 1851

Mayhew, Henry, *The Great World of London*, Part IX, London, 1856

Miles, E. and Miles, Lieutenant Lawford, *An Epitome, Historical and Statistical, of the Royal Naval Service of England*, London, 1841

Mill, John Stuart, *On Liberty*, London, 1859

Nolan, Michael, *A Treatise of the Laws for the Relief and Settlement of the Poor*, Vol. III, Joseph Butterworth & Son, 1825

Raithby, John (ed.), *Statutes of the United Kingdom of Great Britain and Ireland Vol. V*, London, 1814

Sharp, William, *Life of Percy Bysshe Shelley*, Walter Scott, 1887

Shipp, John and Chichester, H. Manners (eds), *Memoirs of the Extraordinary Military Career of John Shipp*, T. Fisher Unwin, 1890

Sims, Richard, *A Manual for the Genealogist, Topographer, Antiquary and Legal Professor*, London, 1856

Smiles, Samuel, *Brief Biographies*, Ticknor & Fields, 1861

Smiles, Samuel, *Lives of the Engineers: George and Robert Stephenson*, John Murray, 1862

Southey, Robert, *Life of Nelson*, New York, 1831

Stanley, Maude, *Clubs for Working Girls*, Macmillan & Co., 1890

Whitaker, Joseph, *An Almanack for the Year of Our Lord 1894*, London, 1894

Wilson, John Iliff, *The History of Christ's Hospital*, London, 1821

Modern Works

Salvation Army Year Book, London, 1980

Bagley, J.J. and A.J., *The State and Education in England and Wales, 1833–1968*, Macmillan, 1969

Barker, Juliet, *The Brontës*, Phoenix Giant, 1995

Barnardo, Mrs and J. Marchant, *Memoirs of Dr Barnardo*, Hodder & Stoughton, 1907

Behlmer, George K., *Child Abuse and Moral Reform 1870–1908*, Stanford University Press, 1982

Beresford, John (ed.), *The Diary of a Country Parson: The Revd. James Woodforde 1758–1781*, Oxford University Press, 1924

Blake, Nicholas and Lawrence, Richard, *The Illustrated Companion to Nelson's Navy*, Chatham Publishing, 1999

Block, Brian P. and Hostettler, John, *Hanging in the Balance: A History of the Abolition of Capital Punishment in England*, Waterside Press, 1997

Blocker, Jack S., Fahey, David M. and Tyrell, Ian R., *Alcohol and Temperance In Modern History: A Global Encyclopedia*, ABC-CLIO, 2003

Bourdillon, Anne Francis Claudine, *Voluntary Social Services: Their Place in the Modern State*, Methuen, 1945

Bourke, Joanne, *Working-Class Cultures in Britain 1890–1960: Gender, Class and Ethnicity*, Taylor & Francis, 2009

Brand, Jack, *Local Government Reform in England 1888–1974*, Croom Helm, 1974

Brunton, Deborah, *The Politics of Vaccination: Practice and Policy in England, Wales, Ireland and Scotland 1800–1874*, University of Rochester Press, 2008

Carlebach, Julius, *Caring for Children in Trouble*, Routledge and Kegan Paul, 1970

Childs, Michael J., *Labour's Apprentices: Working Class Lads in Late Victorian and Edwardian England*, Hambledon Press, 1992

Christian, Peter and Annal, David, *Census: The Expert Guide*, TNA, 2008

Cole, Hubert, *Beau Brummel*, Granada Publishing, 1977

Cook, T.G. (ed.), *Local Studies and the History of Education*, Methuen & Co., 1972

Cowie, Evelyn E., *Education*, Methuen Educational Ltd, 1973

Cox, J. Charles, *The Parish Registers of England*, Methuen & Co., 1910

Cox, Marjorie, *A History of Sir John Deane's Grammar School Northwich*, Manchester University Press, 1975

Cruickshank, Marjorie, *Children and Industry: Child Health and Welfare in North-West Textile Towns During the Nineteenth Century*, Manchester University Press, 1981

Cunningham, Hugh, *Children and Childhood in Western Society since 1500*, Pearson Education, 2005

Dent, Harold Collett, *Secondary Education for All: Origins and Development in England*, Taylor & Francis, 1949

Dickinson, H.W., *Educating the Royal Navy; Eighteenth and Nineteenth Century Training for Officers*, Routledge, 2007

Duckworth, Jeannie, *Fagin's Children: Criminal Children in Victorian England*, Hambledon, 2002

Dwork, Deborah, *War is Good for Babies and Other Young Children: A History of the Infant and Child Welfare Movement in England 1898–1918*, Tavistock Publications Ltd, 1987

Dyhouse, Carol, *Girls Growing Up in Late Victorian and Edwardian England*, Routledge, 2013

Edmonds, E.L., *The School Inspector*, Routledge and Kegan Paul, 2002

Finlayson, Geoffrey B.A.M., *Seventh Earl of Shaftesbury 1801–1885*, Eyre Methuen, 1981

Fletcher, W.G.D. (ed.), *Shropshire Parish Registers, Diocese of Hereford*, Vol. VIII, Shropshire Parish Register Society, 1911

Foreman, Amanda, *Georgiana, Duchess of Devonshire*, HarperCollins, 1999

Fowler, Simon, *Workhouse: The People; The Places; The Life Behind Doors*, TNA, 2007

Fowler, Simon, *Tracing Your Naval Ancestors*, Pen & Sword, 2011

Gérin, Winifred, *Charlotte Brontë*, Oxford University Press, 1977

Gibson, Clare, *Army Childhood: British Army Children's Lives and Times*, Shire Publications Ltd, 2012

Glass, David V. (ed.), *Social Mobility in Britain*, London, 1954

Glover, Richard, *Peninsular Preparation: The Reform of the British Army 1795–1809*, Cambridge University Press, 1963

Select Bibliography

Gregg, Pauline, *A Social and Economic History of Britain, 1760–1970*, 6th edn, G. Harrap & Co. Ltd, 1971

Hammond, J.L. and Barbara, *The Village Labourer*, 2 vols, Guild Books, 1948

Heyman, Neil, *World War One*, Greenwood Press, 1997

Higgs, Edward, *A Clearer Sense of the Census*, HMSO, 1996

Hill, J.R. (ed.), *Oxford Illustrated History of the Navy*, Oxford University Press, 2002

Hislam, Percival A., *The Navy Shown to the Children*, T.C. and E.C. Jack, *c.* 1920.

Holmes, Richard, *Soldiers*, Harper Press, 2012

Hopkins, Eric, *Childhood Transformed: Working Class Children in Nineteenth Century England*, Manchester University Press, 1994

Horn, Pamela, *The Victorian and Edwardian Schoolchild*, Alan Sutton, 1989

Horn, Pamela, *The Victorian Country Child*, Alan Sutton, 1990

Horn, Pamela, *Young Offenders: Juvenile Delinquency 1700–2000*, Amberley Publishing, 2010

Humphreys, Margaret, *Empty Cradles*, Corgi Books, 1995

Humphries, Robert, *Poor Relief and Charity 1860–1945: the London Charity Organisation Society*, Palgrave Macmillan, 2001

Illingworth, W.H., *History of the Education of the Blind*, Sampson Low, Marston & Co., 1910

James, Peter (ed.), *The Diary of James Woodforde, Vol. 14, 1794–1795*, Parson Woodforde Society, 2004

Jones, E.D., 'Elementary School Log Books', *National Library of Wales Journal*, Vol. 1, No. 3, Summer 1940

Jones, Kathleen, *The Making of Social Policy in Britain 1830–1990*, Athlone Press, 1992

Kershaw, Roger and Pearsall, Mark, *Family History On the Move*, TNA, 2006

Kershaw, Roger and Sacks, Janet, *New Lives for Old: The Story of Britain's Child Migrants*, TNA, 2008

Kitchen, Jonathan S., *The Employment of Merchant Seamen*, Croom Helm, 1980

Levene, Alysa, *The Childhood of the Poor: Welfare in Eighteenth-Century London*, Palgrave Macmillan, 2012

Macfarlane, Eric, *Education 16–19: In Transition*, Routledge, 1992

Mackenzie, John M., 'Empire and Metropolitan Cultures', in Andrew Porter (ed.), *Oxford History of the British Empire: The Nineteenth Century*, Oxford University Press, 2009

Mason, Herbert B., *The Encyclopaedia of Ships and Shipping*, The Shipping Encyclopaedia Ltd, 1908

May, Trevor, *The Victorian School*, Shire Publications, 1994

Mitchell, Sally, *Daily Life in Victorian England*, Greenwood Publishing, 1996

Mowat, Charles Loch, *The Charity Organisation Society 1869–1913: Its Ideas and Work*, Methuen, 1961

Murdoch, Lydia, *Imagined Orphans: Poor Families, Child Welfare, and Contested Citizenship in London*, Rutgers University Press, 2006

Owen, David, *English Philanthropy 1660–1960*, Oxford University Press, 1965

Perkin, Joan, *Victorian Women*, John Murray, 1993

Picard, Liza, *Dr Johnson's London*, Phoenix Press, 2001

Rogers, Colin Darlington, *The Family Tree Detective*, 4th edn, Manchester University Press, 2008

Rogers, Colin Darlington and Smith, John Henry, *Local Family History 1538–1914*, Manchester University Press, 1991

Rose, Claire, *Making, Selling and Wearing Boys' Clothes in Late Victorian England*, Ashgate Publishing Ltd, 2010

Rose, Lionel, *Massacre of the Innocents: Infanticide in Britain 1800–1939*, Routledge and Kegan Paul, 1986

Rose, Lionel, *The Erosion of Childhood: Childhood Oppression in Britain 1860–1918*, Routledge, 1991

Rosen, David, *Child Soldiers: A Reference Handbook*, ABC-CLIO, 2012

Springhall, John, *Youth, Empire and Society: British Youth Movements 1883–1940*, Croom Helm, 1977

Sondhaus, Lawrence, *Navies in Modern World History*, Reaktion Books, 2004

Southam, Brian, *Jane Austen and the Navy*, Hambledon and London, 2005

Stanley, Dorothy (ed.), *The Autobiography of Henry Morton Stanley*, Houghton Mifflin, 1909

Stephens W.B. and Unwin, R.W., *Materials for the Local and Regional Study of Schooling 1700–1900*, British Records Association, 1987

Stephens, W.B., *Sources for English Local History*, Cambridge University Press, 1994

Swift, Roger (ed.), *Victorian Chester: Essays in Social History 1830–1900*, Liverpool University Press, 1996

Symonds, Richard, *Far Above Rubies: The Women Uncommemorated by the Church of England*, Gracewing, 1993

Tate, W.E., *The Parish Chest*, 3rd edn, Cambridge University Press, 1979

Wagg, Henry J. and Thomas, Mary G., *A Chronological Survey of Work for the Blind*, National Institute for the Blind, 1932

Wardle, David, *English Popular Education 1780–1975*, Cambridge University Press, 1976

Webb, Sidney and Beatrice, *English Poor Law Policy*, Longmans, Green & Co., 1910

Webb, Sidney and Beatrice, *English Local Government: Statutory Bodies for Special Purposes*, Longmans, Green & Co., 1922

Webb, Sidney and Beatrice, *English Local Government: English Poor Law History*, 2 vols, Longmans, 1927

Wilding, Paul (ed.), *In Defence of the Welfare State*, Manchester University Press, 1986

Wilkes, Sue, *Narrow Windows, Narrow Lives: The Industrial Revolution in Lancashire*, History Press, 2008

Wilkes, Sue, *Regency Cheshire*, Robert Hale, 2009

Wilkes, Sue, 'Required Reading', *Jane Austen's Regency World*, Issue 47, 2010

Wilkes, Sue, *The Children History Forgot*, Robert Hale Ltd, 2011

Wilkes, Sue, 'Raikes' Progress', *Jane Austen's Regency World*, Issue 54, 2011

Wilkes, Sue, *Tracing Your Canal Ancestors*, Pen & Sword, 2011

Wilkes, Sue, *Tracing Your Lancashire Ancestors*, Pen & Sword, 2012

Williams, E.N., *Life in Georgian England*, B.T. Batsford Ltd, 1962

Wohl, Anthony S., *Endangered Lives: Public Health in Victorian Britain*, Methuen & Co., 1984

Online Sources

Baxby, Derrick, 'The End of Smallpox', *History Today*, Vol. 49, Issue 3, 1999: www.historytoday.com/derrick-baxby/end-smallpox

Bell, John Robert, 'The Provision of Nursery Education in England and Wales to 1967 with special reference to North-East England', doctoral thesis (2011), Durham University: http://etheses.dur.ac.uk/1401/

Bradley, Kate, 'Juvenile delinquency and the evolution of the British juvenile courts, c.1900–1950', *Institute of Historical Research*, 2008: www.history.ac.uk/ihr/Focus/ welfare/articles/bradleyk.html

Clark, Gregory, 'The Charity Commission as a Source in English Economic History', *Research in Economic History*, 1998: www.econ.ucdavis.edu/faculty/gclark/papers/ reh.pdf

Cockburn, J.S. and King, H.P.F. and McDonnell, K.G.T. (eds), 'The Education of the Working Classes to 1870', *A History of the County of Middlesex: Volume 1. Physique, Archaeology, Domesday, Ecclesiastical Organization, The Jews, Religious Houses, Education of Working Classes to 1870, Private Education from Sixteenth Century, 1969*, pp. 213–40: www.british-history.ac.uk/report.aspx?compid=22123

Croft, Janet, 'The Hen that Laid the Eggs: Tolkien and the Officers Training Corps', 2011: www.academia.edu/1684221/The_Hen_that_Laid_the_Eggs_Tolkien_and_the_Officers_Training_Corps

Fishman, James J., *Charitable Accountability and Reform in Nineteenth Century England: The Case of the Charity Commission*, 2005, Pace Law Faculty Publications, Paper 108: http://digitalcommons.pace.edu/lawfaculty/108

Gillard, D., *Education in England: a brief history*, 2011: www.educationengland.org. uk/history

Gooderson, Philip, 'Terror on the Streets of Late Victorian Salford and Manchester: The Scuttling Menace', *Manchester Region History Review*, Vol. 11, pp. 3–11, 1997: www. hssr.mmu.ac.uk/mcrh/mrhr

Jolly, Sandra, 'The Origins of the Manchester and Salford Reformatory for Juvenile Criminals 1853–1860', *Manchester Region History Review*, Vol. 15, pp. 2–8, 2001:www. hssr.mmu.ac.uk/mcrh/mrhr

Morrison, Andrew N., *Thy Children Own Their Own Birth: Diasporic Genealogies and Descendants of Canada's Home Children*, e-thesis, Nottingham University, 2006, http://etheses.nottingham.ac.uk/276/1/Thy_Children_Own_Their_Birth.pdf

Roberts, J., 'The significance of Circular 1486 – The Service of Youth', *The Encyclopedia of Informal Education*, 2004: www.infed.org/youthwork/circular1486.htm

Smith, Mark, 'The Making of Popular Youth Work', *Developing Youth Work: Informal education, mutual aid and popular practice*, Open University Press, 2001: www.infed.org/archives/developing_youth_work/dyw2.htm

Smith, M.K., 'Maude Stanley, girls' clubs and district visiting', *The Encyclopaedia of Informal Education*, 2001: www.infed.org/thinkers/stanley.htm; last update 29 May 2012

Smith, M.K., 'Waldo McGillicuddy Eagar and the making of boys' clubs', *The Encyclopedia of Informal Education*, 2004: www.infed.org/thinkers/eagar.htm

Building On History: The Church in London: www.open.ac.uk/Arts/building-on-history-project/resource-guide/source-guides/ResearchingSchools.pdf

Gerald Massey: http://gerald-massey.org.uk/massey/index.htm

History of Education in Wales: http://history.powys.org.uk/history/common/educ5.html

Royal Naval Museum Library: www.royalnavalmuseum.org/info_sheets_navy_league.htm

INDEX

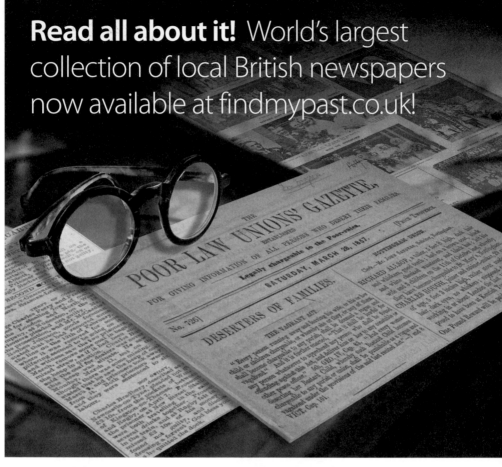